T0304260

Mastering the Business of Global Trade

Negotiating Competitive Advantage Contractual Best Practices, Incoterms®, and Leveraging Supply Chain Options

THE GLOBAL WARRIOR SERIES
Series Editor: Thomas A. Cook

Mastering the Business of Global Trade: Negotiating Competitive Advantage Contractual Best Practices, Incoterms, and Leveraging Supply Chain Options, Thomas A. Cook (2014)

Thomas A. Cook

Mastering the Business
of Global Trade

Negotiating Competitive Advantage
Contractual Best Practices, Incoterms®,
and Leveraging Supply Chain Options

CRC Press
Taylor & Francis Group
Boca Raton   London   New York

CRC Press is an imprint of the
Taylor & Francis Group, an **informa** business

A PRODUCTIVITY PRESS BOOK

CRC Press
Taylor & Francis Group
6000 Broken Sound Parkway NW, Suite 300
Boca Raton, FL 33487-2742

© 2014 by Taylor & Francis Group, LLC
CRC Press is an imprint of Taylor & Francis Group, an Informa business

No claim to original U.S. Government works

Printed on acid-free paper
Version Date: 20140227

International Standard Book Number-13: 978-1-4665-9578-1 (Hardback)

Visit the Taylor & Francis Web site at
http://www.taylorandfrancis.com

and the CRC Press Web site at
http://www.crcpress.com

To Sergeant Dan W. (Gunny Man!), who saved my life. Rest peacefully.

Contents

Preface

Contract management, logistics, understanding Incoterms®, and leveraging supply chain options in global trade are all integral and base foundations for trade in every corner of the world. A company's opportunity for success in global trade is determined by how it manages agreements and influences every component of its import and export sale or purchase.

This book will teach not only the key elements of what every international businessperson must know, but also, more importantly, the use of negotiation skills and leveraged options, along with Incoterms, to work supply chains for competitive benefits.

This will allow for more trade, more deals, higher returns, and a reduction in commercial risks.

At the end of the day, landed costs determine pricing and profits. We dedicate a lot of space and dialogue in the book to understanding how landed cost modeling works and how to use these business models to leverage supply chain options.

As the world enters 2014, ever-increasing elements of global business include trade compliance and risk management. This book provides great insight for the reader on how Incoterms impact compliance and risk and then offers the critical options for avoidance and best practices.

Managing global supply chains is all about striving for efficiency, driving out cost, and increasing profits. The reader will learn how to manage these areas by better understanding how negotiating better contracts can impact these both adversely and favorably.

Mitigating risk and establishing sound risk management protocols in an organization go a long way toward assuring that the company stays out of trouble and do not bear unnecessary cost. Learning and working Incoterms is a risk management and loss control method in global business to impact opportunity.

It is also critical to note that Incoterms, a set of terms created by the International Chamber of Commerce (ICC) that are regularly employed in commercial transactions, have little to no meaning in a global transaction without an interface that includes all the numerous components of a global trade such as freight, payment, insurance, tax issues, revenue recognition, and contractual dispute resolution, just to name a few. Additionally, global supply chain managers typically use freight forwarders and customhouse brokers to manage their import and export freight and logistics. The book outlines how to manage these relationships and maximize value in service agreements.

The book establishes a very simple but comprehensive roadmap for both the neophyte and the more experienced global supply chain executive to follow and then to master. The key to this book is leveraging the global supply chain and gaining competitive advantage.

Acknowledgments

The author expresses appreciation for information flow and valuable resources obtained from the following parties:

American Management Association
American River International
American Shipper
Bureau of National Affairs
Cargo Business News
Census Bureau/Department of Commerce
Travis Cook
International Chamber of Commerce (ICC)
The Internet (Thank God!)
Journal of Commerce
United States Council for International Business (USCIB)
United States Customs Border and Protection (CBP)
United States Department of Commerce (DOC)
Kelly Raia
Reuters
The World Academy

About the Author

Thomas A. Cook is a seasoned logistics, international trade and supply chain executive. Tom is the author of more than 300 articles and 12 published books on global trade and related subjects. Tom's reach into global corporations is deep, with extensive experience in guiding companies on supply chain management and Incoterms. Tom's work is internationally recognized with a global reach spanning six continents.

Tom is Managing Director of Blue Tiger International in New York, a prominent and exclusive management consulting firm specializing in customized supply chain and management solutions. (www.bluetigerintl.com)

Tom's bestseller, *Managing Global Supply Chains (Auerbach2008)* ... is considered by many to be one of the most comprehensive guides to best practices in global supply chain management in both the academic and commercial world. It's focus on trade compliance, security and dealing with Terrorism, became the 'go to' reference guide for trade practitioners, following the Events of 9/11. Tom is available for inquiries at thomasalancook@gmail.com or aritac4@aol.com.

Note

This book is not a legal document, nor is the advice portrayed legal in nature. It is a reference guide and commentary put forth by an experienced trade professional to assist companies in how they manage Incoterms® and conduct business in global trade.

1

Role of Contracts in Global Trade

Contracts of sale purchase orders and transactional agreements are foundations for expected deliverables and performance on the part of both parties in global trade. They become the basis for what was intended and agreed upon and how both parties are supposed to act in an international transaction. When a deal goes wrong, the contract becomes the focus; if it is not aligned with what everyone had as its intentions, it will typically be more harmful than helpful to both parties. This chapter provides some central guidelines for international executives to follow to basically stay out of trouble and achieve better results.

CONTRACTS IN GLOBAL TRADE

Simply said, companies want to sell and buy products and services on a global basis. Contracts are made to reflect the agreements between sellers and buyers.

Consider the following typical scenario. A company based in Toledo, Ohio, has found a source in Taipei, Taiwan, for a component that it requires in the manufacturing process. A purchasing manager in the plant begins a negotiation process to acquire that component. A salesperson in the manufacturing plant in Taipei enters the negotiation to sell the purchasing manager in Toledo what he needs.

They negotiate on the following key issues:

- Products and specifications
- Quality control issues
- Samples
- Delivery schedules

- Pricing
- Incoterms®
- Freight and logistics

But do they address additional issues, such as

- Intellectual property rights
- Duties and taxes
- Transportation insurance considerations (marine cargo coverage)
- Product liability
- Warranty
- Product dispute resolution
- Managing customs issues

And the list can go on and on, depending upon the products involved and all the nuances and complexities involved in the specific supply chain.

The major consideration here is: How experienced are the parties managing the contract of sale or purchase, and are they well prepared, well educated, and well trained to make sure they are protecting the interests of their company not only in reducing risk and cost but also in leveraging the contractual terms to their company's best interest?

This book examines all the issues executives need to consider to maximize supply chain sales, purchases, and operations when they are engaged in global trade. This is first best reviewed by looking at a case study and then by examining the necessary steps to take in managing global contracts to reduce risk and cost and to better world trade.

CASE STUDY: WHEN CONTRACTS (OR LACK OF) FAIL

A few years back, I was involved with a pharmaceutical company based in Europe with a large North American subsidiary. For purposes of this example, we will refer to them as Genrex. This North American subsidiary was new to export and found a very receptive market in Latin America, more specifically in Brazil. Over a few short years, export sales to Brazil had grown to over US$20 million. Genrex had established a strategic plan of first selling through approved third-party agent/distributors. After several years of establishing a base in a specific country, the goal was to then set up its own sales and distribution presence.

In Brazil after high growth for five years and successful market penetration, Genrex executed a contractual 180-day notice to its local agent/distributor of its intent to structure its own presence in Brazil. This was not a surprise to the agent, as Genrex had discussed this from the very beginning. After 180 days, Genrex had established its own offices and began the process of handling the first of 20 inbound 40-foot containers coming from the North American Warehouse in Chicago. Genrex Brazil was now set up to be the importer of record in Recife where the freight was going to land.

When Genrex began to work with its customs broker to handle the clearance, it was advised to produce the necessary import permits and product registrations. At that point, it realized that those documents and control thereof were still in the hands of the former agent/distributor. Left out of its initial contract and agreement were details as to who would control these licenses after the contract had been terminated. As a result, local laws prevailed, and Genrex's agent was the owner of these critical licenses. Genrex hired a local attorney, but all the attorney could do was negotiate a resolve, which turned out to add several hundred thousand dollars to the costs of setting up its own presence.

If Genrex had dealt with this issue proactively in its initial contract, the consequences and costs would have been manageable and reasonable.

In the long-term, everything was worked out. But in the short-term:

- Those first 20 containers were delayed by six weeks. Customers were not happy.
- Storage charges became excessive and ate at transactional profits.
- The cost of the settlement enveloped almost 50% of anticipated first year net revenue to Genrex's new Brazilian office.
- Genrex management in Europe had a major loss of confidence in the export sales division in Chicago.
- Promotions, bonuses, and perk packages were negatively impacted that year.

But what could have been done to prevent this error?

- All Genrex management should have taken responsibility for this Brazilian initiative in the form of basic skill set training in the fundamental issues of setting up a foreign subsidiary.
- Consulting expertise and counsel should have been obtained with both international and local expertise in Brazil to make sure Genrex's interests were being protected.

- A risk management profile should have been performed of this business initiative before proceeding, and action plans should have been created to avoid or mitigate potential risks.
- There should have been proactive dialogue with the original agent/distributor to identify long-term objectives, and then a structured agreement should have been drafted to release all local rights to Genrex.

Contracts become a blueprint for the understandings and agreements between both parties. They do not afford functionality of the relationship. They hopefully get filed away and never opened again. Typically when they need to be opened it is a result of a dispute gone badly.

What really sets the stage for good contracts is the following:

- Transparency of what both parties are trying to accomplish
- Trust
- Doable capabilities
- Responsible structure

TRANSPARENCY OF WHAT BOTH PARTIES ARE TRYING TO ACCOMPLISH

In our practice we often troubleshoot contracts between two foreign entities in which we have no idea exactly what is being agreed upon. Additionally, we read wordings that are obscure and unclear, which leaves more questions unanswered. These contracts will usually result in problems that leave both parties vulnerable. We recommend the following:

- Establish a language for contract use that both parties can respond to. English is typically the first option here since it is the most established international contractual language.
- Clearly outline both parties' responsibilities and expectations.
- Keep the wording simple and to the point.

Example

NOT GOOD

The buyer needs blueprints on a timely basis from the seller before goods are received by the buyer from the seller. It is imperative that these documents be received ahead of the shipment so the buyer can prepare the arriving facility.

BETTER

The seller will be responsible to provide engineering blueprints 90 days before the equipment arrives at overseas destinations.

- Wording should be as specific as possible with all the necessary detail to meet performance acceptability.

Example

NOT GOOD

All packing lists need to conform to buyers' purchase order requirements and be in the most traditional format.

BETTER

All packing lists should be in English, should be double spaced, and should contain specific quantities, unit measures in metric, colors, and size order with individual extended pricing and country of origin marking details.

- Keep in mind that translations into English and from English into certain languages leave gaps. Certain words cannot be translated, and often similar words are used. While the words may be similar they potentially present different meanings. This is typical in some Latin American, Asian, and Middle Eastern languages when compared with English. This may mean an intended word may require accompanying detailed explanations.

TRUST

This may be the most important aspect of contract management.

Americans and Western cultures are more likely to buy based upon a company's reputation, global size/presence, name recognition, or product, for example. The balance of the world needs more to first establish "trust" before entering into a "deal."

The best way to explain this is to consider a purchasing manager at a beverage company in Cleveland, Ohio, buying from the Pepsi Corporation. The purchasing manager at the beverage company in Venice, Italy, buys from Mario, the salesperson at Pepsi in Rome. The basis of the latter relationship is what will drive the ultimate decision of who to buy from.

While I would argue that in all business relationships "trust" is a critical component, in the international arena its relevance and salience are questioned quite a bit. I would go as far as to say that the seller has to spend more time internationally in certain markets to work on that relationship first before focusing on the product or service sale. Trust will be developed in the following ways:

- Commit to learning the other parties' culture and show respect.
- Learn basic and rudimentary language of the other parties: hello, good-bye, thank you, please.
- Plan on first establishing the relationship before attempting to hard-sell or negotiate.
- Plan on a commitment of time, social activities (e.g., golf, soccer, bull fights, camel races), dinners, and other social bonding events.

The balance will go in favor of both interests when a bond or trust is accomplished. The contract will be much easier to deal with when that basic bond is in place. It will also be the first action of dependency when certain issues come up, which are best resolved when two parties can raise their issues and come to a compromised resolution based upon their mutual trust for one another.

CAPABILITIES THAT CAN BE DELIVERED

In some of the international contractual disputes we become involved with, once we have the contract in view and interview both parties we can easily see how a mishap was inevitable.

For example, we worked in a dispute resolution case where the purchaser was a U.S.-based company in Sacramento, California. It entered into a manufacturing agreement with a company based in Taipei, Taiwan, to produce a certain type of high-volume, high-end water pump.

The Sacramento company had lost a production source in India over quality issues a few months earlier and now was under the gun to find an alternative low-cost supplier and begin production and shipping quickly. The agreement spelled out that the supplier was responsible for providing several product samples and prototypes. In a number of quality control tests back in Sacramento, the products did not meet basic standards. The purchaser's engineering group provided further enhanced instructions and assisted leading new samples and prototypes. This met minimum quality specifications, but just barely and not consistently.

The order was given to produce against the new prototypes with some minor modifications. Under time pressures, the Taiwanese manufacturer produced product and made several rush shipments. Because of the time constraints, many shipments went directly to end users. At the end of six months, about 50% of the recipients had quality issues. The buyer had a Letter of Credit (L/C) in place to draw down on in the event of quality issues, which they acted on. So the dispute began.

This was a no-win for both parties. After interviewing them both and reading the contract, we saw that the agreement was doomed to fail. However, this was not because of the contract, but because, in this case the buyer did not exercise enough due diligence to assure that the manufacturer in Taiwan was able to meet the quality control standards. In its rush to move this process along, it accepted minimum standards and did not require more samples and prototypes before full manufacturing was authorized. There was more of a "hope-for-the-best" approach than best practices or more responsible, patient, management. Both parties needed to practice due diligence, prudence, good judgment, patience, and general common sense prior to finalizing the agreement.

In this example, the buyer usurped every sensible protocol and standard operating procedure to deal with the pressure of not being able to supply product. The result was now worse than what might have been potential other options. Generally cutting corners in the world of global trade will prove to be disastrous. Both parties need to do whatever is available and reasonable to assure each other can perform.

RESPONSIBLE STRUCTURE

The structure of the deal has to work for both parties, and it is important that both parties enter into the agreement being able to earn profits and deliver internal margins.

With the exception of companies taking a stance in a specific market or transaction that is a loss leader, both parties should always make sure the other is making money. Otherwise, the deal will fail—not just for one but for both.

Here is our checklist of questions and issues to consider when looking at a contract in an international transaction:

- Are both parties able to meet the deliverables, obligations, and expectations?
- Are profits and margins being maintained?
- What are the terms of sale?

- How and what mechanisms are in place to assure timely payment? Is there a currency risk?
- How will your bank play a role in the transaction and offer assistance in reducing financial exposure?

- Who is responsible for arranging freight and paying for it? Will it be prepaid or collect? Are you in control of service provider and carrier options? Are the freight charges competitive?
- What risks are involved in the transactions: property, cargo, liability, personnel, auto, etc.? Are the risks quantified and managed? Are they being assumed or transferred to a third-party insurance company? What are the qualifications of the brokers and underwriters that are engaged? Do any local insurance requirements need to be considered?
- A critical risk involves intellectual property rights (IPR) issues with patents, trademarks, trade secrets, formulizations, and assists. This is outlined in Chapter 7 in more detail. This has to be thought

out in advance because the negative ramifications could leave little ability to mitigate them. The use of legal support here is of heightened importance.

- Do any tax issues need to be addressed and factored into the decision-making process?
- Are revenue recognition protocols in place that consider regulatory bodies such as the Securities Exchange Commission, the Internal Revenue Service, or the International Financial Reporting Standards and possibly the Sarbanes–Oxley (SOX) Guidelines.
- Jurisdiction of contract? How will disputes be settled? Is arbitration a favored option?
- Are Incoterm options being leveraged?
- Who is responsible for trade compliance controls, based both upon Incoterms doctrines and local laws?

MANAGING INTERNATIONAL CONTRACTS: BEST PRACTICES AND NECESSARY DELIVERABLES

Our first recommendation for managing international contracts is not to assume that you know what you are doing in every situation. Global trade is captivating for most participants because it is always a work in process, ever changing with new challenges every day. It is a moving target with nuances at every turn with both slight and major differences in the various cultures and countries we will do business with.

Our guidelines for best practices follow the following steps:

1. Make sure senior management is actively engaged in all international initiatives. The risks, costs, and consequences could be impactful, and their support, blessing, and leadership are better obtained up front and throughout the globalization process.
2. A committee made up of all the parties with vested interests should be formed to get everyone's buy-in who are stakeholders in the international initiatives.
3. The committee makeup will vary from each company but generally would include managers from the following areas of profit and cost:

   - Sales
   - Purchasing
   - Manufacturing
   - Engineering
   - Operations
   - Warehousing and traffic
   - Compliance
   - Legal
   - Financial
   - Customer service
   - Supply chain and logistics
   - Research and development
   - Information technology

4. The committee must set an agenda outlining the following:

   a. Guidelines that follow the mantra and mission of the company as a whole into how those personnel negotiating contracts will manage that process from a cultural perspective, ideology, and mind-set into actual contract structure.
   b. Decide what role each member will play and the individual expectations and contributions.
   c. Create a blueprint, standard operating procedures, and protocols on how the company will manage global supply chain contracts. Identifying first what will not be acceptable, then what absolutely needs to be contained, and then what are negotiable areas and the parameters or discretion each person can offer are finalized when senior management must become involved to authorize variations that fall out of the committee's scope and authority level.
   d. The committee can also arrange for internal contract management training, dispersion of the contract standard operating procedures, and the various authority levels given to various levels of personnel.
   e. The committee will also work with either internal or external audit teams that review contracts to assure compliance with

committee guidelines. The more independent the auditor, the more likely the results will be unbiased and also in the best interest of the company.

The committee can set a template for the auditor to follow and make sure both expected and unexpected audits occur on a quarterly basis but not less than at least once per annum. For public companies the audit process is most likely a necessary evil to comply with SOX regulations and best practice protocols.

Auditing of global supply chain contracts makes for a best practice and can meet SOX protocols. The committee can also establish relationships with third-party expertise and external resources to raise the bar of expertise and skill set in contract management, particularly on local levels in foreign countries.

THIRD-PARTY OPTIONS

One of the important functions of the committee and the point person on contract management is to obtain support from external expertise.

Support can come in numerous forms, but there are two general recognized areas: consultants and law firms.

Consultants

Firms such as Booz & Company, McKinsey, KPMG, Accenture, PwC, AT Kearney, and American River International are among the elite that can provide very functional advice on how to construct and manage contracts in international business. They have the following:

- Tenure
- Experience
- Resources
- Contract management skill sets
- Access to worldwide local knowledge
- Potential connections to make things happen locally

Law Firms

Firms such as Doyle and Doyle, Sandler Travis, and Braumiller and Schulz specialize in international contracts. They provide all the same capabilities as previously outlined but additionally can

- Provide legal counsel and representation
- Litigate

It is important to note that proactive use of consultants and law firms that are qualified in international contracts can avoid a lot of the potential future nightmares and problems that are likely to occur in overseas expansion.

2

Freight, Logistics, and the Global Supply Chain

Companies competing in global trade who manage the logistics process do very well. They employ and engage professional in-house and outsourced staffs that comprehend how to best move freight internationally.

This chapter explores how logistics plays an integral role in the global supply chain and how Incoterms® impact logistics management in world trade.

Logistics are the engine that moves freight from sellers to buyers all over the globe. No logistics can happen without both parties agreeing to who is responsible to arrange and pay for the transportation that moves goods from point A to point B.

MANAGEMENT 101: THE GLOBAL SUPPLY CHAIN

Importers and exporters depend heavily on the professional support pro-vided by third-party expertise to move freight in the global supply chain.

Their expertise is quintessential to the movement of goods and services worldwide. The primary objectives in the movement of goods and services globally are safe, timely, and cost-effective deliveries.

The goal of logistics is to make these happen on a consistent, determinable and predictable basis. Using the correct Incoterms can also facilitate this to the benefit of both shippers and consignees worldwide. Shippers and consignees rely upon the expertise of their freight forwarder, customhouse broker, and third-party transportation provider to provide counsel and advice as to what Incoterms mitigate their risks and can best leverage opportunities to commercial benefit. That expertise is a very critical element of the expectation from principal companies to their transport providers. And this is a global expectation, whether you are based in and operate from Saudi Arabia; South Africa; South Bend, Indiana, USA; or the Sudan. If you use a freight forwarder, you expect it to comprehend Incoterms and know how to apply that expertise to the benefit of your logistics and shipment activity.

MANAGING INCOTERMS OPTIONS WITH FREIGHT FORWARDERS, CUSTOMHOUSE BROKERS, AND TRANSPORTATION INTERMEDIARIES

Principal import and export companies want to leverage their logistics and freight "spend." Additionally, they want to gain competitive advantage. But many companies who compete globally lack the expertise necessary in the area of freight, logistics, and the shipping of their goods, products, and services in world markets.

Freight forwarders and related companies have their place in the global supply chain as the support mechanism to the companies of the world in how freight moves internationally. They have developed an expertise in all aspects of international trade inclusive of Incoterms. There is a very reasonable expectation that quality experienced freight forwarders can guide their customer through the maze and challenges of global shipping, including Incoterms.

Transportation providers can lend Incoterms resources and expertise as follows:

- Advanced knowledge of Incoterms
- Global reach through office or agency network for local Incoterms knowledge and applications
- Global resources to execute various Incoterms options

Advanced Knowledge of Incoterms

A quality freight forwarder's sales, customer service, and operations should all have a basic working knowledge of Incoterms and the changes that were made in the 2010 edition. Larger providers typically will identify key personnel who are Incoterms experts providing internal Incoterms advice to the staff and also external advice to the principal import and export customers. Customers can rely on this expertise to navigate through the 13 Incoterms options of Edition 2000 and the 11 Incoterms options of Edition 2010. Keep in mind that some companies are still utilizing Incoterms 2000 in their global contracts.

Global Reach through Office or Agency Network for Local Incoterms Knowledge and Applications

While Incoterms are recognized as a global standard, some local and regional applications will vary. Often this information is critical in how freight moves through the supply chain and ultimately what Incoterms options are chosen. Freight forwarders and related transportation providers have a global reach through either an owned office structure, an agency network, or some combination of the two. All three are effective as long as the parties are reliable and competent. Forwarders rely on this structure to provide local expertise on all matters related to global import and export operations and procedures, customs formalities, dealing with carriers, and so forth.

Incoterms impact the decisions that are made in choosing providers and what they do for us in handling our import and export shipments. For example, if you are a manufacturer based in Buffalo, New York, and you decide to source raw materials for your manufacturing process in the Philippines and various components in China, you have various options in how you purchase from those suppliers. When you ask for prices from the suppliers, as an option you ask for three various terms of sale: Ex Works, free on board (FOB) outbound gateway, and cost, insurance, and freight (CIF) inbound gateway. Simultaneously, you ask your freight forwarder and customhouse broker as well to provide freight costs using the same Incoterms options. Now, once you receive the three quotes from the two suppliers in the Philippines and China, you are in a leveraged position to comparison shop.

After detailed analysis you have determined in communication and coordination with my forwarder and broker that a better option would place you in a more competitive position by purchasing through Ex Works the supplier's facilities and controlling the shipment from that point forward until it arrives at your manufacturing plant in Buffalo.

The role of the provider was twofold:

- Provide information that afforded you to compare costs with different Incoterms
- Assist in making the shipment happen

In another example, you are an exporter of fine chocolates and candies in Geneva, Switzerland. Your distributor in Mexico has found a new customer with a chain of sweet shops in Mexico and a distribution warehouse in Monterrey. While the customer has a great sales network, the sweet shop owners are not very sophisticated from a global supply chain capability perspective. They are interested in product from Switzerland but are very reticent about handling the import formalities and process in Mexico. They request a delivery duty paid (DDP) Incoterms; therefore, they are taken out of the import process, and the goods are cleared and delivered to their warehouse, with all export, logistics, and import formalities handled by the supplier.

The chocolate manufacturer is more than happy to handle the shipment this way, as it is planning to recover all its costs in the price and payment terms. It also uses the services of a very competent freight forwarder in Geneva, who handles other shipments on its behalf shipped DDP to various European countries, the United Sates, and even Japan. When it finally receives the purchase order from the company in Mexico, it contacts its forwarder to handle the shipment. The forwarder reaches out to its agent in Monterrey, where the goods will eventually be cleared and delivered. It is advised that it requires import permits, product registrations, and a local equivalent of a Tax ID number showing incorporation as a Mexican company.

These steps not only add significant cost to the import process but may not even be achievable, particularly with the responsibility of producing a local Tax ID number and showing incorporation in Mexico. In many countries around the world, import customhouse brokers can clear goods in their own name and become Importer of Record, but this is very difficult, if not impossible in Mexico. When the salesperson handling the new transaction is advised of this situation, he reaches out to the new customer in Monterrey to determine if it could amend the Incoterms to place the onus on it for import clearance in Mexico. The Mexican company is reluctant to handle this aspect of the transaction and now is threatening to cancel the purchase order.

The freight forwarder in Geneva is now aware of the dilemma. It provides a very workable resolution. Through its agent in Monterrey, it contacts the customer directly and offers to handle the import process on the customer's behalf. It will handle the entire license and permit process—the *piedmentos*—and will manage the import clearance and deliver process on the customer's behalf. It even offers to bill the exporter for the services, or the customer can pay it to the freight forwarder directly. The importer would have paid these costs in any scenario, as the exporter would have recovered these in its sales process and payment terms originally offered.

In this case the forwarder and agent in Monterrey have provided a very easy resolution to the choice of Incoterms, DDP, and have converted them to a CIP Term, but with local services making the DDP on a de facto basis in a situation that is unique to certain places in the world like Mexico, where the import process is best controlled by the importer or their hired local customhouse broker.

Global Resources to Execute Various Incoterms Options

Incoterms options require the exporter or importer to handle certain aspects of the entire shipping process:

- Pick-up
- Packing, marking, and labeling
- Consolidation

- Loading
- Domestic freight
- Export clearance
- International freight
- Import clearance
- Booking and paying carriers
- Banking
- Trade compliance responsibilities
- Duties, taxes, GST, and VAT payments
- Warehousing
- Deconsolidation
- Inland freight

The forwarder/broker/transport provider has the expertise on a global scale to manage all these responsibilities. The choice of Incoterms impacts all these areas of responsibility—either for the exporter or the importer. Most principal import and export companies totally rely on their provider to manage these tasks on their behalf and guide them through the maze of Incoterms options that reduce their risks and provide commercial advantage.

Consider another example of what a provider may offer in terms of INCO expertise. A German equipment manufacturer has made a product sale to a customer in Nairobi, Kenya. The customer is requesting a delivered at place (DAP) shipment delivered to its warehouse just outside of Nairobi. It will handle the clearance and payment of duties and taxes but requires the quoted price to include freight from origin in Frankfurt, Germany.

When the seller is getting ready to prepare the details of an export quote and to develop a pro forma export invoice with an outline of costs, it reaches out to its freight forwarder in Hamburg, Germany. The freight forwarder, in turn, reaches out to its agent in Kenya. Both agree that the clearance and local delivery should be controlled by the importer. They are concerned about the potential of graft and corruption in the import process that might require payments to officials to move the freight successfully from the inbound gateway at the port of Mombasa to the final destination in Nairobi.

As a reference point, every country in the world, at various ports and places at certain times, has various aspects of graft, corruption, in-kind payments, and gratuities to make things happen in the import and export process—some more than others, some with more certainty than others. This scenario is used only as an example and not a statement about all shipments moving in Kenya.

The forwarder in Hamburg, being knowledgeable about shipping to this part of the world and tied into the local information, strongly urged the seller or exporter to amend its Incoterms to a DAT price, where the goods get delivered at the terminal in Mombasa and not to final destination. This advice will reduce the risk to the seller in what might have ended up being the more difficult leg in this export transaction—Mombasa to Nairobi. This is now eliminated from the selling responsibility and handed over to the buyer, who may be in a much better position to mitigate risk and maximize the delivery process.

Advice, counsel, and prudent information on Incoterms, risks, and costs are what a relationship with a quality transportation provider are all about.

The following article was reprinted with permission from *Inbound Logistics* magazine, a U.S.-based professional monthly publication covering numerous transportation domestic and international topics from all aspects of managing supply global chains. This article addresses the use of the FOB Incoterms in an interesting and insightful way.

Managing Inbound Transportation: All on Board FOB˙

Joseph O'Reilly

Tire importer TBC Corporation converts its inbound transportation to free-on-board terms and rolls out a supply chain transformation.

Given global trade's complexity and volatile pace of change, it's hard to conceive how simply altering a few letters on an ocean bill of lading (BOL)

˙ O'Reilly, J. Managing Inbound Transportation: All on Board FOB. *Inbound Logistics*. 2011. Accessed from http://inboundlogistics.com/cms/article/managing-inbound-transportation-all-on-board-fob.

could radically change an organization's supply chain bearing. In the sea of everyday acronyms, Incoterms are adrift with countless other meanings. But on a BOL they mean everything.

Modifying Incoterms—the International Chamber of Commerce's commercial standards used to communicate the tasks, costs, and risks associated with transporting and delivering goods—isn't nearly as simple as playing alphabet roulette. It requires a deep commitment to supply chain business process change, often at the behest of a third-party partner or the directive of new leadership—sometimes both.

This was the reality for Palm Beach Gardens, Florida-based TBC Corporation, a subsidiary of Sumitomo Corporation of America, one of Japan's major integrated trading enterprises. TBC is the nation's largest vertically integrated marketer of tires for the automotive replacement market, with retail operations under the Tire Kingdom, Merchant's Tire & Auto Centers, National Tire & Battery, and Big O Tires brands. The company also operates as a wholesaler to regional tire chains and distributors throughout North America.

When Jim Markey came on board in 2005 as vice president of logistics, he discovered a supply chain approach that was counter-intuitive to his previous experience managing transportation and logistics for various tire manufacturers, including Yokohama.

"TBC procured most of its shipments from suppliers on a Delivered Duty Paid (DDP) basis," Markey recalls. "TBC does a lot of customer-direct container shipping, and the total cost of delivering goods to the customer was included in the price."

Because TBC's suppliers are tire experts, not shipping experts, freight costs were not being managed as efficiently as they could have been. "I argued that the volatility in ocean freight rates—which account for 10 percent of our total cost—makes it more sensible to directly control that spend," Markey explains.

"When working with suppliers, you have to keep an ear to the ground and understand market trends," Markey says. "Why not bite the bullet and control costs, rather than negotiate with suppliers?"

In 2009, TBC partnered with Atlanta-based non-vessel operator (NVO) American Global Logistics (AGL) to help convert its inbound shipping terms to free-on-board (FOB) and proactively manage its transportation costs.

A NEW NVO ORDER

Companies that buy on a landed cost basis pay the price of the goods and the transportation. When freight rates rise, the total swells accordingly. But when they drop, there's no guarantee suppliers will prorate that cost.

"We've seen swings of $1,500 per container within six months for shipments to the East Coast," says Chad Rosenberg, CEO of American Global Logistics. "When you're moving several thousand containers a year, that fluctuation creates considerable opportunity for cost savings."

AGL specializes in moving furniture from Asia to the United States. But the tire industry also fits well within its value proposition. The intermediary banks on large accounts that place a premium on service, which isn't the typical NVO model.

AGL's average client moves more than 1,000 40-foot equivalent units every year—more in line with what a steamship line does than an NVO.

"We bring value to companies that ship containers direct to many customers, rather than several thousand containers to one distribution center," says Rosenberg. "These shippers and their customers have specific demands, delivery windows, and challenges."

TBC was a good fit for AGL because it runs a complex operation, and ships all over the United States and North America. It also gave AGL a clean slate to work with.

"We evaluated our best practices and TBC's needs, then worked from origin to destination to offer documentation, visibility, and carrier selection recommendations," Rosenberg says. "TBC gave us the opportunity to provide a total solution that might not have been possible if we were working with a more mature inbound practitioner."

Controlling inbound transportation is an established trend among direct importers with large-item quantities that fill containers. But companies are growing more sophisticated.

"Tire and furniture industry end users are now dictating how freight moves, as well as negotiating with vendors to be the importer of record," Rosenberg explains. "They want the control, but not the liability and risk."

This is exactly what TBC aspired to do. FOB terms ensure suppliers use carriers "nominated by the buyer," as *Incoterms 2010* stipulates. Cost and risk are divided when the goods are onboard the vessel, and the seller must clear them for export.

"As a tire distributor with a relatively high liability risk for the product, we try to limit being the importer of record," says Markey. "We arrange for our suppliers to pay all expenses involved in moving product to us—for example, insurance—apart from the freight cost. We haven't completely unbundled the FOB; we take a hybrid approach."

While there is occasional resistance from suppliers that count on TBC's volume to leverage their own discounted rates with carriers, there are generally opportunities for compromise.

"In the past, we have offered AGL's rates to our suppliers," Markey says. "It's still an arm's-length deal, but it helps soften some concerns about taking away their freight. You can't do that unless you deal with an NVO that has attractive pricing."

FOB FYI

While Rosenberg acknowledges that he has never entered an FOB conversion where cost wasn't the top priority, managing inbound transportation at point of origin unleashes a flood of efficiencies downstream in the supply chain.

"Shippers want to dictate carrier selection, transit and idle time, and transport mode," he says. "They can have visibility to all those decisions by controlling the flow of goods."

For example, consignees can operate a drop-and-hook system if they have enough volume and control over who transports the freight. When vendors dictate transportation, it becomes more complex, almost necessitating live unloads. Once they load the container at the point of origin, the invoice is on the way.

Companies such as TBC derive great value integrating with NVOs, especially in terms of direct input regarding bookings and shipment tracking.

"We have been able to integrate that information all the way to accounts payable," says Markey. "When we started out, AGL sent us paper invoices. Now, data enters directly into our system daily. The system provides granular data that helps us quickly and easily slice and dice ocean freight and drayage costs, or bills for detention per diem."

AGL provides visibility to this information on its website. It also has an iPhone application customers can use to track a hot shipment. This level of transparency opens up even more opportunities to reduce costs.

"We just constructed a 1.1-million-square-foot warehouse in Charleston, S.C.," Markey says. "We would typically have included drayage as part of the ocean freight rate, but we've broken that cost out so we can negotiate with trucking companies independently, and focus on service as much as cost. That gives us more flexibility unloading and moving containers, and helps us avoid accessorial charges."

In the ocean trade, volatility is a given. Even with rates stabilizing recently as a consequence of surplus oceangoing capacity and continuing recessionary dips in trade, other factors keep logisticians such as Markey busy.

In 2009, the Obama Administration imposed a 35-percent duty on certain types of tires coming out of China, which makes importing cost-prohibitive for many manufacturers and distributors.

"Chinese production is being re-sourced to Japan—where we originally procured tires—and to countries in Southeast Asia," notes Markey.

TBC now receives shipments from Japan, Indonesia, Thailand, and India. Markey has been busy exploring how the company must adapt when the Panama Canal expansion opens. He was involved in the decision to locate the new DC in Charleston. Change is fluid within TBC's supply chain.

Working with AGL has enabled the importer to cut costs by capitalizing on its buying leverage and managing inbound freight on an FOB basis. But it's the value-adds and non-commoditized service intangibles—be it a hot alert on an iPhone or a better drayage contract—that make this partnership a competitive differentiator.

The article points out how manipulation of the Incoterms can provide real value in this very true example from a company that depends upon imports into the United States from the Far East as its lifeblood of business. It demonstrates how control over the freight purchase by using Incoterms that provide that control to the buyer clearly affords them opportunity to reduce costs that impact as much as 10% of their total landed costs. It also points out how a company that pays attention to all the details and components of the "spend" to bring goods to point of use or point of value (i.e., the landed costs) can make a favorable difference in competitive advantage.

Case studies in this chapter demonstrate examples taken from our archives of how companies can impact costs and risk by controlling the correct Incoterms. The company in the article in Palm Beach Gardens, Florida, clearly took the time and developed the expertise to understand what steps it could take to leverage the choice of Incoterms to commercial advantage. It also worked with its transportation providers and carriers to secure competitive freight rates. Additionally, it brought all its suppliers and vendors into agreements that they all derived benefit from to create win–win sales and purchase scenarios, which impacted global transactions favorably for all parties.

Congratulations to the management team at TBC for insightfulness and the capability to make good Incoterms choices to make its business grow, thrive, and sustain.

3

Incoterms: Foundation of Global Trade

A key to mastering global trade is to master the foundation issues. Incoterms® are one of those issues and are often misunderstood or overlooked. This chapter provides the basic profile and overview of the International Commercial Terms and outlines all the underlying issues in global trade and how Incoterms impact all global transactions. We must first dissect, analyze, and understand what we eventually desire to control, leverage, and master.

FUNCTIONAL DEFINITION AND USE

Incoterms are

- Point in time and trade
  - Responsibility
  - Liability

- Transfer
  - Seller <-> Buyer
  - Importer <-> Exporter
- Costs and Risks

Incoterms are interpreted at a point in time and trade between a seller and a buyer in international business where the responsibility and liability pass between the parties. The original intent of these terms was to provide a uniform and consistent reference point for exporters and importers to use when determining when and where this exchange took place. It was imperative to understand this point in time and trade as it attempted to provide a reference point in defining costs and risks to both parties. As Incoterms evolved through the years to the current 2010 edition, these points are still valid, though the structure, options, and meanings have altered.

In the past and now, understanding these costs impacts decision-making regarding various aspects of the transaction, such as price, logistics, payment options, and title transfer. Managing these decisions eventually impacts a company's ability to make the trade and transactions profitable, competitive, and ultimately sustainable. The focus of the balance of this book is to provide how Incoterms relate to all these peripheral areas of an international business relationship, so that your company can stay out of trouble. More importantly, however, it shows how to best leverage options that place your company in the most competitive arena.

When Incoterms were updated in 2010, I came to a much greater awareness that Incoterms are not an "end-all" to an international commercial transaction but rather are a starting point or reference point for the seller and buyer to utilize to manage cost and risk. Incoterms are a serious issue. I always provide the warning that they must be read in a *detailed way*. What I mean is that you have to read the prologue, opening pages, definitions, and so forth before you read the leading Incoterms reference page. Then you must continue to read the following pages to obtain full details and their intent and use.

It is imperative when you read the *Incoterms 2010* book that you are focused and disciplined. It is not a single page. It is the sum of all the pages, words, explanations, and intents that can be grasped only by thorough and comprehensive reading, analysis and contemplation. I have also found that you may need to read it several times, maybe 10 times before you get it. I also have learned about specific Incoterms, by reading about other terms where references are made back and forth, that make gray areas a little clearer.

This book will demonstrate clearly that

- There are wide misconceptions about Incoterms.
- Most companies and global personnel do not know how to navigate Incoterms.
- Most companies and personnel begin to grasp Incoterms only once a problem has raised its ugly head and certainly not proactively.
- The companies and individuals that master Incoterms then master global trade.

Some examples of the misconceptions of Incoterms are as follows:

- They are part of the law in most countries.
- They are a complete global transaction from sale through to payment and defining aspect of a sale or purchase.
- They calculate when "title or ownership" transfers between the parties.
- They have merit in domestic transportation.
- While they attempt to identify "risk," they clearly regulate insurance responsibilities.
- They identify what parties are responsible for trade compliance responsibilities to the government agencies regulating the export–import transaction.
- They define origin and delivery points by default.
- They provide a clear costing model to both the seller and buyer.
- FOB has use in our domestic business model in all countries.

All these examples demonstrate areas in which Incoterms are thought to be a solution. However, more likely they are really only a reference point, and a lot more should be considered and ultimately done to protect cost and risk to both parties. When we say *done*, we mean actions should be taken by both or either party in how the transaction is constructed and agreed to, by contract (typically sales or purchase order). Both parties have numerous options on how the deal is constructed. How they construct the deal will truly determine costs and risks. This book provides the blueprint to see how best we elect those options that put our company in the most leveraged, competitive scenario. In exports typically sales personnel take leads to an eventual export order.

In imports, typically purchasing takes the lead on purchase orders. It is at that time in the process of the global trade that this critical element of Incoterms comes into play. Incoterms are often a very misunderstood aspect of trade. Many global supply chair personnel supported by company protocols relate Incoterms to insurance, freight, transfer of title, ownership, and revenue recognition, when in fact they are connected to all these issues with a dotted line but are very much "independent" functions that impact sales and purchase agreements very differently. The following issues crop up when creating a purchase or sales order:

- Terms of sale
- Terms of payment
- How freight is handled
- How insurance and risk are managed
- When and how title or ownership is transferred
- How and when "revenue" gets recognized
- Who is responsible for trade compliance issues
- Legal jurisdiction
- How disputes are settled
- How company tax issues (IRS or equivalent) are mitigated
- Packaging, marking, and labeling
- Intellectual property rights (IPRs)

The connection among all these issues is that they impact cost and risk for the buyer and seller, importer and exporter, and potentially all the parties engaged in the transaction. They impact the ultimate profit for the transaction and in the long-term set the stage for future potential or demise. Additionally, we recognize that Incoterms both by design and default are really only a reference point in an international transaction. The seller and buyer must look at the nuances of the transaction and write their contractual agreements to mirror these nuances and make a best attempt to proactively "handle" the matter within the written language of the documentation.

That means that Incoterms are not necessarily an "end all" but only a starting point for gaining common ground in a trade or transaction. The final agreement is supposed to reflect the Incoterms plus a clearer indication of what else would need to be agreed to. The following summarizes some of the contractual issues that are covered in more detail throughout the following chapters in this book.

Terms of Sale

The terms of sale are the Incoterms where risk and costs are distinguished as a point in time where that transfer occurs between the seller (the exporter) and the buyer (the importer). ExWorks, free on board (FOB), cost, insurance, and freight (CIF), and delivery duty paid (DDP) are the most common terms used in global trade. The Incoterms outline responsibility and liability boundaries between sellers and buyers (exporters and importers) as a standard of cost and risk in a contractual obligation typically found in sales or purchase orders. Incoterms are set by choice, default, or trade practice. In any method they become part of the agreement between two or more parties that deal with a multitude of issues involved with logistics, insurance, and the passage of risk and costs.

Terms of Payment

How money is transferred between the buyer and the seller is how we determine payment methods: for example, drafts, L/Cs, or consignment. This is regardless of what Incoterms is used. But as this will appear in Chapter 5, we show how payment will impact risk to an exporter well beyond the Incoterms used.

How Freight Is Handled

Freight is addressed in the Incoterms, but because we can make other arrangements in the actual sales or purchase agreement we will tend to impact ultimately how freight is handled in an international transaction. For example, we can always make freight prepaid or collect. We can always amend Incoterms to include loading or movement to a forwarder, for example.

How Insurance and Risk Are Managed

Risk is determined by the Incoterms chosen. However, when other parameters are raised in how a contract is ultimately structured, this can impact how risk is perceived and realized to either the seller or the buyer. An example outlined in detail in Chapter 5 entails a FOB export sale where the buyer has payment terms after the goods arrive at its facility overseas. The goods are lost or damaged, and the customer refuses to make payment in full, citing that some of the goods arrived lost or damaged. The exporter now has a risk of loss or damage after delivery on-board an ocean-going vessel, contrary to the intent of the Incoterms FOB because they have not yet received payment.

When and How Title or Ownership Is Transferred

Title is not controlled by Incoterms. It has to be addressed elsewhere in the contract of sale or purchase. We recommend that "title" or "ownership" not be passed to the buyer until payment in full has been achieved against the seller's performance to deliver.

How and When Revenue Gets Recognized

This is discussed in Chapter 6 in detail. Revenue recognition is different in every country, and the controlling body that impacts accounting regulations—for example, IRS, SEC, QI, DGDDI, EU, or HM are revenue-generating agencies of some countries, to name a few governing bodies. The issue gets more convoluted for companies with similar ownership shipping internationally between common parties.

Who Is Responsible for Trade Compliance Issues

Incoterms do state which party to the transaction is responsible for either export or import formalities. This could be part of the overall trade compliance responsibilities, which differ greatly from one country to another. The events of 9/11 have greatly impacted the trade compliance and security guidelines for shipping to and from the United States. The 2010 Incoterms edition was greatly enhanced when it included trade compliance and security initiatives into its definitions. More specifically, this relates to the importer's security filing (ISF) for inbound freight into the United States from overseas origins. It requires the seller in the foreign country of origin to provide information to the buyer in the United States in regard to customs clearance date prior to the goods being loaded on-board the ocean-going vessel destined for a U.S. Port of Entry. The new Incoterms now includes these security concerns as part of a seller's or buyer's responsibility in the transaction.

Legal Jurisdiction

All contracts should have a provision not influenced by the choice of Incoterms that outlines what jurisdictions the contract is written in and what regulatory bodies are involved in managing the contractual obligations. Examples of countries that would be influenced by local laws are the Arab Republic of Egypt, the United States, United Kingdom, and the People's Republic of China.

How Disputes Are Settled

All contracts need to have provisions on where disputes will be settled. This usually will tie into jurisdiction, but not necessarily so. For example, a contract between a Belgian and an Italian company may have contractual wording that settles disputes in arbitration in Zurich, Switzerland. An export from France to Japan may entail both parties agreeing that if a dispute arises it will be settled in Japan. Settlement is a negotiated issue that eventually both parties must agree on rather than committing it to writing as part of their sales or purchase contract/agreement. This area has no direct relationship to the Incoterms used.

How Company Tax Issues (IRS or Equivalent) Are Mitigated

Taxes are determined typically by the country or governing body where the transaction is occurring. This is covered in more detail in Chapter 6. If they become part of a sale or purchase contract, that would typically be referring to who has the obligation to pay value-added tax (VAT), goods and service tax (GST), or other related charges. There are also tax issues relating to how the government taxes a company for profits, such as the Internal Revenue Service in the United States, which is potentially impacted by how sales and purchases are structured inclusive of the use of Incoterms. While the Incoterms used address this in their intent to provide cost and risk to certain point in time, most companies have learned from experience that they are better off in most contracts to outline in detail who is responsible for any taxes or duties—particularly those where refunds are available, such as with VAT and GST. Tax issues in global trade are typically complex, with lots of interpretation and leeway as to how the regulations apply. It is critical to obtain tax assistance from professionals such as lawyers, accountants, and consultants. A decision on one end of a transaction on what Incoterms to use may impact the tax implications for the other party, making collaboration between sellers and buyers imperative.

Packaging, Marking, and Labeling

Packing, marking, and labeling are discussed in Incoterms, but the issue is really not made as clear as it should be. First of all, Incoterms do not address stowage or handling at all. They do mention packing to comply with any requirements under the contract of sale and those fit for transportation, but they do not define either one. Parties to the contract of sale or purchase need to outline in detail exactly what the shipper needs to do to properly pack, mark, and label the goods for the transit and customs access to that market. This is discussed in more detail in Chapter 7. When transport conveyances such as ocean and air containers are used, it is important to add guidance and instruction on cargo stowage, blocking, and bracing.

Intellectual Property Rights

The protection of patents, trademarks, and other proprietary rights is not addressed by Incoterms. It is necessary for those entering the sales or purchase agreement to address these very specifically. Companies engaged in global trade also must be aware of how local governments deal with IPR issues and how they support the protection of IPR matters for foreign entities doing business in their country. This is covered in more detail in Chapter 5 and is another important component of global trade that is not addressed by Incoterms.

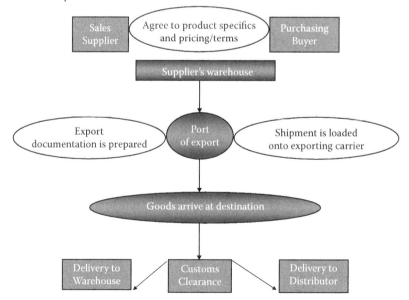

Pictorial outlines the basic flow of a global transaction.

Additionally, all the related parties to the transaction will be impacted by the choice of the Incoterms, such as the following:

- The banker

- The insurance company
- The carriers

- Service providers, such as third party, freight forwarders, and customhouse brokers

- Truckers
- Warehouse workers

The list is expanded on by the nature of the transaction, trade lanes, and commodity and product nuances, for example. All of these impact the right choice of Incoterms, but all can be affected both favorably and adversely. These related companies are all impacted in various ways. For example, a banker who is managing a Letter of Credit on an export transaction has to review the presented documents prior to making payment to the beneficiary party. The quality of those documents relates to individual parties to the transaction "cutting" those documents according to the sales contract or purchase order, which should include the Incoterms agreed. The Incoterms will outline who would be the responsible party to "cut" those documents and assure banking compliance. Both the bank and the exporter–importer could face various risks, such as no delivery, nonpayment, and fiduciary exposure to the bank, for an L/C transaction that becomes mishandled. Typically, customer-based routed transactions, where the buyer controls the outbound freight forwarding and choice of forwarder and carrier, could present certain exposures to the seller (exporter) when it has a hard time getting paid because documents were not done correctly or a shipment does not make delivery on time when the seller depended upon the buyer's choices of provider and carrier to perform. An insurance company may have certain exposures under the shipper's cargo policies where it believed that risk transferred along with the Incoterms interpretation but actually was extended because the shipper did not get paid after affecting delivery.

WHAT WE NEED TO KNOW ABOUT INCOTERMS
TO OBTAIN BETTER COMMERCIAL ADVANTAGES

Paris: Home of the ICC and Incoterms

Background and History

Incoterms were recently updated in September 2010, which took effect on January 1, 2011. To move forward on understanding how best to manage Incoterms for the purpose of creating competitive advantage, we need to review the history.

Incoterms in the modern form first showed up in 1921. The International Chamber of Commerce, located in Paris, France, took the lead in bringing a global solution to the meaning of these terms, which at that time had different meanings in the various countries that partook in global trade. FOB in the United States meant one thing, and in Germany it meant another. CIF in China had one interpretation, and in Brazil it had another. Uniformity was sorely lacking.

The Original Drafting Group Members at the ICC in Paris had the vision that the world was going to get smaller and that global trade would dominate business. There was a very definite need to provide a "standard" in numerous international business issues—contracts, banking, and customs and trading terms, to name a few areas. Incoterms addressed the area of trade and taking common words (e.g., FOB, CIF) and brought them to some global standard.

In 1948, when the United Nations (UN) began to first develop, the ICC used its clout to create some authority for a standard and uniformity to be established for and distribute for the benefit of the trading world. Today the foundation exists so that most countries that belong to the UN will use and recognize Incoterms in their international transactions.

It is important to note that there are no recognized rules or governance that require Incoterms to be used in the international arena. They have become a recognized favored option in international business and are well managed by the ICC in Paris. The terms become part of law and legal jurisdiction when they become part of an international contract of sale or purchase that does have legal standing.

The first set of Incoterms, which were created in 1936, remained in use for almost 20 years before their second publication in 1953. Additional amendments and expansions followed in 1967, 1976, 1980, 1990, and 2000. The eighth and current version—*Incoterms 2010*—was published on January 1, 2010, and went into effect on January 1, 2011. Does that mean every company needs to convert to the 2010 edition now? The answer is no. But what is important as we transition from the 2000 to the 2010 edition is that in our contracts of sale and purchase we reference which set we are using—either 2000 or 2010. We will discuss later in this chapter, under "Best Practices," that most companies should integrate the 2010 Incoterms into their supply chains within 18 to 24 months and should ensure that their suppliers, customers, and service providers are all notified when the change takes effect.

Chapter 4 outlines how best to incorporate "training" of the new Incoterms into the company's standard operating procedures, protocols, and governance. Public companies in the United States need to be aware that there are numerous doctrines under Sarbanes–Oxley (SOX) requiring incorporation of the new Incoterms in an expedited and comprehensive fashion. This is further discussed in Chapter 5. Keep in mind that we need to gain a comprehensive understanding of Incoterms to create opportunities on leveraging them.

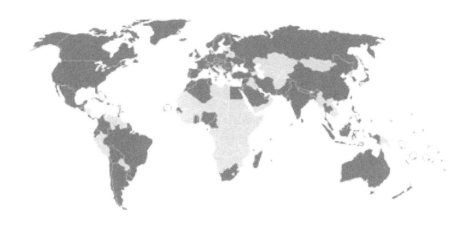

INCOTERM MEMBER COUNTRIES

UN Convention on Contracts for the International Sale of Goods

The United Nations has adopted a treaty that over 70 countries, including the United States but not Great Britain, that offers uniform international sales regulations. It does not incorporate Incoterms into its guidelines but references the "shipping terms" to be used in international contracts of sale and purchase and identifies, for example, FOB and CIF. As of August 2010, this treaty had been ratified by the 77 countries that account for the majority of global trade.

The UN Convention on Contracts for the International Sale of Goods (CISG) allows exporters to avoid choice of legal jurisdiction as the CISG offers accepted substantive rules on which contracting parties, courts, and arbitrators may rely on which was developed by the UN Commission on International Trade Law (UNCITRAL) and was signed in Vienna in 1980. Following ratification by 11 countries in 1980, CISG has been regarded as a success for UNCITRAL because the convention has since been accepted by countries worldwide.

Countries that have ratified the CISG are referred to within the treaty as "Contracting States." Unless excluded by the express terms of a contract, the CISG is deemed to be incorporated into (and supplant) any otherwise applicable domestic laws with respect to a transaction in goods between parties from different Contracting States. Of the uniform law conventions, the CISG has been described as having a huge and favorable impact on global trade offering uniformity and a legal reference point for companies trading globally.

CISG has been successful in global trade as it allows uniformity, legality, and at the same time flexibility in member states to use only portions where applicable. A number of countries that have signed the CISG have made declarations and reservations as to the treaty's scope, though the vast majority (55 of the current 76 Contracting States) has chosen to accede to the convention without any reservations.

Lawyers who are involved in global contracts and traders who enter into sales and purchase agreements with complexity are urged to become familiar with CISG and its application to their business models for themselves or their clients. There is more reference material on CIGS in the Appendix to this book.

Issues in World Governance

Hundreds of agreements are made that are applicable on a multilateral basis. Some, but not all, impact some aspects of global trade. They also will impact the decision-making options we have when choosing how we construct all the agreements and contracts in our global supply chains. This will eventually lead us to the details involved with what are the best Incoterms options we have to gain commercial advantage in our import and export transactions.

Any person engaged in global trade has to have a working knowledge of all the country-specific and political mandates that will potentially impact the various factors affecting the business issues in that part of the world. Business is all about making decisions. The more informed we are and the better we are able to evaluate all aspects of the international business arena including government regulations and politics, the better position we are in to make quality decisions. Many of these decisions we make involve how we construct contractual sales or purchase agreements, of which a key ingredient is the Incoterms.

We now have 11 options. Free trade agreements, treaties, government organizations, protocols, and conventions all affect how "trade" is accomplished. When we choose a specific Incoterm, this places certain responsibilities and liabilities on either party as the importer or the exporter to the transaction. Our choice of Incoterms may introduce uncertain risk or create opportunity. We need to know the difference to make the best decision for our supply chain to function at its best.

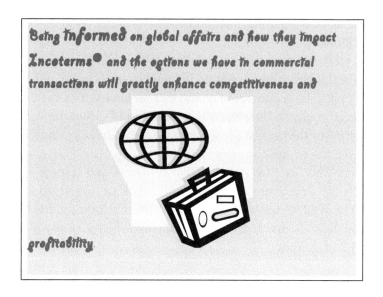

Being informed on global affairs and how they impact Incoterms® and the options we have in commercial transactions will greatly enhance competitiveness and profitability.

Governmental Profiles

World Customs Organization (WCO)

WCO aids the national economic wealth and social protection of its members by promoting honest, transparent, and predictable customs. Established in 1952 as the Customs Co-operation Council, the WCO is an independent intergovernmental body whose mission is to enhance the effectiveness and efficiency of customs administrations. With 151 member governments, it is the only inter governmental worldwide organization competent in customs matters.

Organization for the Prohibition of Chemical Weapons (OPCW)

The mission of OPCW is to implement the provisions of the Chemical Weapons Convention to achieve the OPCW's vision of a world free of chemical weapons and a world in which cooperation in chemistry for peaceful purposes for all is fostered. In doing this, their ultimate aim is to contribute to international security and stability, general and complete disarmament, and global and economic development.

Convention on International Trade in Endangered Species of Wild Flora and Fauna (CITES)

CITES was formed in 1975 and now has a membership of 152 countries, which act by banning commercial international trade in an agreed list of endangered species and by regulating and monitoring trade in others that might become endangered.

Montreal Protocol

The Montreal Protocol on Substances that Deplete the Ozone Layer is a landmark international agreement designed to protect the stratospheric ozone layer. The treaty was originally signed in 1987 and stipulates that the production and consumption of compounds that deplete ozone in the stratosphere are to be phased out.

Organization for Economic Cooperation and Development (OECD)

The OECD groups 30 countries in an organization that, most importantly, provides governments a setting in which to discuss, develop, and perfect economic and social policy. They compare experiences; seek answers to common problems; and work to coordinate domestic and international policies that increasingly, in today's global economy, must form a web of even practice across nations.

Wassenaar Arrangement

This agreement was established to contribute to regional and international security and stability by promoting transparency and greater responsibility in transfers of conventional arms and dual-use goods and technologies, thus preventing destabilizing accumulations. Participating states, France included, will seek, through their national policies, to ensure that transfers of these items do not contribute to the development or enhancement of military capabilities that undermine these goals and are not diverted to support such capabilities.

When we choose an Incoterm, this agreement above all could potentially impact both the risks and costs for the importers and exporters who engage in trade that crosses international borders.

Some acts occur in one country and impact all countries that do business with that country.

The Lacey Act

The Lacey Act (16 U.S.C. 3371 et seq., the Act) as amended makes it unlawful to import, export, transport, sell, receive, acquire, or purchase in interstate or foreign commerce any plant, with some limited exceptions, taken or traded in violation of the laws of the United States, a U.S. state or a foreign country. On September 2, 2009, the U.S. Department of Agriculture (USDA) Animal and Plant Health Inspection Service (APHIS) published a notice in the Federal Register announcing a revised enforcement phase in plan for the act's requirement for a plant product import declaration (see 74 Fed. Reg. 45415 for details); (USDA: Animal and Plant Health Inspection Service). The revised plan identifies a list of products and the associated Harmonized Tariff Schedule (HTS) Chapter or Heading for which the requirement for a Plant Product Declaration Form (PPQ 505) is anticipated to be enforced.

Nuclear Non-Proliferation Treaty (NPT)

Participation in the Nuclear Non-Proliferation Treaty

The Treaty on the Non-Proliferation of Nuclear Weapons is a landmark international treaty whose objective is to prevent the spread of nuclear weapons and weapons technology, to promote cooperation in the peaceful uses of nuclear energy, and to further the goal of achieving nuclear disarmament and general and complete disarmament. Opened for signature in 1968, the treaty entered into force in 1970. On May 11, 1995, it was extended indefinitely. A total of 190 parties have joined the treaty, including the five nuclear-weapon countries of the United States, Russia, the United Kingdom, France, and China (also the five permanent members of the United Nations Security Council). More countries have ratified the NPT than any other arms limitation and disarmament agreement, a testament to the treaty's significance. Four non-parties to the treaty are known or believed to possess nuclear weapons: India, Pakistan, and North Korea have openly tested and declared that they possess nuclear weapons, while Israel has had a policy of opacity regarding its own nuclear weapons program. North Korea acceded to the treaty in 1985, but never came into compliance, and announced its withdrawal in 2003. The NPT consists of a preamble and 11 articles. Although the concept of "pillars" is not expressed anywhere in the NPT, the treaty is nevertheless sometimes interpreted as a *three-pillar* system, with an implicit balance among them:

1. Nonproliferation
2. Disarmament
3. The right to peacefully use nuclear technology

The NPT is often seen to be based on a central bargain. According to the treaty: "the NPT non-nuclear-weapon states agree never to acquire nuclear weapons and the NPT nuclear-weapon states in exchange agree to share the benefits of peaceful nuclear technology and to pursue nuclear disarmament aimed at the ultimate elimination of their nuclear arsenals." The treaty is reviewed every five years in meetings called Review Conferences of the Parties to the Treaty of Non-Proliferation of Nuclear Weapons. Even though the treaty was originally conceived with a limited duration of 25 years, the signing parties decided, by consensus, to extend the treaty indefinitely and without conditions during the Review Conference in New York City on May 11, 1995.

In 2012 this treaty remains a very difficult global protocol to enforce and maintain governance over. Any company that manufacturers nuclear or nuclear-related products and sells to global markets is impacted by the edicts and regulatory implications under this global treaty. This might impact an Incoterms decision in the following way.

An American company based in Salt Lake City, Utah, manufactures power adapters for regulating nuclear power equipment in nuclear power plants. It has just received an order from a company in Russia for five units. This product is controlled by the U.S. Department of Commerce Export Regulations. The manufacturer goes through the necessary process to obtain an export license. After a rigorous export license application, the license is obtained. The license requires that the exporter obtain proof of delivery to the specific consignee listed in the export license. The manufacturer, after careful deliberation, decides to use the DDP Incoterms because that will provide the best control over the export and import process to assure that delivery is made under the export license requirements.

The treaty causes U.S. government action, which then causes an export license protocol. That process requires control over the delivery process. Control over the delivery process causes a decision to be made to use the DDP Term. There is a direct and indirect link between a global treaty and the choice of Incoterms between a seller and a buyer. While other options exist, this choice is believed to present the best opportunities to mitigate the risks associated with failure of the manufacturer to meet U.S. government export license protocols put in place for the following reasons:

- The nature of the product
- The destination
- The consignee
- The logistics of how freight moves in this supply chain
- Export license requirements

The business executives who make these arrangements—from marketing to sales to customer service to operations to logistics, and including legal and finance—all need to have this basic knowledge of world affairs so they can apply it to the very detailed decisions on how freight is moved globally. There is "connectivity" in the company that needs to take place, with everyone backing each other up to both avoid risk and assure profitable global operations.

An example of a major disaster for a U.S. company can be found in Gibson Guitars.* Based in Nashville, Tennessee, as reported by several news sources it is being carefully watched by many trade professionals and practitioners. In 2011, federal agents raided the Gibson Guitar Corporation in Nashville for the second time in several years. A Gibson facility was raided, although it's believed to be related to a prior raid at the same facility in November 2009, for possible violations of the Lacey Act. The Lacey Act is a federal environmental law that prohibits importing endangered plants and wildlife. It was amended in 2009 to also include wood products.

---

* Sources include http://www.joc.com, http://www.cbp.gov, and http://www.inboundlogistics.com.

During the raid in 2011, federal agents seized materials, files, and computers from the plant on allegations that a rare ebony wood from Madagascar was illegally used at the factory. No charges were ever filed.

Wednesday morning, several hundred employees at the facility were first evacuated.

"We were just in our department and one of the supervisors just come in [sic] and said everybody get out and we just shut the machines off and headed out the door," one employee who did want to be identified said.

They were later told to go home after being allowed to reenter the building to collect their belongings.

The Gibson Guitar facility in Memphis was also raided by federal authorities Wednesday morning.

In a statement released after the event, Gibson said they are "fully cooperating with agents of the U.S. Fish and Wildlife Service as it pertains to an issue with harvested wood."

The statement continued, "Gibson is a chain of custody certified buyer who purchases wood from legal suppliers who are to follow all standards. Gibson Guitar Chairman and CEO sits on the board of the Rainforest Alliance and takes the issue of certification very seriously. The company will continue to cooperate fully and assist our federal government with all inquiries and information."

I believe that Gibson will be eventually be exonerated and a resolve will be made favorable to the company. But the case itself clearly makes the point about chain of custody as well as responsibility and liability, which we know that Incoterms help dictate. The choice of the Incoterms has a potential impact on how this situation will play out and, in future situations, will be a very delicate area where these types of wood products crossing international borders are involved. It brings into the Incoterms "equation of options"—that the nature of the product, where it originates from, and the rules around its sale and use could impact the decision on which Incoterms a seller and buyer might consider.

In this case, Gibson may have elected to take itself out of the inbound supply chain and found a domestic source that had already imported the goods or purchased the goods on a DDP basis, where the seller would have taken the risks and costs of customs clearance in the United States. As ultimate consignee, Gibson may still have had some responsibility and risk but may have been removed from some of the cross fire.

Any party selling or involved in the supply chain of goods protected under various government regulations needs to think out the Incoterms option very carefully, as the risks of government scrutiny could be much greater than the potential rewards. In some instances, Incoterms providing "control" may be warranted to assure that all aspects of the transaction are done correctly: for example, documentation, classification, origination, record-keeping, valuation. In other instances, the choice of the Incoterms would provide others control so they bear the responsibility and risks, where that party may be more suitable to handle. In either case, one needs to factor in a lot more information when certain tenuous products are involved.

Australian Quarantine and Inspection Service (AQIS) Laws

Another example looks at Australian import regulations governed under its AQIS regulatory laws. The AQIS is primarily concerned with ensuring that dangerous or illegal goods don't enter Australia. While dangerous goods include items such as weapons and explosives, "dangerous" can also mean food, plant material, and animal products that can harm the environment or agriculture in Australia. It is important to know the customs regulations prior to importing anything into Australia, as AQIS officers screen all flights, passengers, baggage, mail, and cargo before materials are allowed into the country. If you export to Australia, your basic knowledge of these laws may impact how you sell or what Incoterms you choose.

Items You Must Declare When Importing or Traveling or Shipping to Australia

According to AQIS, you must declare the following items as they may be prohibited in Australia: dried fruit and vegetables; instant noodles and rice; packaged meals; herbs and spices; herbal and traditional medicines, remedies, tonics and herbal teas; snack foods, biscuits, cakes and confectionery; black tea, coffee and other beverages; infant formula (must be accompanying a child); airline food/snacks; dairy products (fresh and powdered) including milk, cheese, and "non-dairy" creamers, and airline food containing dairy, including milk, yogurt, and sandwiches containing cheese; all whole, dried and powdered eggs, egg products that contain more than 10 percent egg as an ingredient, homemade egg products including noodles and pasta that are not commercially manufactured; all uncanned meat from all animal species, sausages, salami, sliced meats, airline food, pet food, rawhide articles, and handicrafts including drums; cereal grains, popping corn, raw nuts, pine cones, birdseed, unidentified seeds, some commercially packaged seeds, ornaments including seeds; all fresh and frozen fruit and vegetables; mammals, birds, birds' eggs and nests, fish, reptiles, amphibians, and insects, feathers, bones, horns, tusks, wool, animal hair, skins, hides and furs, stuffed animals and birds; shells and coral (including jewelry and souvenirs); bee products including honey, beeswax, and honeycomb; used animal equipment including cages, biological specimens; craft and hobby lines made from animal or plant material; used sporting and camping equipment, used freshwater watercraft or fishing equipment; potted/bare rooted plants, cuttings, roots, bulbs, corms, stems, and other viable plant material, banana products; souvenirs made with or filled with straw, wooden articles and carvings including painted or lacquered items, items that include bark, artifacts, handicrafts, and souvenirs made from plant material, palm fronds or leaves, straw products, bamboo, cane or rattan basket ware and furnishings, potpourri, coconut shells, Christmas decorations, wreaths and ornaments, dried flowers and arrangements, and fresh flowers and leis.*

Example

A Taiwanese food manufacturer sells dry packaged Asian noodles to a customer in Perth, Australia. The buyer in Perth, wants little to do with the import hassles of buying on a DDP basis.

DDP requires the exporter to handle the import formalities. The Taiwanese exporter now has to be very concerned with this Australian import business process it will undertake as the product is listed in the items to be declared when shipping.

The Taiwanese seller will be responsible and also potentially liable for any issues related to import process, permits, packaging, marking, labeling, and quality control from Australian customs or its AQIS officers.

The manufacturer has options here:

1. It can attempt to negotiate other Incoterms so it will not be responsible for the import process, such as but not limited to DAP. The buyer may or may not agree to this option.
2. It can develop an expertise on Australian import regulations by using a quality freight forwarder who has this expertise in Australia, and which would have the resources to make sure the import process and all related matters such as documentation, permits, packing, and labeling are all done in accordance with Australian AQIS regulations.

---

* From government regulations in Australia.

While this option has risks, these could be minimized by exercising due diligence and arranging service-provider options that can provide value in this area. Additionally, law firms, consultants, and government agencies can assist in this regard.

Global Governance Guidelines for Incoterms

International executives need to follow these guidelines in respect to managing their global governance responsibilities:

- Exercise due diligence and reasonable care in deciding which Incoterms to use when certain factors come into play with respect to treaties, conventions, governments, and organizations.
- Acknowledge that no supply chain is automatically exempt from any level of global governance and that it impacts every global supply chain to some extent.
- Resource development and allocating time into everyone's schedule for information flow of world affairs and politics is a necessary mandate. An excellent example of this would be a French printing company that is shipping to the Middle East and North Africa, where it has a huge market share. This company would need to be paying attention to all the political fires burning: Libya, Egypt, Tunisia, and Syria, and of course all the issues with Israel. Concerns with ability to conduct business, ability to get paid, ability to arrange safe transportation, ability to communicate effectively, and the ability to travel to see the customer would be some of the many issues facing anyone doing business in that part of the world.
- Recognize that at the end of the day any political issues may potentially impact the decisions we make on whom we sell to and how we going about making that sale happen.
- We will always create sales or purchases that reduce risk or create opportunity.
- This will ultimately influence which Incoterms we choose and how the choice impacts risk, costs, and profitability.

What We Need to Know about *Incoterms 2010*

Incoterms 2010 now is written by defining 11 rules and reducing the previously used 13 rules in *Incoterms 2000*. The 2010 edition introduced two new rules, Delivered at Terminal (DAT) and Delivered at Place (DAP), which replace four rules of the prior version, Delivered at Frontier (DAF), Delivered Ex Ship (DES), Delivered Ex Quay (DEQ), and Delivered Duty Unpaid (DDU).

In the 2000 edition, the rules were divided into four categories (E, F, C, and D), but the new 11 predefined terms of *Incoterms 2010* are subdivided into two categories based only on method of delivery. The larger group of seven rules applies regardless of the method of transport, with the smaller group of four being applicable only to sales that solely involve transportation over water.

Rules for Any Modes of Transport

The seven rules defined by *Incoterms 2010* for any modes of transportation are in summary form:[*]

EXW: ExWorks (named place of delivery): The seller makes the goods available at its premises. This term places the maximum obligation on the buyer and minimum obligations on the seller. The ExWorks term is often used when making an initial quotation for the sale of goods without any costs included. EXW means that a seller has the goods ready for collection at its premises (works, factory, warehouse, plant) on the date agreed upon. The buyer pays all transportation costs and also bears the risks for bringing the goods to their final destination. The seller doesn't load the goods on collecting vehicles and doesn't clear them for export. If the seller does load the goods, it does so at the buyer's risk and cost. If parties wish the seller to be responsible for the loading of the goods on departure and to bear the risk and all costs of such loading, this must be made clear by adding explicit wording to this effect in the contract of sale.

FCA: Free Carrier (named place of delivery): The seller hands over the goods, cleared for export, into the disposal of the first carrier (named by the buyer) at the named place. The seller pays for carriage to the named point of delivery, and risk passes when the goods are handed over to the first carrier.

CPT: Carriage Paid To (named place of destination): The seller pays for carriage to the named place of destination. Risk transfers to buyer upon handing goods over to the first carrier.

---

[*] From the United States Council for International Business, http://www.uscib.org.

CIP: Carriage and Insurance Paid to (named place of destination): The containerized transport/multimodal equivalent of CIF. Seller pays for carriage and insurance to the named place of destination, but risk passes when the goods are handed over to the first carrier.

DAT: Delivered at Terminal (named terminal at port or place of destination): Seller pays for carriage to the terminal, except for costs related to import clearance, and assumes all risks up to the point that the goods are unloaded at the terminal.

DAP: Delivered at Place (named place of destination): Seller pays for carriage to the named place, except for costs related to import clearance, and assumes all risks prior to the point that the goods are ready for unloading by the buyer.

DDP: Delivered Duty Paid (named place of destination): Seller is responsible for delivering the goods to the named place in the country of the buyer and pays all costs in bringing the goods to the destination including import duties and taxes. This term places the maximum obligations on the seller and minimum obligations on the buyer.

Rules for Sea and Inland Waterway Transport

The four rules defined by *Incoterms 2010* for international trade where transportation is entirely conducted by water are as follows:[*]

FAS: Free Alongside Ship (named port of shipment): The seller must place the goods alongside the ship at the named port. The seller must clear the goods for export. FAS is suitable only for maritime transport and not for multimodal sea transport in containers (see *Incoterms 2010*, ICC publication 715). This term is typically used for break bulk, heavy-lift, or bulk liquid cargoes.

FOB: Free On Board (named port of shipment): The seller must load the goods on-board the vessel nominated by the buyer. Cost and risk are passed from seller to buyer when the goods are actually on-board of the vessel. The seller must clear the goods for export. The term is applicable for maritime and inland waterway transport only but not for multimodal sea transport in containers (see *Incoterms 2010*, ICC publication 715). The buyer must instruct the seller on the details of the vessel and the port where the goods are to be loaded, and there is no reference to, or provision for, the use of a carrier or forwarder.

---

[*] From the United States Council for International Business, http://www.uscib.org.

CFR: Cost and Freight (named port of destination): Seller must pay the costs and freight to bring the goods to the port of destination. However, risk is transferred to the buyer once the goods are loaded on the vessel. CFR applies to maritime transport only and insurance for the goods are not included. This term was formerly known as CNF (C&F).

CIF: Cost, Insurance and Freight (named port of destination): Exactly the same as CFR except that the seller must, in addition, procure and pay for the insurance. Maritime transport only.

The four terms from the 2000 edition of Incoterms that were eliminated are DAF, Delivered at Frontier; and DES, Delivered Ex Ship; DEQ, Delivered Ex Quay; and DDU, Delivered Duty Unpaid. DAF, DES, and DEQ were rarely used and had a place in international trade years ago when freight was moved differently. DDU, however, had great use and a real value in global trade transactions. It has been replaced by DAP. The switch from DDU to DAP is an ongoing process for a lot of companies who operate globally. In Chapter 2 when we look at best practices we will review how best to manage these changes and incorporate them into supply chain management.

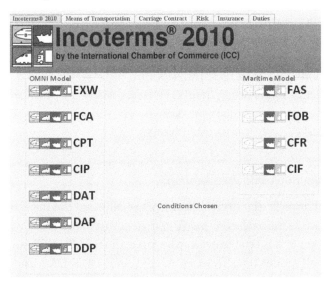

2000 versus 2010

The Incoterms Appendix points to a drafting group of 10 individuals who collaborated to make a favorable impact on global trade by redesigning the *Incoterms 2010* to make them more contemporary and easier to use for world traders. We are sure the process was timely, arduous, and complicated. They had to listen to people, governments, lawyers, trade professionals, global corporations, and vested interests. The drafting group is to be lauded for a great effort and numerous accomplishments and betterments with the 2010 edition.

To some extent, what was expected was accomplished. But I, along with a host of professionals in this field, have recognized that many functional-level problems still exist or were newly created as a result of this new publication. This book will attempt to help the reader navigate through these terms so they can use them for leverage and benefit.

As time passes and the new terms are tested in business, trade, and the courts, we will be in a better position to review maybe in another three to four years just how this drafting group did. We hold out for great promise, as many of the changes are a very clear benefit to global trade. The following list reflects a summary of the changes made in the 2010 edition that we need to review in more detail:

- Placing the book into two sections
- FOB "on-board"
- Domestic use
- Security-related clearances and information
- Clearly defined terminal handling charges responsibility
- "Goods sold in transit" transactions
- Redefinition of ocean freight, FOB responsibilities of seller and buyer
- Better defined cargo insurance
- Specific Incoterms nuance changes

Placing the Book into Two Sections

A good change by the drafting committee afforded the new edition to be set into two sections. *Incoterms 2010* is structured into these two sections: those for sea and inland waterway only (i.e., FAS, FOB, CFR, and CIF) and those for all modes (i.e., EXW, FCA, CPT, CIP, DAT, DAP, and DDP). It is important to note the following:

- Transactions by air, rail, truck, and nonvessel need to be referencing Incoterms in the first section allowing multimodal transport. If these sections also allow sea and inland waterway, they would also be a potentially good choice across the board, allowing a broader term to be used and then possibly avoiding confusion. The terms-specific details need to be reviewed to assure that this will work in your supply chain.

The perfect example here would be the term of sale used by a supplier in Genoa, Italy, that plans to ship by air from Rome, Italy, to a customer in Seoul, South Korea. That seller uses a commercial invoice stating FOB Rome, Leonardo da Vinci Airport. This would be a misuse of an Incoterm designed for sea and inland waterway only. But if the company had a policy for exports from its plant in Genoa that used FCA, this would have application for both air and sea and help avoid this type of error.

- Do we see a potential future in the next Incoterms update, where these specific terms relegated to sea and inland waterway only will be eventually eliminated? (See Table 3.1.)

FOB On-Board

The FOB term in this new edition underwent numerous changes. The one being discussed here references the issue of *on-board* versus *when the goods pass the ship's rail* in the 2000 edition. That point in time where responsibility and liability pass from the seller to the buyer in the 2000 edition could clearly be observed when the cargo passed the ship's rail moving onto the vessel. In the real world, we all know that a majority of sea freight moves in ocean containers, typically 20- and 40-foot varieties. But we also know that a considerable amount of freight moves by break bulk, roll on/roll off, or by other modes.

Freight in those situations will move across the rail, but potentially, at a later time and distance, will be moved and secured into position. So the question is raised as to what then does *on-board* mean? Is it when it passes the rail, stevedored into position, secured, and so forth? The information flow always reminds us that Incoterms are a reference point and not an end-all in an international commercial transaction.

In the case of FOB on a break bulk shipment, this would mean that the purchase order from the buyer should clearly express what they require from the shipper in loading the goods on-board the vessel. Or the seller or shipper clearly describes on the commercial invoice what it will plan to do to meet the on-board requirement.

TABLE 3.1

Incoterms Shipping Guide

	Loading on Truck (Carrier)	Export-Customs Declaration	Carriage to Port of Export	Unloading of Truck in Port of Export	Loading Charges in Port of Export	Carriage to Port of Import	Unloading Charges in Port of Import	Loading on Truck in Port of Import	Carriage to Place of Destination	Insurance	Import Customs Clearance	Import Taxes
EXW	No	No	No	No	No	No	No	No	No	No	No	No
FCA	Yes	Yes	Yes	No	No	No	No	No	No	No	No	No
FAS	Yes	Yes	Yes	Yes	No	No	No	No	No	No	No	No
FOB	Yes	Yes	Yes	Yes	Yes	No	No	No	No	No	No	No
CFR	Yes	Yes	Yes	Yes	Yes	Yes	No	No	No	No	No	No
CIF	Yes	Yes	Yes	Yes	Yes	Yes	No	No	No	Yes	No	No
DAT	Yes	Yes	Yes	Yes	Yes	Yes	Yes	No	No	No	No	No
DAP	Yes	Yes	Yes	Yes	Yes	Yes	Yes	Yes	Yes	No	No	No
CPT	Yes	Yes	Yes	Yes	Yes	Yes	Yes	Yes	Yes	No	No	No
CIP	Yes	Yes	Yes	Yes	Yes	Yes	Yes	Yes	Yes	Yes	No	No
DDP	Yes	Yes	Yes	Yes	Yes	Yes	Yes	Yes	Yes	No	Yes	Yes

For example, an exporter from Sydney sells a 60-foot sailing yacht to a buyer in Singapore. The terms of sale are FOB Sydney, and the goods will be shipped on an ocean-going vessel direct from Sydney Harbor to the port of Singapore. The FOB term means that the seller delivers once the goods are placed on the vessel. But functionally this is not as easily as it seems. The nature of the shipment places the yacht in a cradle, spanning some 70 feet long by 20 feet wide and 38 feet high, and weighing some 32 tons. The cradle will be nestled and secured on deck before the ship sails by the Sydney longshoreman and stevedores engaged by the ocean freight carrier or steamship line. If the intent of the buyer to have the seller make delivery once the goods are on-board, in final position, and then secured by lashing by the professionals and approved by the captain of the vessel, then they need to build those terms in their purchase order and have the seller (exporter) in Sydney agree to those terms. Additional costs for all this labor should be reflected in the overall FOB price between the two parties: typically prepaid by the seller and recouped when payment is received.

The bottom line here is that both parties must be wary of an ocean-going FOB transaction where noncontainerized freight is being handled, and they must specify the intent of their expectations on just what they want on-board to mean in that transaction or agreement. As time passes and we see litigation and cases adjudicated, we will learn more about this interpretation. Meanwhile, use this term cautiously on break bulk freight.

Domestic Use

I believe that the original architects of Incoterms placed the intent that they were designed for goods passing through international borders—and not for internal country shipments or for domestic transportation needs.

The 2000 edition stated that the intent was for goods crossing international borders but allowed for domestic utilization. It is important to note that while it allowed for domestic, that was not a "license" to utilize for domestic. But the cover of the 2010 edition added the words "Domestic and International Trade." This has changed how companies engaged in global trade view and use Incoterms. Many companies have begun to incorporate them into their overall sales strategies and procedures for both domestic and international transactions.

Many countries around the globe benefit from Incoterms in domestic use. But it has an uncertainty attached to its application for domestic trade in the United States.

In the United States, prior to 2004 the UCC, governance in all 50 states in the United States except Louisiana had provisions in their shipping terms FOB was a "place" most widely used FOB origin or FOB destination. Very simplified, FOB origin meant the price paid to a buyer was that you come and pick the freight up. FOB destination meant price paid included delivery to the agreed destination.

In 2004, these provisions were recommended to be abolished from the UCC. The problem with that is not many states adopted this change, so a quandary exists that this UCC provision of FOB origin and destination still have application in most states in the United States. And it is still accepted in practice as a shipping term in most American domestic contracts.

It is still acceptable for a U.S. company to use this UCC provision for FOB origin and destination in its domestic sales or purchase contracts. However, recognize that at some point it is likely to be eliminated formally. When? We do not know. This particular issue does not necessarily impact domestic shippers in other countries around the globe.

In the United States, it is okay to use *Incoterms 2010* for domestic sales, but we must realize that the complications of how Incoterms have been designed make the FOB term mostly not viable. I believe that the main reason for the change of Incoterms to include "domestic" was because of considerations in the European community and not the United Sates. The FCA term has domestic viability in the United States, but this whole subject must be carefully and judiciously thought out to ensure that any changes work both internally and externally with suppliers and customers.

ExWorks and DAP are also excellent options. ExWorks could replace FOB origin, and DAP could replace FOB destination with some minor differences. But technically any *Incoterms 2010* could be used.

The key is using the Incoterms that meet both parties' intent and that they both agree to, recognizing the risks and costs associated for both. It is also very important to note that the 2010 FOB Incoterms should not be used for domestic trade as the intent per the section is in the wording for sea and inland waterway only, unless you will be using those water modes for inland transportation, which is typically unlikely.

All companies need to tread carefully when choosing *Incoterms 2010* for domestic use. There are logistic, financial, and legal considerations in moving from the standard UCC terms to *Incoterms 2010*.

I am determined by practice and current typical situations in corporate America. UCC still has validity and *Incoterms 2010* has validity with some gray areas, so move forward, thinking out options that work best for your supply chain. And acknowledge that you now have options.

Security-Related Clearances and Information Are Addressed

The events of 9/11 have increased significantly how goods transit through the world transportation infrastructures. Having said that, shipments to and from the U.S. have been more greatly impacted.

- There are stringent security requirements on goods coming into the United States for declaring information to U.S. Customs Border and Protection (CBP), prior to loading on-board the vessel. Two regulations, CSI and ISF, mandate information flow to CBP electronically before the conveyance departs for the United Sates port of entry.
  - Terms such as FCA and CIP specify that the seller will be responsible for providing security information to the buyer.
  - The buyer must in a timely manner advise the seller of any security information requirements.
  - The seller must, were applicable in a timely manner, include security-related information.

What is the Security Filing?

The Security Filing, formerly known as the "10+2" initiative, is a Customs and Border Protection (CBP) regulation that requires importers and vessel operating carriers to provide additional advance trade data to CBP pursuant to Section 203 of the SAFE Port Act of 2006 and section 343(a) of the Trade Act of 2002, as amended by the Maritime Transportation Security Act of 2002, for non-bulk cargo shipments arriving into the United States by vessel.

Importer Requirements:

      U.S.-bound Cargo (Includes FTZ and IT): requires the electronic filing of an Importer Security Filing (ISF) comprised of 10 data elements.

      Transit Cargo (FROB, IE, and TE): requires the electronic filing of an Importer Security Filing (ISF) comprised of 5 data elements.

Carrier Requirements:

      Vessel Stow Plans required for arriving vessels with containers.
      Container Status Messages required for containers arriving via vessel.

The European Union has also implemented advanced notification criteria that will have an effective date at some point closely mirroring the U.S. ISF regulations.

From Order to Delivery

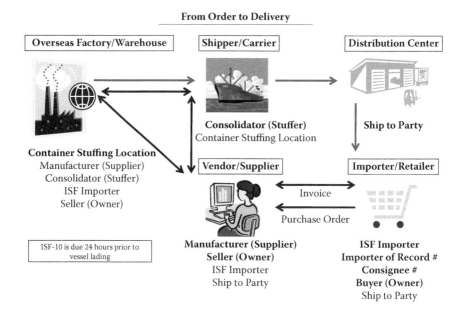

Terminal Handling Charges Responsibility Clearly Defined

There have been always points of contention in Incoterms regarding various port and accessorial charges such as unloading, handling, demurrage, and container service charges, all of which might impact the costs of an export–import transaction, particularly regarding who is responsible for paying. When you read the terms such as CIP, DAP, and DAT closely, you can determine that the responsibility for delivery cost is clearly spelled out.

For example, under DAT the exporter (seller) is responsible for all costs up to delivery at the named arrival location. If that location is the terminal, such as for an ocean freight shipment, then the seller/exporter would be responsible for unloading and for any costs to move the goods to affect delivery.

When handling specialized commodities, heavy lift, break bulk, etc., both parties must be very diligent to outline the delivery location, details, and all related expectations to avoid any potential problems.

DAT has been a first-class improvement to *Incoterms 2000* because it requires the exporter/seller to bring the goods to an inbound gateway, to unload them from the conveyance, and to bring them to a point in a "terminal" where the goods can be cleared and picked up by the importer/buyer. Up until that point all risks and costs are accounted for by the exporter/seller. DAT goes much more deeply than does CIP, CIF, CFR, or CPT, where delivery occurs once on-board the conveyance but transportation is arranged to the overseas inbound gateway. Questions have always arisen as to what happens to the terminal or demurrage costs after arrival. The new DAT Incoterms make this clear and concise. They have tidied up a term that held some ambiguity for a long time.

"Goods Sold in Transit" Transactions Addressed

The 2010 edition addresses "goods sold in transit" much more responsibly and clearly than the 2000 edition. In commodity sales such as bulk petroleum products, coffee, cocoa, and rubber, it is likely that goods might begin their transit to a destination without yet being sold. Or because goods like these are "traded," they could be sold several times over before reaching the ultimate consignee. Incoterms address these issues by requiring the seller to procure the contracts of carriage in the new trade. You can see this in the A3 provisions of CFR, as an example.*

When a transaction is in place and the "freight is on the water," both parties must work closely in the new sales contract to secure a transition because when a loss occurs and is discovered after arrival, time and location of the transition from one agreement to the other becomes a decisive point in pursuing an insurance claim.

Ocean Freight and FOB Responsibilities of Seller and Buyer Redefined

In the 2000 edition under the FOB term, delivery occurs once the goods pass the ship's rail of the vessel. In the 2010 edition, delivery occurs once the goods are loaded on-board. The new issue developed with the FOB wording lies in FOB > B5 transfer of risks. This section recognizes the contemporary issue of freight not making the vessel it was booked for and being rolled over to a new sailing.

Under the 2010 edition the basic understanding is that if the seller delivers to the carrier on schedule but the carrier does not move the freight due to circumstances out of the seller's control, and the seller properly notifies the buyer, then delivery has occurred and all risks going forward are now accounted for by the buyer.

Buyers, their agents, freight forwarders, insurance brokers, and underwriting companies need to pay attention here, as this changed the point in time for transfer of responsibility previously asserted in prior Incoterms to a much earlier point than ever before. With more and more freight being "bumped,"

---

* See *Incoterms 2010.*

this risk could prove huge. When the earthquake and tsunami of 2011 hit Japan, picture the freight sitting at Japanese ports that was delivered to carriers but not yet loaded on-board vessels. This could have dramatically impacted cargo liability and just who was ultimately responsible for any loss or damage. It will be interesting to watch how the courts deal with these FOB claims as they develop in the next few years.

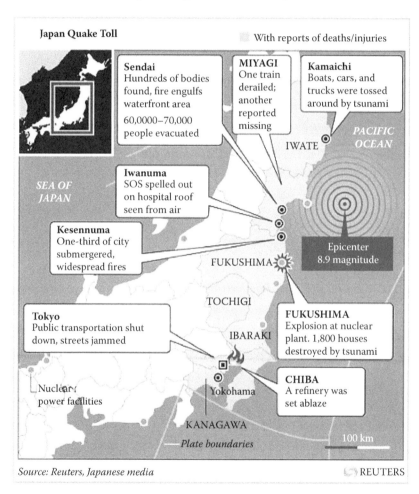

Japan Quake Toll — With reports of deaths/injuries

Sendai — Hundreds of bodies found, fire engulfs waterfront area 60,0000–70,000 people evacuated

MIYAGI — One train derailed; another reported missing

Kamaichi — Boats, cars, and trucks were tossed around by tsunami

PACIFIC OCEAN

IWATE

Iwanuma — SOS spelled out on hospital roof seen from air

SEA OF JAPAN

Kesennuma — One-third of city submergered, widespread fires

FUKUSHIMA

Epicenter 8.9 magnitude

TOCHIGI

Tokyo — Public transportation shut down, streets jammed

IBARAKI

FUKUSHIMA — Explosion at nuclear plant. 1,800 houses destroyed by tsunami

Nuclear power facilities

Yokohama

CHIBA — A refinery was set ablaze

KANAGAWA

Plate boundaries

100 km

Source: Reuters, Japanese media   REUTERS

There were also hundreds of other ports impacted that had cargoes awaiting shipment to and from these Japanese ports. *Forces majeure*, or acts of God, occur all the time, but usually not to this magnitude. A lot of cargo, which were sold on an FOB basis, missed vessel sailings "as booked" as a result of this disaster. Importers, exporters, bankers, insurance brokers, underwriting companies, carriers, freight forwarders, and third-party transportation providers all have been working diligently to mitigate the problems associated with these quakes and tsunamis in Japan. It will be interesting to watch and observe how these get sorted out and how the new interpretations of FOB from *Incoterms 2010* will be viewed by the trade professional community.

Cargo Insurance Better Defined

Cargo insurance in the world of international trade has always provided a mystery and solution for the more than 300 years it has existed. Incoterms make a best attempt to address cost and risk. Insurance is a critical issue to both mitigate risk and maximize profit and is covered in great detail in Chapter 7. What I want to outline here is the betterment made in the 2010 edition where insurance is provided by the seller for the benefit of the buyer such as we observe in the CIF and CIP *Incoterms 2010*.

In the 2000 edition, the seller procures insurance on behalf of the buyer, but only on "minimum cover." This means that the seller goes into an insurance market place such as Lloyds of London and among numerous choices can elect the least expensive coverage with the least amount of protection available. The 2000 edition offers a warning to the buyer, but only if he or she reads, understands, and then acts on that information could he or she be further protected. It created a huge risk to the buyer.

In the United States many importers who had inbound terms of CIF, once and only once that they had a loss or damage on an import transaction and attempted to recover from the underwriter did they then notice their predicament—an uninsured claim!

The insurance purchase by the buyer impacts not only the scope of coverage, with certain underlying terms and conditions, but also the quality of the insurance company being utilized. What is the rating of that underwriter, what is its financial condition, does it have representation in the country of destination, how are claims paid—all these are related issues that would come back to haunt the seller once a claim has occurred. Like anything in business, you don't know the value until you are in crisis.

Thank the drafting committee for adding better wording to these terms, which now offer openly a better option for the insurance purchase by the seller to at least look at the coverage and possibly provide better policy terms and conditions. As an example, under CIF, both the 2000 and 2010 editions on the cover page of the term address *minimum cover*, but in the 2010 edition on p. 110 A#, the subsequent instructions and guidelines outline options in considering broader coverage. This becomes a very important risk management tool that can potentially provide greater protection and indemnification for loss or damage to goods in transit from an external cause covered under policies supplied by exporters for the benefit of their customers or buyers (importers). Keep in mind that a cargo claim can eat up profits, spoil relationships, and cause greater harm than any good. Making sure the proper cargo insurance is in place is as important a responsibility as booking the freight with the right steamship line.

London has always been the leader in worldwide cargo insurance through the famous institution Lloyd's of London. Over centuries, Lloyd's has developed standard cargo insurance terms as a global reference for all underwriters to use when outlining cargo risks and coverage offered. Institute Cargo Clauses A, B, and C are outlined in the following sections.

Minimum Cover
Institute Cargo Clauses C

These clauses provide the minimum cover against risks, but the price is lower.

Institute Cargo Clauses (C) are generally used for shipment of bulk cargo and cover loss of, or damage to, the goods reasonably attributable to*

- Accident to the conveyance, such as crashing of aircraft, fire, explosion, stranding, grounding, sinking or capsizing, overturning or derailment of land conveyance
- Collision or contact of the vessel, craft or conveyance with any external object other than water
- Discharge of cargo at a port of distress
- Loss of, or damage to, the goods caused by jettison and general average sacrifice
- General average expenditure and salvage charges

Normally, insurance companies will indemnify a cargo owner against the aforementioned certain occurrences.

Intermediate Cover
Institute Cargo Clauses B

Institute Cargo Clauses (B) incorporate (C) *and* provide cover for loss of or damage to the subject matters insured reasonably attributable to

---

* Reproduced from Roanoke Trade Services, Long Beach, California, http://www.roanoketrade.com.

any of the perils covered by Institute Cargo Clauses (C), as well as against additional risks, such as

- Earthquakes, volcanic eruptions, or lightning
- Washing overboard
- Entry of water (i.e., sea, lake, or river) into the vessel, hold, conveyance, container, or place of storage
- Total loss of any package lost overboard or dropped during loading or unloading operation

Normally, insurer will indemnify a cargo owner against the aforementioned certain occurrences. Where necessary, supplementary risk cover can be added, such as regarding malicious damage, nondelivery, theft, and pilferage.

Greater Protection

"All Risks"—Institute Cargo Clauses (A)

With the development of trade, the demand grew to cover extraneous risk. The practice of adding such risks to the cover afforded by the Standard Marine Policy so developed to embrace all the transit risks under one omnibus wording.

Institute Cargo Clauses (A) incorporates (B) *and* provides the most coverage to traders at the highest premium price.

Practically, these clauses cover the cargo for "all" risks of physical loss or damage, except, for instance, wars and strikes. These exclusions may however be reinstated by including appropriate clauses.

Specific Incoterms Nuance Changes

Pictures with Each Incoterms

Every leading page with the new Incoterms has a graphic showing place of delivery. I am a big proponent of visual aids, but I get concerned when viewing the graphic on some of the terms because it is truly not representative of the likely intent on how business executives will use the term.

The best example of this is DAP, which many agree really has replaced DDU. DAT brings the goods to the arrival facility unloaded and awaiting pick-up by the buyer. The graphic shows this. The likely point will be a terminal on arrival at the inbound gateway. DAP could also be the inbound gateway or at some other named point, such as the final destination. I understand that the drafters considered a DAD term—Delivered at Destination—but it was declined.

IF DAP is the replacement for DDU, than the likely delivery place will be an inland point away from the arriving port and terminal, and I think a graphic could have been created showing these more likely inland options.

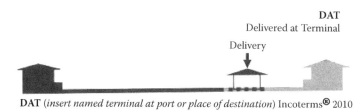

DAT (*insert named terminal at port or place of destination*) Incoterms® 2010

DAT (*insert named place of destination*) Incoterms® 2010

Gaining Competitive Advantage on Inbound Logistics

BEST PRACTICES: MAKING THE RIGHT CHOICES

Ten Action Steps

1. Engage senior management.
2. Establish a point person and a team approach.

3. Learn Incoterms and establish an Incoterms guru.
4. Integrate Incoterms in every corner of the organization.
5. Partner with providers.
6. Plan the best options and leverage sales and purchases.
7. Educate suppliers, customers, and vendors.
8. Develop and use technology options.
9. Develop competitor-friendly options: network.
10. Develop resources.

Engage Senior Management

The only way change will occur in most larger and even smaller companies is when senior management is informed of the issues and believes that the company will be best served in the long-term. Typically, in all companies cost is associated with positive change. Senior management will always be involved in "spend." Change also requires infrastructure and personnel issues, which senior management can most favorably impact. Many companies are littered with fiefdoms, silos, and areas of individualized territories that are difficult to broach. Senior management has the best opportunity to get past these artificial barriers and cause better cohesion between internal working units. Senior management can also exercise a "hammer approach" when necessary.

Establish a Point Person and a Team Approach

An individual person irrespective of the company size will need to take "ownership" of managing Incoterms inside the organization. That individual will best be served by organizing a committee made up of all the individuals and divisions that are "stakeholders" in the global supply chain. These might include the following:

- Sales
- Purchasing

- Logistics, traffic, and freight
- Operations, distribution, and warehousing
- Manufacturing
- Legal
- Finance and accounting
- Customer service
- Technology and information technology (IT) services

That "point" person along with the committee would be charged with the following:

- Evaluate all the stakeholders in the global supply chain and make sure they have a word in what the committee does.
- Evaluate all the issue in their global supply chain that impacts Incoterms use.
- Assure that the company has "benchmarked" itself against other operators in their industry or scope of business or size.
- Guide and establish protocols for specific personnel, sales or purchasing, company or divisional nuances regarding Incoterms use.

- Establish a line of accountability and responsibility both into senior management and into company operations at all levels.
- Establish a direct line of communication into tax, legal, and finance for Incoterms issues that impact these corporate areas of concern.
- Establish a direct line of communication into the company's technology group or providers to determine how technology can play a role in the management of Incoterms matters.
- Be able to create standard operating procedures (SOPs) in the use and application of Incoterms throughout the organization, with a need for an ability to tailor and customize the SOPs for individual needs without compromising consistent and standardized applications.
- Develop internal training and instructional regiments in the organization on what are and best use of Incoterms.
- Engage outside counsel, advisors, or consultants to support the committee's initiatives.
- Establish communication capabilities to address information flow internally to all aspects of the organization.

In addition, reach out to vendors, providers, suppliers, customers, and potentially government authorities.

Committees provide an excellent platform for team initiatives that will typically produce the best results when managing projects inside and within corporations. Committees can also span divisions, various entities, countries, and the globe.

Learn Incoterms and Establish an Incoterms Guru

One person has to become the "go-to" person for Incoterms in an organization of any size. That person would need to:

- Establish some degree of skill set in Incoterms
- Have access to Incoterms professionals for clarification, edification, and practical counsel

That person may not necessarily be the Incoterms point person or committee chair but might even be a subordinate who has shown interest and identified a capability in Incoterms. This person would attend all Incoterms training and updates and take the Advanced Incoterms class offered by the World Academy (http://www.theworldacademy.com), the ICC (http://www.iccwbo.org), and the United States Council for International Business (http://www.uscib.org). This person could also be made available to conduct in-house training exercises or manage third-party training initiatives. An additional responsibility of this person could be the actual internal coordination of Incoterms utilization and practice coordinated with the committee and the point person.

Integrate Incoterms in Every Corner of the Organization

Incoterms impact every aspect of an organization, from sales to purchasing, from warehousing to legal, from finance to customer service, from manufacturing to traffic. A committee that engages all the stakeholders will help with this effort, and it is very important that all personnel who have anything to do with the global supply chain be involved with:

- Understanding the basics of Incoterms
- How Incoterms impact what they have as company responsibilities
- How Incoterms impact the other aspects of their company interfaces
- How to make better decisions that leverage supply chain variables with Incoterms utilization

Companies that assure total Incoterms compliance with all personnel and divisions in every nook and cranny of sales, purchasing, and logistics are those that have the best-run global supply chains producing the best opportunity for growth and profits.

Partner with Providers

Our expertise in global trade points to the fact that a clear majority of companies, upward of 95%, use the services of freight forwarders, customhouse brokers, or third-party service providers in the operation of their international sales and purchase programs mainly in the freight and logistics arenas. This is covered in more detail in Chapter 6. This is a very important relationship that develops among the principal shippers, importers, and exporters and their providers. It will make or break the success of the supply chain.

When the principal shipper, importer, or exporter views the relationship as a "partnership" instead of just a "vendor," there is a dramatic improvement in the performance level of the provider in being able to deliver on promises and commitments. Partnership mind-sets allow for better communication, information flow, and ease of operational adherence. It also affords a better opportunity for problem resolution or mitigation. As problems are always likely, it is important to note that how we resolve these likely issues is critical to the overall relationship. They are likely to happen, and how they are dealt with will impact performance of both parties. A partnership mind-set affords the best opportunity for success.

Plan the Best Options and Leverage Sales and Purchases

When we are discussing *best practices,* we are mitigating risk and maximizing opportunity. Developing a strategy and plan of action then becomes an integral part of our business process in managing Incoterms. We are trying to discover which are the best Incoterms to use to give us advantage in our export sales or our import purchases.

In the various chapters that follow are numerous examples and overviews of how best to leverage Incoterms. An example that my colleague Rennie Alston (an accomplished licensed customhouse broker and trade professional) uses relates to goods being shipped to the United States and how importers value the goods for declaration to U.S. Customs and Border Protection (CBP).

Foreign Inland Freight Can Be a Nondutiable Charge

In every country, various factors affect the compliant reporting values for imported merchandise. CBP defines proper value based on five different methods of valuation. The most common method of valuation is *transaction value*, which is defined as the price paid or payable between a buyer and seller of imported merchandise. Valuation factors also must be added to such cost to properly ascertain a valuation sum consistent with CBP regulatory standards.

CBP assesses the dutiable value concept on all charges including the cost of the merchandise and all charges to get the goods packed and to a point of an on-board status on a vessel, vehicle, or aircraft destined for the United States. Many importers associate their customs declared value on this concept as the term of sale as FOB to include foreign inland freight as a proper element of their declared value.

Many purchasing options available to buyers of imported merchandise are often reflected in the selected Incoterms. This is another example of why personnel engaged in managing various aspects of the global supply chain need to be instructed on the basic tenement of Incoterms.

Many importers purchase under ExWorks or ex-factory terms and are incorrectly declaring a U.S. import value inclusive of foreign inland freight. This practice results in the assessment of an incorrect entered value as the cost of foreign inland freight is not included under the terms of an ex-factory transaction as per 19CFR 152.103 (a) 5 (i), which states: *If the price actually paid or payable by the buyer to the seller for the imported merchandise does not include a charge for foreign inland freight and other charges for services incident to the international shipment of merchandise, those charges will not be added to the price.*

There also exist areas in which terms other than ex-factory may also qualify for the exclusion of foreign inland freight in such cases as when such cost are itemized separately and occur after the goods are shipped on a through bill of lading and are placed with the carrier as referenced in CFR 152.103 (a) 5 (ii).

Many importers are not aware of this regulatory position and are declaring foreign inland freight for their import transaction declarations resulting in an overpayment of duties for all dutiable entries. This issue is worth a detailed review and analysis to determine if in fact your firm is eligible for a revenue recovery process in the form of a possible protest of liquidation as well as a proactive adjustment to declared value computations to save your firm millions of dollars in unnecessary duty amounts.

Keep in mind that it is a penalty or fine as much for paying too much duty as for not paying enough. Customs around the world expect the "importer of record" to declare the "correct value" based upon the import rules of that country. Importers understanding how this aspect applies can take advantage not only of how to make a purchase and declare the correct values to stay out of trouble but more importantly also to how to reduce the landed cost for a competitive edge.

Educate Suppliers, Customers, and Vendors

The global supply chain includes the principal seller or buyer, and the sales agreement, the purchase order, commercial invoice, and contract all include the parties who work with us in the logistics, handling, clearing, and movement of funds. It is imperative that they be included in our process of deciding the best Incoterms since they will also be impacted by that decision. What you want is a decision that is in the best interest of all parties. This may require some compromise.

Do Not Operate in a Vacuum

We need to keep in mind that the supplier, vendor, and customer need to take part in the decision-making process. They must *be educated, informed, and made aware* of the issues that impact that decision-making process. Over the last 30 years, I have witnessed successful supply chains: they engage all parties to the transaction, proactively, with transparency and compromise.

Develop and Use Technology Options

In the early 1990s, technology was a very small part of global trade. Today it is a big component and an even more important factor impacting supply chain efficiency and performance. What it took five people to do in an hour to move freight in 1990 can be done by one person today in 10 minutes. Around the world today more and more freight moves globally "paperless" or certainly with a minimum amount of paper. Not only does that create supply chain savings, but more and more companies go "green."

Reducing paper, documentation, protecting the environment, and eliminating waste are the future.

Technology's advantages are

- Efficiency
- Compliance benefits
- Record-keeping components

- Government requirements
- Reports for management oversight
- Performance measuring
- Better communications
- Better quality control

Technology can be incorporated into Incoterms management in numerous ways.

Some Incoterms applications with technology options are as follows:

- Companies can place the desired Incoterms right into sales agreements or purchase orders as they are administered.
- Incoterms options can be decided based upon parameters of an agreement and can pop up automatically to the individual involved in the transaction. For example, the product, the customer, and countries of sale or purchase when factored could impact the choices of Incoterms on a preprogrammed automatic basis.
- Additionally, parameters can be set up in sales and purchase order databases to point to preferred Incoterms options or to alert users when the wrong Incoterms options are being considered.
- Technology can be programmed with SOPs that mirror corporate or company-wide Incoterms protocols and strategies.

Companies engaged in global trade need to invest into technology solutions, which can be sourced independently from software companies or acquired from transport providers who offer access to their IT capabilities.

Develop Competitor-Friendly Options: Network

Networking is a vital aspect of every individual in the global supply chain with management oversight responsibilities. It allows a beneficial interface with friendly competitors who share intelligence, contacts, and best practices. Learning occurs on the back of their experience. Trade associations, public seminars, and government outreach initiatives are all options for networking.

The United States Council for International Business (USCIB), http://www.uscib.org

The United States Council for International Business promotes open markets, competitiveness and innovation, sustainable development and corporate responsibility, supported by international engagement and prudent regulation. USCIB's vision and strength are provided by an active membership of leading corporations and organizations, while our unique global network helps turn the vision into reality. USCIB also provides a range of business services, including the ATA Carnet for temporary exports, to facilitate overseas trade and investment.

The World Academy, http://www.theworldacademy.com

The World Academy provides training programs and seminars for the following:

Trade Associations
Global Trade Organizations
In Association with Pre-existing Teaching Centers
Public Seminars
Customized In-house Training Programs
Specially Designed and Tailored Training Activities

Topics covered in classes and workshops include all phases of Import/Export logistics and compliance including hazardous materials (HAZMAT), letters of credit, harmonized tariff schedules, Incoterms, and other topics needed to compete in today's global trade arena, such as sales and sales management classes.

American Management Association (AMA), http://www.amanet.org
Seminars

Sharpen skills and stay ahead of the competition with AMA's leading-edge seminars in 21 distinct subject areas. With over 140 workshops to choose from in 40 cities across the country, AMA offers training to meet every individual's needs.

Professional Association of Import/Export Compliance Managers (PACMAN), http://www.compliancemaven.com
About PACMAN

Our Mission Statement:
To provide a formal structure of corporate executives engaged in import and export compliance management for mutual solution development, more compliant and secure global supply chain management and career advancement opportunities.

Deliverables:

- To develop a free exchange of ideas in import/export compliance management
- To provide a testing and certification capability for all professional members
- To develop a database of resources, such as websites, literature, and regulations for all members

- To provide a lobbying presence in Washington
- To provide a medium to gain access to senior government officials in the BIS, U.S. Customs, DOT and State Departments, ITAR, CDC, USDA/FDA, etc.
- To provide web-based and telephone "help-lines" for questions and inquiries
- To provide a forum for research, education, and training on import/export compliance management
- To grow the membership and overall forum, to be a positive advocate in overall global trade and international business
- Career development opportunities
- Compliance technology capability
- Develop dialogue with carriers for more compliant and secure transportation services
- Develop better trade relations with various government agencies
- Develop in-house capability for establishing SOP's on compliance management
- In-house education and training systems

The International Trade Administration (ITA), http://www.trade.gov
ITA strengthens the competitiveness of U.S. industry, promotes trade and investment, and ensures fair trade through the rigorous enforcement of our trade laws and agreements. ITA works to improve the global business environment and helps U.S. organizations compete at home and abroad. ITA supports President Obama's recovery agenda and the National Export Initiative to sustain economic growth and support American jobs.

ITA is organized into four distinct but complementary business units:

U.S. and Foreign Commercial Service—Promotes U.S. exports, particularly by small and medium-sized enterprises, and provides commercial diplomacy support for U.S. business interests around the world.

Manufacturing and Services—Strengthens U.S. competitiveness abroad by helping shape industry-specific trade policy.

Market Access and Compliance—Assists U.S. companies and helps create trade opportunities through the removal of market access barriers.

Import Administration—Enforces U.S. trade laws and agreements to prevent unfairly traded imports and to safeguard the competitive strength of U.S. businesses.

International Chamber of Commerce (ICC), http://www.iccwbo.org

ICC is the voice of world business championing the global economy as a force for economic growth, job creation, and prosperity.

Because national economies are now so closely interwoven, government decisions have far stronger international repercussions than in the past.

ICC—the world's only truly global business organization—responds by being more assertive in expressing business views.

ICC activities cover a broad spectrum, from arbitration and dispute resolution to making the case for open trade and the market economy system, business self-regulation, fighting corruption or combating commercial crime.

ICC has direct access to national governments all over the world through its national committees. The organization's Paris-based international secretariat feeds business views into intergovernmental organizations on issues that directly affect business operations.

The world's most influential business lobby group.

—*Financial Times*, 2008

Networking

Supply chain executives must be consistently committed to networking. Anywhere from 3 to 10 percent of one's time can be structured into creating networking opportunities. Networking creates:

- Camaraderie
- Information flow
- Benchmarking
- Resource development

All these foster an environment in which to learn, grow, and positively act for mutual benefit to the company and the executive.

Develop Resources

No matter how experienced an individual is in supply chain management, it is necessary to process a great deal of information every day to successfully operate in global business.

The key element to success is to develop resources from numerous areas so that when circumstances come up they have variable options to find out what their solutions are. Many consider resource development their "gateway" to managing all their responsibilities successfully. The old adage that you are as good as who you associate with could easily be amended to say you are as good in business as your contacts and resources.

Key U.S. and Globally Based Associations

- Professional Association of Import/Export Compliance Managers (PACMAN)—Elizabeth, NJ, http://www.compliancemaven.com
- Transportation Intermediaries Association (TIA)—Alexandria, VA, http://www.tianet.org
- The National Customs Brokers & Forwarders Association of America (NCBFAA)—Washington, DC, http://www.ncbfaa.org
- The National Industrial Transportation League (NITL)—Arlington, VA, http://www.nitl.org
- American Management Association (AMA)—New York, NY, http://www.amanet.org
- The United States Council for International Business (USCIB)—New York, NY, http://www.uscib.org
- The Institute for Supply Management (ISM)—Tempe, AZ, http://www.ism.ws
- Council of Supply Chain Management Professionals (CSCMP)—Lombard, IL, http://www.cscmp.org

Global Organizations

- Federation of International Trade Associations (FITA)—Washington, DC, http://www.fita.org
- Casa Eagle Pass de Mexico A.C. Piedras Negras Coahuila Mexico
- North American International Trade Corridor Partnership San Nicolas de los Garza Nuevo Leon Mexico
- REPEX—Regroupement Des Professionnels De L'Exportation, Montreal, Quebec, Canada
- The European Free Trade Association—Brussels, Belgium, http://www.efta.int/about-efta/the-european-free-trade-association.aspx
- Asian Food Trade Association—China and California, http://www.asianfoodtrade.org

Key Periodicals

One must develop a number of resources that provide timely information on competitors, vendors, service providers, governmental issues, and industry trends. I read over 60 magazines, newsletters, and periodicals every month. What follows is a recommended sampling that is useful for import and export supply chain executives.

- *Export Practitioner*—Telephone: (202) 463-1250, http://www.exportprac.com
- *Exporter*—Telephone: (212) 269-2016, http://www.exporter.com
- *Export America*—Telephone: (866) 512-1800, http://www.exportamerica.doc.gov
- *Logistics Management*—Telephone: (847) 390-2377, http://www.Logisticsmgmt.com
- *American Shipper*—Telephone: (212) 233-3589, http://www.americanshipper.com
- *Global Logistics & Supply Chain Strategies*—Telephone: (516) 829-9210, http://www.glscs.com
- *Inbound Logistics*—Telephone: 212-629-1560, http://www.inboundlogistics.com
- *Journal of Commerce*—Telephone: (888) 215-6084, http://www.joc.com
- *Traffic World*—Telephone: (888) 215-6084, http://www.trafficworld.com
- *Air Cargo World*—Telephone: (202) 661-3387, http://www.aircargo.com

- *AFSM International*—Telephone: (239) 275-7887, http://www.afsmi.org
- *Shipping Digest*—Telephone: (888) 215-6084, http://www.shippingdigest. com
- *Managing Imports and Exports (MIE)*—Telephone: (800) 524-2493, http://www.theworldacademy.com

An array of other quality options might fit your specific needs better.

Recommended Schools in Import/Export Supply Chain Management
- The World Academy—Telephone: (800) 524-2493, http://www. theworldacademy.com
- PACMAN Association—Telephone: (631) 396-6800, http://www. compliancemaven.com
- World Trade Institute—Telephone: (888) PACE-WTI, http://www. wti.pace.edu
- American Management Association—Telephone: (212) 586-8100, http://www.amanet.org
- Global Training Center—Telephone: (800) 860-5030, http://www. xportnow@aol.com
- Farmingdale State University—Telephone: (631) 420-2246, http:// www.farmingdale.edu
- Global Maritime and Transportation School—Telephone: (516) 773-5161, http://www.usmma.edu/gmats

Key International Websites
- 1travel.com: http://www.onetravel.com
- A UK service for small businesses that provides preliminary information on trade: http://www.dti.uk/ots/explorer/rade.html
- ACW (Air Cargo Week): http://www.aircargoweek.com
- Addresses & Salutations: http://www.bspage.com
- AES Direct (Automated Export System): http://www.aesdirect.gov
- Africa Online: http://www.africaonline.com
- AgExporter: http://www.fas.usda.gov
- *Air Cargo World*: http://www.aircargoworld.com
- *AIRCARGO News*: http://www.air-cargo-news.com
- Airforwarders Association: http://www.airforwarders.org
- Airline Toll-Free Numbers and Websites: http://www.princeton.edu/ Main/air800.html

- American Association of Port Authorities (AAPA): http://www.aapa-ports.org
- American Computer Resources, Inc.: http://www.the-acr.com
- American Countertrade Association (ACA): http://www.countertrade.org
- American Institute for Shippers' Associations (AISA): http://www.shippers.org
- *American Journal of Transportation (AJOT)*: http://www.ajot.com
- American River International: http://www.worldest.com
- American Shipper: http://www.americanshipper.com
- American Short Line and Regional Railroad Association (ASLRRA): http://www.aslrra.org
- American Stock Exchange: http://www.amex.com
- American Trucking Association (ATA): http://www.trucking.org
- ASXTraders: http://www.ASX.com
- ATA Carnet (Merchandise Password): http://www.uscib.org
- ATMs Around the World: http://www.fita.org/marketplace/travel.html#atm
- Aviation Consumer Action Project: http://www.acap1971.org
- *Aviation Week:* http://www.aviationnow.com
- Blue Tiger International, http://www.bluetigerintl.com
- Bureau of Industry and Security (BIS): http://www.bis.doc.gov
- Bureau of National Affairs, International Trade Reporter Export Reference Manual: http://www.bna.com
- Business Advisor: http://www.business.gov
- Business Traveler Info Network: http://www.business-trip.com
- Career China: http://www.dragonsurf.com
- Cargo Systems: http://www.cargosystems.net
- Cargovision: http://www.editorial@cargovision.org
- Census Bureau, Foreign Trade Division: http://www.census.gov/foreign-trade/www
- Central Europe Online: http://www.centraleurope.com
- Chicago Stock Exchange: http://www.chicagostockex.com
- Chinese News (in English): http://www.einnews.com/china
- Classification Schedules: http://www.census.gov/ftp/pub/foreign-trade/www/schedules.html
- *Commerce Business Daily*: http://www.cbdnet.gpo.gov
- *Commercial Carrier Journal (CCJ)*: http://www.etrucking.com

- Commercial Encryption Export Controls: http://www.bxa.doc.gov/Encryption/Default.htm
- Compliance Consulting of Importers/Exporters: http://www.compliancemaven.com
- Correct Way to Fill Out the Shipper's Export Declaration: http://www.census.gov/ftp/pub/foreign-trade/www/correct.way.html
- Country Risk Forecast: http://www.controlrisks.com/html/index.php
- Create Your Own Newspapers: http://www.crayon.com
- Culture and Travel: http://www.ciber.bus.msu.edu/busres/static/culture-travel-language.htm
- Currency: http://www.oanda.com
- Daily Intelligence Summary: http://www.dtic.mil/doctrine/jel/doddoct/data/d
- Database at the UN World Bank: http://www.worldbank.org/data/onlinedatabases/onlinedatabases
- Department of Transportation: http://www.dot.gov
- Diverse languages of the modern world: http://www.unicode.org
- DOT's Office of Inspector General: http://www.oig.dot.gov
- Dr. Leonard's Healthcare Catalog: http://www.drleonards.com
- Dun & Bradstreet: http://www.dnb.com
- *Economic Times (India)*: http://www.economictimes.com
- *Economist*: http://www.economist.com
- Electronic Embassy: http://www.embassy.org
- Embassies & Consulates: http://www.embassyworld.com
- Embassy Web: http://www.embassy.com
- European Union (EU): http://www.europa.eu.int
- Excite Travel: http://www.excite.com/travel
- Export Administration Regulations (EAR): http://www.ntis.gov/products/type/database/export-regulations.asp
- Export Assistant: http://www.cob.ohio-state.edu
- Export Hotline: http://www.exporthotline.com
- Export-Import Bank of the United States (Ex-Im Bank): http://www.exim.gov
- Export Legal Assistance Network (ELAN): http://www.fita.org/elan
- Export Practitioner (Export Regulations): http://www.exportprac.com
- Far Eastern Economic Review: http://www.feer.com
- Federal Register Notice on the Status of AES and AERP: http://www.access.gpo.gov

- Federation of International Trade Associations (FITA): http://www.fita.org
- *Financial Times:* http://www.ft.com
- For female travelers: http://www.journeywoman.com
- Global Business: http://www.gbn.org
- Global Business Information Network: http://www.bus.indiana.edu
- Global Information Network for Small and Medium Enterprises: http://www.gin.sme.ne.jp/intro.html
- Global Law & Business: http://www.law.com
- Glossary of Internalization and Localization terms: http://www.bowneglobal.com/bowne.asp?page=9&language=1
- Glossary of Ocean Cargo Insurance Terms: http://www.tsbic.com/cargo/glossary.htm
- Government Resources: http://www.ciber.bus.msu.edu/busres/government.htm
- Hong Kong Trade Development Counsel (TDC): http://www.tdctrade.com
- iAgora Work Abroad: http://www.iagora.com/pages/html/work/index.html
- IMEX Exchange: http://www.imex.com
- Import Export Bulletin Board: http://www.iebb.com
- Inbound Logistics: http://www.inboundlogistics.com
- Incoterms 2000: http://www.iccwbo.org/home/menu_incoterms.asp
- Independent Accountants International: http://www.accountants.org
- Information on Diseases Abroad: http://www.cdc.gov
- Inside China Today: http://www.einnews.com
- Intellicast Weather (4-day forecast): http://www.intellicast.com/LocalWeather/World
- Intermodal Association of North America (IANA): http://www.intermodal.org
- International Air Transport Association (IATA): http://www.iata.org
- International Association for Medical Assistance to Travelers (IAMAT): http://www.iamat.org
- International Business: Strategies for the Global Marketplace Magazine: http://www.internationalbusiness.com
- International Chamber of Commerce (ICC): http://www.iccwbo.org
- International Commercial Law Monitor: http://www.lexmercatoria.org
- International Economics and Business: dylee.keel.econ.ship.edu/econ/index.html

- International Executive Service Corps (IESC): http://www.iesc.org
- International Freight Association (IFA): http://www.ifa-online.com
- International Law Check: http://www.law.comindex.shtml
- International Maritime Organization (IMO): http://www.imo.org
- International Monetary Fund (IMF): http://www.imf.org
- International Society of Logistics (SOLE): http://www.sole.org
- International Trade Administration (ITA): http://www.ita.doc.gov
- International Trade Shows and Business Events: http://www.ciber. bus.msu.edu/busre
- International Trade/Import-Export Jobs: http://www.internationaltrade. org/jobs.html
- International Trade/Import-Export Portal: http://www.imakenews.com
- Intershipper: http://www.intershipper.com
- IWLA: http://www.warehouselogistics.org
- *Journal of Commerce Online:* http://www.joc.com
- Latin Trade: http://www.latintrade.com
- Libraries: http://www.libraryspot.com/librariesonline.htm
- Library of Congress: http://www.loc.gov
- Local Times Around the World: http://www.times.clari.net.au
- Logistics Management & Distribution Report: http://www. manufacturing.net/magazine/logistic
- London Stock Exchange: http://www.londonstockexchange.com
- Mailing Lists: http://www.ciber.bus.msu.edu/busres/maillist.htm
- *Marine Digest:* http://www.marinedigest.com
- Market Research: http://www.imakenews.com
- Matchmaker site: http://www.ita.doc.gov/efm
- Medical Conditions Around the World: http://www.cdc.gov/travel/ blusheet.htm
- More Trade Leads: http://www.ibrc.bschool.ukans.edu
- NAFTA Customs: http://www.nafta-customs.org
- National Association of Foreign Trade Zones: http://www.NAFTZ.org
- National Association of Purchasing Management (NAPM): http:// www.napm.org
- National Association of Rail Shippers (NARS): http://www. railshippers.com
- National Business Travel Association: http://www.biztraveler.org
- National Customs Brokers & Forwarders Association of America (NCBFAA): http://www.ncbfaa.org

- National Institute of Standards and Technology (NIST): http://www. nist.gov
- National Law Center For Inter-American Free Trade: http://www. natlaw.com
- National Motor Freight Traffic Association (NMFTA): http://www. nmfta.org
- New Records Formats for Commodity Filing and Transportation Filing: http://www.customs.ustreas.gov
- *New York Times:* http://www.nytimes.com
- North American Industry Classification System (NAICS): http:// www.census.gov/epcd/www/naics.html
- Office of Anti-Boycott Compliance: http://www.bxa.doc.gov/ AntiboycottCompliance
- Online Chambers of Commerce: http://www.online-chamber.com
- Online Newspapers: http://www.onlinenewspapers.com
- Original Notice/Bureau of Census re: a classification of the definition of the exporter of record for SED: http://www.access.gpo.gov
- Overseas Private Investment Corp. (OPIC): http://www.opic.gov
- Pacific Dictionary of International Trade and Business: http://www. pacific.commerce.ubc.ca/ditb/search.html
- PACMAN: http://www.compliancemaven.com
- Passenger Rights: http://www.passengerrights.com
- PIERS (Port Import/Export Reporting Service): http://www.PIERS.com
- Ports and Maritime Service Directory: http://www.seaportsinfo.com
- Professional Association of Import/Export Compliance Managers: http://www.compliancemaven.com
- Resources for International Job Opportunities: http://www.dbm. com/jobguide/internat.html
- Reuters: http://www.reuters.com
- Russia Today: http://www.russiatoday.com
- SBA: http://www.sbaonline.com
- SBA Office of International Trade: http://www.sba.gov/oit
- SBA Offices and Services: http://www.sba.gov/services
- Schedule B Export Codes: http://www.census.gov/foreign-trade/ schedules/b
- Search Engine: http://www.google.com
- Service Corps of Retired Executives (SCORE): http://www.score.org
- Shipping International: http://www.aajs.com/shipint

- *Shipping Times (Singapore)*: http://www.business-times.asia1.com.sg/shippingtimes
- SIC Codes: http://www.trading.wmw.com/codes/sic.html
- Small Business Administration (SBA): http://www.sba.gov
- Small Business Association: http://www.sbaonline.gov
- Small Business Development Centers (SBDC): http://www.sba.gov/sbdc
- Statistical Data Sources: http://www.ciber.bus.msu.edu/busres/statinfo.htm
- STAT-USA & NTDB: http://www.stat-usa.gov
- Telephone Directories on the Web: http://www.teldir.com
- *The Expeditor*: http://www.theexpeditor.com
- *The Exporter*: http://www.exporter.com
- The Global Business Forum: http://www.gbfvisa.com
- The Import-Export Bulletin Board: http://www.iebb.com/sell.html
- The International Air Cargo Association (TIACA): http://www.tiaca.org
- *The Times*: http://www.londontimes.com
- The Trading Floor: http://www.trading/wmw.com
- The World Academy: http://www.TheWorldAcademy.com
- Tokyo Stock Exchange: http://www.tse.or.jp
- Trade and Development Agency (TDA): http://www.tda.gov
- Trade Compass: http://www.tradecompass.com
- Trade Information Center (TIC): http://www.ita.doc.gov/td/tic
- Trade Law Web site: http://www.hg.org/trade.html
- Trade Net: http://www.tradenet.gov
- Trade Point USA: http://www.tradepoint.org
- Trade Statistics: http://www.ita.doc.gov/media
- Trading Floor Harmonized Code Search Engine: http://www.trading.wmw.com
- Traffic World: http://www.trafficworld.com
- Transportation Intermediaries Association (TIA): http://www.tianet.org
- Transportation Jobs & Personnel: http://www.quotations.com/trans.htm
- Travlang: http://www.travlang.com
- UN Conference on Trade and Development: http://www.uncadtrains.org
- UN International Trade Center (ITC): http://www.intracen.org
- Unibex: http://www.unibex.com
- United Nations (UN): http://www.un.org

- United States-Mexico Chamber of Commerce: http://www.usmcoc. org/nafta.html
- Universal Travel Protection Insurance (UTPI): http://www.utravelpro. com
- U.S. Business Advisor: http://www.business.gov
- U.S. Census Bureau: http://www.census.gov
- U.S. Census Bureau Economic Indicators: http://www.census.gov/ econ/www
- U.S. Census Bureau Foreign Trade Division Harmonized Tariff Classification Schedule: http://www.census.gov/foreign-trade/www/ schedules.html
- U.S. Council for International Business (USCIB): http://www.uscib.org
- U.S. Customs Services: http://www.cbp.gov
- U.S. Department of Commerce (DOC): http://www.doc.gov
- U.S. Department of Commerce Commercial Service: http://www. export.gov/com_svc/
- U.S. Department of Commerce International Trade Administration: http://www.ita.doc.gov
- U.S. Export Assistance Centers (USEAC): http://www.export.gov/ eac.html
- U.S. Export Portal: http://www.export.gov
- U.S. Federal Maritime Commission (FMC): http://www.fmc.gov
- U.S. Foreign Trade Zones: http://www.ia.ita.doc.gov/ftzpage
- U.S. Government Glossary and Acronym of International Trade Terms: http://www.joc.com/handbook/glossaryofterms.shtml
- U.S. Patent and Trademark Office (USPTO): http://www.uspto.gov
- U.S. State Department Travel Advisory: http://www.travel.state.gov
- U.S. Trade Representative (USTR): http://www.ustr.gov
- USA/Internet: http://www.stat-usa.gov
- USDA Foreign Agricultural Service (FAS): http://www.fas.usda.gov
- USDA Shipper and Export Assistance (SEA): http://www.ams.usda. gov/tmd/tsd
- USDOC Trade Information Center: http://www.trade.gov/td/tic
- Various Utilities and Useful Information: http://www.ciber.bus.msu. edu/busres/statics/online-tools-utilities.htm
- *Wall Street Journal*: http://www.wsj.com
- Wells Fargo: http://www.wellsfargo.com
- World Academy: http://www.theworldacademy.com

- World Bank Group: http://www.worldbank.org
- World Chambers of Commerce Network: http://www.worldchambers.com
- World Customs Organization (WCO): http://www.wcoomd.org
- World Factbook: http://www.odci.gov/cia/publications/factbook/index.html
- World Intellectual Property Organization (WIPO): http://www.wipo.int
- World Newspapers On-line: http://www.virtourist.com/newspaper
- World Trade Analyzer: http://www.tradecompass.com
- World Trade Centers Association (WTCA): http://www.iserve.wtca.org
- *World Trade Magazine*: http://www.worldtrademag.com
- World Trade Organization (WTO): http://www.wto.org
- World Wide Shipping: http://www.ship.com
- WorldPages: http://www.worldpages.com

Developing resources that provide timely updates not found in printed material is a key component of Incoterms management (ITM). An example of information is from CBP on the costs involved in fees for imported merchandise into the United States. One such fee, MPF, is profiled next, and this information is taken from the CBP website (http://www.cbp.gov). The fee adds cost to the import process or increases landed cost spend.

U.S. Merchandise Processing Fee Increase

(10/26/2011) Recent trade legislation, H.R. 2832, was signed into law on October 21, 2011, changing the merchandise processing fee (MPF) rate for formal entries from 0.21% (.0021) to 0.3464% (.003464), effective October 1, 2011. The minimum and maximum fees, $25 and $485 respectively, did not change. CBP is currently in the process of modifying our automated systems to accept the new MPF rate of 0.3464%. We do not have an estimated completion date at this time; however, we will notify the trade as soon as possible via the Cargo Systems Messaging Service, when filers may begin transmitting entry summary information with the new MPF rate.

For entries filed on or after October 1, 2011, until the CBP system changes take effect with the 0.3464% rate, CBP will bill the importer for the increase in MPF. CBP will disregard differences of less than $20.

The only sure method of timely information is from sources that update daily. This makes websites such as http://cbp.gov excellent go-to locations for the most up-to-date and critical information for making the best decisions for the responsibilities of exercising best practices and leveraging risks and costs.

Incoterms are a choice best made with timely and comprehensive information.

SENIOR MANAGEMENT: EXECUTING A BEST PRACTICE STRATEGY

Incoterms Management

As outlined in this chapter, senior management's engagement in Incoterms is critical to running a successful global supply chain. Senior managers must take a leadership position to ensure that middle managers and operational staff comply with SOPs and best practices in what we refer to as ITM. For senior managers of public companies this is not optional but required.

The following outline demonstrates a higher-level strategy of, for example, chief executive officers, chief operating officers, presidents, and divisional senior executives to implement and follow:

1. Develop ITM into your business processes.
2. Learn the basics of Incoterms.
3. Develop resources for Incoterms expertise.
4. Understand how Incoterms decisions impact the global supply chain and break down fiefdoms.
5. Create integration management into Incoterms decision-making.
6. Learn leverage options in general, and then apply to the specifics in your global supply chain metrics.
7. Establish service provider, supplier, vendor, and other business relationship communications and SOPs.
8. Integrate technology into the Incoterms management process.
9. Create policy guidelines for Incoterms options and trade compliance management. For public companies, SOX Incoterms management is critical.
10. Engage Incoterms lobbying to increase and enhance change to your company's benefit.

Develop ITM into Your Business Processes

Reduce risk and maximize advantage. Gain a senior management commitment. ITM is the new buzz for successfully developing an expertise in Incoterms within an organization and developing processes to gain leverage and competitive advantage in your global supply chain. A commitment from senior management recognizing the importance of Incoterms as a skill set and ability to reduce risk and enhance and impact profits favorably is a corporate behavior that will prove necessary and valuable for long-term sustainability.

Companies allocate funds into personnel, training, and infrastructure. Firms and organizations develop all kinds of protocols and procedures to manage their day-to-day marketing, sales, and operations. Incoterms need to be prioritized among these management decisions and brought into corporate culture, behavior, and decision-making like in any other area of importance.

Learn the Basics of Incoterms

Senior managers do not necessarily need to understand Incoterms with the same detail as mid-level managers and operational staff, but they do need to know the following:

- Incoterms impact risk and cost.
- Companies can choose options that either increase or lower risk and costs.
- Staff making these decisions need to be educated and trained, and monies need to be allocated to this endeavor.

Develop Resources for Incoterms Expertise

Senior managers need to allocate funds and internal resources such as access to chief information officers (CIOs) and their staffs for the purpose of obtaining the wealth of information so better decisions about Incoterms and supply chain management can be made.

Understand How Incoterms Decisions Impact the Global Supply Chain and Break Down Fiefdoms

Senior managers need to budget time to interface with operational personnel and observe and scrutinize their Incoterms decisions to assure that their impacts on the global supply chain meet with long-term company objectives. An example might be just how Incoterms options that may benefit logistics choices could unfavorably impact corporate tax issues impacting P&L and balance sheet concerns. Senior management might need to break down the fiefdoms between logistics and finance to come up with compromises that meet both operational concerns and fall in line with company directives and policies. Senior managers in U.S.-based public companies are also typically charged with Sarbanes–Oxley compliance and would also incorporate Incoterms considerations in setting policy decisions in the global supply chain.

Create Integration Management into Incoterms Decision Making

Senior managers need to create a platform within a corporation that not only breaks down walls of distrust but also creates a balance of integration and cooperation between divisions, disciplines, and the various entities that operate the company's global supply chain.

Learn Leverage Options in General, and Then Apply to the Specific Scenarios in Your Global Supply Chain Metrics

Senior managers need to motivate operational personnel to obtain and review and execute Incoterms decisions based upon hard-core information, data, and resources obtained from accounting, freight payment companies, consultants, transportation providers, and carriers. These metrics need to be studied hard and comprehensively, and senior managers should lead the way to decision-making that combines these data with the esoteric more "feely" data that one compiles in making the best Incoterms decisions for the company.

Establish Service Provider, Supplier, Vendor, and Other Business Relationship Communications and Standard Operating Procedures

Senior managers need to lead value proposition management with all those support companies that helps or supports the company in managing all the aspects of their import and export operations. They should stress the value of open, direct, and no-nonsense communications that favorably impact business communications between principals and their vendors/suppliers. And they should encourage the implementation of

SOPs between all parties setting up lines of accountability and responsibility. This will assure compliance to best practice levels.

Integrate Technology into the Incoterms Management Process

Information technology can play a very important role in risk management, supply chain operations, and Incoterms management. Senior management needs to set direction and encourage the interface between the IT staff and those who operate the global supply chain to establish common areas of cooperation and utilization. Senior managers need to make sure that IT and supply chain know what each other has as needs and capabilities, and these two should meet somewhere to their mutual benefit. IT can play a huge role in creating tools and options for better Incoterms use that reduces risk and opens opportunity for competitive betterments.

Create Policy Guidelines for Incoterms Options and Trade Compliance Management; for Public Companies, SOX Incoterms Management Is Critical

Senior managers have to create an environment that includes trade compliance management in every Incoterms decision. While Incoterms structure includes compliance, it does so only in a peripheral way. Senior management has to set the guideline for compliance as a major factor in the company's decision-making process. For senior managers leading public companies, this is an absolute because the Incoterms choice at the lowest level of that company could have a huge impact on the financial exposures that company may face.

Engage Incoterms Lobbying to Increase and Enhance Change to Your Company's Benefit

Incoterms don't happen by default. The ICC (http://iccwbo.org) in Paris, France, through its leadership and membership, has numerous outlets for companies to exercise influence on how Incoterms are designed, structured, and eventually implemented. Delegates are lobbied by interested parties to make certain decisions that impact how Incoterms influence risk and costs in the global supply chains of the world. By engaging and joining organizations such as the ICC and the United States Council for International Business (USCIB; http://www.uscib.org) in New York, there are numerous venues, committees, and outreach opportunities for companies to lobby those who make Incoterms decisions. So participate and make a difference. The ICC has a complete listing of its member organizations and how to contact them, join in, participate, and make a favorable impact.

GOVERNMENT SECURITY PROGRAMS

Since 9/11, many countries, such as United States, Japan, Europe, Canada, and Mexico, have installed trade compliance and security initiatives for goods and people that move across their borders. This is relevant to Incoterms because the new *Incoterms 2010* specifically outline responsibilities to the seller or buyer to meet security obligations put forth by governments as part of their obligations in the transaction.

Exporters and importers who sell globally need to pay attention to these programs for a number of reasons:

- To meet obligations under their Incoterms
- To create potential advantages in their supply chain
- To assist their governments in thwarting terrorism

Some of the programs work as follows.

United States: C-TPAT

Customs-Trade Partnership Against Terrorism (C-TPAT) is a joint program between U.S. Customs and Border Protection (CBP) and global trade stakeholders. The program is designed to strengthen global supply chains and U.S. border security. The goal is to achieve the highest level of cargo security through close cooperation between CBP and businesses related to U.S. import supply chain cargo handling and movement.*

---

* From the U.S. Customs and Border Protection, http://www.cbp.gov.

C-TPAT is now 10 years old, and those companies involved in assisting companies join the program are very aware of the greater scrutiny CBP is putting on C-TPAT members as they become validated and revalidated. The C-TPAT program has remained a fluid process and has seen numerous changes in the application and validation process.

Prior to 9/11, the extent to which CBP was interested in a U.S. importer's supply chain was via the clearance process. The events of 9/11 obviously changed that, and C-TPAT has gone through many transformations over the past 10 years, as CBP realized the numerous vulnerabilities associated with the U.S. import supply chain. CBP has become aware that through the process of validation and revalidation, C-TPAT members are not conducting thorough international supply chain security assessments—or at least to the standards that CBP would like to see. While most C-TPAT members were conducting a domestic risk security analysis of their own domestic facility, CBP found that it was not doing the same for its international partners and vendors in dealing with risks in relation to its own import supply chain. This has caused concern for CBP and has created additional processes for U.S. importers to address if they want to remain in the program.

It is now highly recommended, although not required, that C-TPAT members perform an international supply chain risk assessment to discover the areas of improvement in the supply chain from point of origin to end delivery. This review becomes an integral part of their security profile. This assessment should be done once a company applies to the C-TPAT program since it is part of meeting the minimum security guidelines for joining C-TPAT. Once in the program, these assessments should be performed annually or else expulsion from C-TPAT is a risk. A strongly recommended 5 step risk assessment program will enable companies to meet these guidelines:*

- Mapping cargo and business partners: This involves monitoring how freight moves from your business partners throughout the supply chain from point of origin to delivery.
- Conducting a threat assessment: Research any potential vulnerability in your supply chain that can result in potential terrorism.

---

* From the U.S. Customs and Border Protection, http://www.cbp.gov.

- Conducting a security vulnerability assessment: With your business partners, identify any potential areas for potential security gaps using the minimum standards guidelines set up by C-TPAT.
- Preparing an action plan to address vulnerabilities: Prepare a written plan to deal with any vulnerabilities that are identified.
- Documenting how the security risk assessment is conducted: Identify the procedures of the assessment, who will be responsible, and how often it will occur.

It is important to remember that no matter how big or small your company is, if you want to remain a member in good standing in C-TPAT, you need to ensure that these risk assessments become an SOP. For an importer to go through the process of applying to the program only to be rejected—or even worse, expelled for not following these steps—is a waste of valuable resources.

Europe: AEO

The countries of Europe in 2005 began a program mirroring some of the principals of C-TPAT and meeting security guidelines tailored to European issues and needing an authorized economic operator (AEO).

One of the main elements of the security amendment of the Community Customs Code (Regulation (EC)648/2005) is the creation of the AEO concept.

On the basis of Article 5a of the security amendments, Member States can grant the AEO status to any economic operator meeting the following common criteria: customs compliance, appropriate record-keeping, financial solvency and, where relevant, security and safety standards.

The status of authorized economic operator granted by one Member State is recognized by the other Member States. This does not automatically allow AEOs to benefit from simplifications provided for in the customs rules in the other Member States. However, other Member States should grant the use of simplifications to authorized economic operators if they meet specific requirements.

Economic operators can apply for AEO status either to have easier access to customs simplifications or to be in a more favorable position to comply with the new security requirements. Under the security framework, which has been applicable since July 1, 2009, economic operators have to submit pre-arrival and pre-departure information on goods entering or leaving the EU. The security type of AEO certificate and the combined one allow their holders to benefit from facilitations with regard to the new customs controls relating to security.

The detailed provisions are laid down in the amendment (by Regulation 1875/2006) of the Implementing Provisions of the Community Customs Code. These provisions were drafted on the basis of experiences from the AEO Pilot conducted in 2006. Regulation(EC)197/2010 has established new time limits for issuing the AEO certificate

Regulation (EC) No 1192/2008 aligns the rules for granting both the AEO certificate for customs simplifications and the single authorization for simplified procedures (SASP). Being an AEO facilitates the process of achieving a single authorization for simplified procedures as the relevant criteria are deemed to be met.

AEO Guidelines

The AEO Guidelines ensure harmonized implementation of the AEO rules throughout the EU, guaranteeing the equal treatment of economic operators and transparency of the rules.

Part One of the AEO guidelines explains the AEO concept based on the adopted legislation, including:[*]

- Explanations about the different categories of AEO
- A specific section dedicated to Small and Medium sized Enterprises (SME) with guidance on how to examine the AEO requirements if the applicant is an SME
- A section giving advice to customs authorities on how to speed up the authorization process

---

[*] From Authorized Economic Operator, Taxation and Customs Union, http://ec.europa.eu/taxation-customs/customs/policy-issues/customs_security/aeo.

- Guidance for both customs authorities and trade on how to facilitate the procedure for parent/subsidiary companies
- A description of the AEO benefits with indications on the relevant AEO category and on the timeframe for the application of particular benefit
- A complete explanation on the concept of "business partners' security"
- An explanation, with concrete examples, for determining the competent Member State where the AEO application has to be submitted
- Guidelines for multinational companies and large businesses
- Guidance on how to perform monitoring after an AEO certificate has been issued

Part Two contains the questionnaire, providing a list of points to assist both customs authorities and AEO applicants in assessing whether or not the AEO criteria are met.

Japan

 Japan Customs

Under guidance from the World Trade Organization, Japan has also structured an AEO program. Following the 9/11 terror attacks on the United States, many countries have joined forces to combat terrorism, and C-TPAT and Container Security Initiatives (CSI), introduced by the United States, have been part of this initiative. The European Union amended the Community Customs Code and its implementing provisions in December 2006. They provide traders (AEOs) that meet the compliance criteria for cargo security with preferential customs procedures. On January 1, 2008, the provisions for the Japanese AEO program entered into force. In addition, it became mandatory for traders to provide customs authorities with advance information on goods brought into or out of the EU customs territory from July 1, 2009. AEO certified companies will be granted a streamlined approach to customs procedures, and our European subsidiaries have already applied for and are preparing for this program.

In Japan, the amended Customs Law was enacted in 2007 with the aim of revising the existing Simplified Export Declaration Procedure. This new law is the Japanese version of the AEO and offers preferential treatment to exporters who meet its high standards of compliance as well as a qualification system to obtain the preferential treatment.*

---

* From AEO, Nippon Express, http://www.nipponexpress.com/about/quality/aeo.html.

Canada Partners in Protection

Partners in Protection (PIP) is a Canada Border Services Agency (CBSA) program that enlists the cooperation of private industry to enhance border and trade chain security, combat organized crime and terrorism, and help detect and prevent contraband smuggling.

It is a voluntary program with no membership fee that aims to secure the trade chain, one partnership at a time. PIP members agree to implement and adhere to high security standards while the CBSA agrees to assess their security measures, provide information sessions on security issues and offer other benefits. Member companies are recognized as being trusted traders, which allows the CBSA to focus its resources on areas of higher or unknown risk.

Through their partnership with the CBSA, PIP members contribute to the security of the supply chain and the facilitation of legitimate trade.*

---

* From Partners in Protection, Canadian Border Services Agency, http://www.cbsa-asfc.gc.ca/security-securite/pip-pep.

4

Landed Cost Modeling

Landed costs need to be successfully integrated into global sales and purchasing because they are the foundation for determining the decisions of where we sell and buy. They allow a "science" to be laid out to a nonscientist to provide analysis for better decision-making in where we buy and how we determine contractual obligations, commitments, and deliverables.

It is both an art and science as to how we go about determining where we source goods globally and how we make our sales more competitive than others. To help us accomplish this goal, we need to understand the accumulation of costs involved in an international transaction to when we are at point of sale, use, or value.

Use of Incoterms® as an option in an agreement between a seller and buyer or an exporter and an importer could have a huge impact on the landed cost. Sellers and buyers need to know how Incoterms impact landed costs so the best options can be used to create competitive advantages.

DEFINITION OF LANDED COSTS

Landed costs are one of the most important aspects of global trade that all parties engaged in importing and exporting need to comprehend thoroughly. They should be a major factor in what determines where we source from globally and, for exports, how competitive our products are in world markets. Free trade agreements (FTAs) play a large role in landed costs. For the past 10 years leading up to 2012 the world has engaged in a number of FTAs. For example, in the United States in 2011 three new agreements were voted into place with Korea, Colombia, and Panama. The North American Free Trade Agreement (NAFTA), among the United

States, Mexico, and Canada, is one of the largest and most successful free trade agreements. FTAs impact landed costs in a huge way, which benefits trade between countries.

Landed cost is the accumulation of costs associated with moving goods from one country to another. It is composed of a number of costs, including the following:

Invoice value

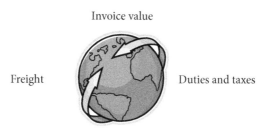

Freight   Duties and taxes

Insurance and finance charges

The major issue is that companies look to source from overseas and look at purchase prices with much lower costs than they could purchase in their domestic markets, but that in itself should not be a final decision-making guide.

The choice of the Incoterms will impact landed costs. Both parties in the transaction need to work out a compromise Incoterms choice that works mutually to each other's advantage.

As discussed in Chapter 3, Incoterms management requires input from numerous parts of a company's structure that would also be impacted by the choice of the Incoterms and could prove valuable in the overall evaluation leading to competitive advantages.

In the United States, for public companies Sarbanes–Oxley (SOX) concerns and mandates will also impact Incoterms options. Landed costs need to be thought out carefully, and those involved in this process need to have a broad perspective of all the costs that impact the final cost of bringing goods from a seller to a buyer to the point of sale, use, or value.

But landed costs equations will require a number of other expenses to be brought into the formula so a sound decision can be made. Some of the additional landed costs fall into the following areas:

- Cost to export from the originating country
- Inland freight from origin to outbound gateway
- Foreign freight from gateway to gateway

- Insurance
- Warehousing
- Inland freight from inbound gateway to the final destination
- Customs clearance
- Import licenses, permits, and registrations

- Ancillary freight charges, demurrage, etc.
- Duties, taxes, value-added tax (VAT), or goods and services tax (GST), etc.

- Handling and related services

- Security fees

COST TO EXPORT FROM THE ORIGINATING COUNTRY: $$$

Every country in the world has an export process that the seller or buyer must go through to move the goods from that country. For example, in the United States certain goods require an export license, issued by the State, Commerce, or Treasury departments. Some are free; others have costs into the thousands of dollars. Some require companies to bear internal costs in determining requirements, evaluating, or processing. Some companies engage outside professionals such as logistics providers, consultants, or law firms to handle the processing, all which could add costs to the overall export process.

Some products from certain countries like Mexico have export fees based upon the value of the goods being exported. In China, goods that are exported have export fees on all export transactions paid to their government agencies. Should a company choose the ExWorks Incoterms in its purchasing agreement, it would have to pay these charges on the outbound logistics of the export. With other Incoterms options, the exporter would pay these costs and may or may not recover these costs in the export sale.

The question to be considered then is: Who is best at going through this export formality—the seller or the buyer? And who would be in a better position to do it in a timely and more cost-effective manner? Both of these questions come into play when products may require a more compliant and secure export formality, such as with export of licensable merchandise.

INLAND FREIGHT FROM ORIGIN TO OUTBOUND GATEWAY: $$

Unless an exporter's manufacturing or distribution warehouse sits alongside an airport or an ocean terminal there will always be an inland freight movement from the origin point to the outbound gateway. The clear majority of these movements travel via truck, but rail, barge, and air could certainly be options. In remote areas of the world and in some third-world or developing nations, this inland mode could be manual labor, donkey, or even a horse-drawn carriage.

In some shipments, the inland move could be 4 miles, 5 kilometers, or 1,000 yards. In some supply chains, as an example goods originating in Sioux City, Iowa, exporting from the Port of Los Angeles could see distances of over 1,000 miles from origin to outbound gateway.

In Australia, goods originating in the Outback could see distances over 2,000 miles to go from origin points to outbound gateways, such as Sydney, Perth, or Melbourne. In Venezuela, goods originating in an inland city such as Cucui could have over 1,000 kilometers before reaching the port city of Puerto Cabello. One would then travel through a dense Amazon jungle with little transportation infrastructure to favorably impact inland freight options. In contrast, I have a client in Long Beach, California, that is located right on the tarmac at Long Beach Airport/Daugherty Field. It manufactures airplane parts and ships directly from that warehousing location. It moves the freight approximately 400 yards in its own vehicles from dock to planeside both for domestic and international shipments.

I have another client located on the Thames River in England. As part of its energy business facility, it has a dock/pier facility for the loading of vessels. The freight moves about 80 meters from storage locale to the pier apron alongside the vessel.

In every case—from 80 meters to 2,000 miles—a cost is associated with the movement from the point of sale to the outbound gateway from within the country of export. In an ExWorks shipment these costs are designed for and are typically for the account of the buyer. In other Incoterm options, these inland freight charges are for the account of the seller, such as FOB, CIF, and DDP.

The questions that are always of concern are, is the exporter recouping these costs in the sales price or are they eating these costs in the "costs of goods sold?" And which party can accomplish these in both a timely and cost-effective manner?

EXPORT PRO FORMA COMMERCIAL INVOICE OUTLINING FOB TERM AND THE ACCUMULATION OF COSTS

TAC COMPANY Exports Abound

12 Benjamin Ave, Hamptons, NY

Phone: 212 345 6789; Fax: 212 345 6781

Export Pro Forma INVOICE

Invoice #[**100**]
Date: August 7, 2013

To:
Star Fishing, Hook DivisionTyson
23 Rue de Housen
1234 Paris, France   Ph# 33 124 56789

PO # 2345
Terms of Sale … CIP Incoterms 2010
Elizabeth, NJ

DESCRIPTION	HOURS	RATE	AMOUNT
23 Hook assemblies, Style 4500 Green IPC 2136789456			23,897 USD
All goods exported according to U.S. EAR regulations. Diversion contrary to U.S. Law.			
Make all checks payable to TAC Company			
Total due in 45 days. Overdue accounts subject to a service charge of 1% per month.		ExWorks	23,897.00 USD
		Inland Freight	527.00 USD
		TOTAL FOB PRICE	24,424.00 USD

The importer would take these costs and now add their additional costs:

- Ocean freight
- Clearance
- Duties, taxes, VAT
- Inland freight to final destination

And these will now bring the importer to a total landed cost calculation.

The Paris-based importer reaches out to its Le Havre–based customhouse broker/freight forwarder, which has an agent in New Jersey, and asks for costs to pick these goods up. It will have a shipment every week. Star Fishing is advised that the inland freight would be approximately $650.00 per transaction. This is over $100.00 more than the manufacturer is charging.

It then asks the manufacturer for a CIP Le Havre quote. It receives a Pro Forma Invoice showing the following:

TAC COMPANY Exports Abound

12 Benjamin Ave, Hamptons, NY

Phone: 212 345 6789; Fax: 212 345 6781

Export Pro Forma INVOICE

Invoice #[**100**]
Date: August 15, 2013

To:
Star Fishing, Hook DivisionTyson
23 Rue de Housen
1234 Paris, France   Ph# 33 124 56789

PO # 2345
Terms of Sale ... CIP Incoterms 2010
Le Havre, France

DESCRIPTION	HOURS	RATE	AMOUNT
23 Hook assemblies, Style 4500 Green IPC 2136789456			23,897 USD
All goods exported according to U.S. EAR regulations. Diversion contrary to U.S. Law.			
Make all checks payable to TAC Company Total due in 45 days. Overdue accounts subject to a service charge of 1% per month.		ExWorks	23,897.00 USD
		Inland Freight	527.00 USD
		Insurance	$500.00 USD
		Ocean Freight	1975.00 USD
		TOTAL FOB PRICE	26,899.00 USD

When compared, the insurance cost is $100 greater, but the overall savings, mostly in the ocean freight area, saves an additional $400 per shipment. This represents a savings of over $20,000 annually in just this one trading lane.

The importer scrutinizes some additional considerations in the overall evaluation:

- Ocean freight times
- Frequency of shipping options
- Which carriers are being stylized
- Reputation of freight forwarder with reference checks
- Claims history

The new shipping option proves to be a viable alternative, and the importer amends the Incoterms from FOB Elizabeth to CIF Le Havre.

The importer in France now applies this process of quoting to all the millions of euros of goods and services it purchases around the world. It estimates that it has reduced landed costs by almost a million euros annually. These savings are passed on to the customers because the importer's price points have now been significantly reduced.

Sales have increased from 6% to almost 11% annually, demonstrating that Incoterms choices impact the competitiveness of global supply chains.

FOREIGN FREIGHT FROM GATEWAY TO GATEWAY: $$$$

One of the largest value components of landed cost is the price of ocean or air freight transportation from outbound gateway of the seller's country to the inbound gateway of the buyer's country. Some examples are John F. Kennedy Airport in New York City to Charles De Gaulle Airport in Paris; ocean freight terminal in Sydney, Australia, to the port of Shanghai, China; from O'Hare Airport in Chicago, Illinois, to Heathrow Airport in London; and from the Port of Genoa, Italy, to the Port of Recife, Brazil.

In some instances, where we have low value freight, the cost of the international leg can be in excess of the value of the cargo. Fortunately, this international leg freight/transportation expense is usually more clearly defined in most sales and purchase agreements. Having said that, where disputes may occur is when air freight becomes an option as a default choice when someone screws up on anticipated delivery schedules. This leaves air freight as a secondary but viable option. The question is then: Was this potential cost budgeted for, and who would be responsible to pay these additional expenses?

Air freight can be as much as 18 to 30 times more expensive than ocean freight on some trade lanes, making dispute resolution an issue on how this may get handled in a sale or purchase on a global basis. These situations, when proactively dealt with in both sales and purchase agreements, are really the best option, so when they do occur both parties will know how it will be handled. Also, having a good working relationship with the buyer or supplier will go a long way in handling disputes favorably.

In the Star Fishing example, in the shipment originating in New York and being sold to the customer in France, the ocean freight costs were the largest component of the import logistics charges. As in this example the best way to deal with this expense favorably is to get quotes using various Incoterms and then to determine which Incoterms provides the best freight rates. As outlined in the previous example, while cost is a key factor other considerations need to be factored in— such as service reliability and frequency of sailings—before coming to a conclusion.

The key area here is acknowledging that Incoterms are options that can both favorably and unfavorably impact a company's landed cost.

MARINE CARGO INSURANCE: $

The only Incoterms that specifically identify the procurement of cargo insurance as part of the responsibilities of the seller are CIF and CIP. In these options the seller or exporter procures cargo insurance on behalf of the buyer's risk of loss and damage from the time the goods began their international transit until when the goods arrive at the inbound gateway in the arrival country. CIF should by design be used only for sea and inland waterway transport, whereas CIP can be used for all modes of transit.

It is important to note that the seller needs to procure cover on only a minimum basis. This should be a red flag to the buyer or importer as the issue could be scope of coverage, underlying terms and conditions, and insurance company, which is utilized. We recommend that those who have the risk control their insurance purchase. But regarding landed cost, this can be another expense variable that could impact competitive advantage.

If a shipment is valued at US$250,000 and insurance is charged at a rate of $.75 per $100 of insured value (IV), the cargo insurance premium is $1875. If one negotiated a rate of $.25 per $100 of IV, the new premium is $625—a difference of $1250, or a savings of almost 66%. If this sale or purchase was made once a month, the annual savings could add up to as much as $15,000, which is a lot of money to leave on the table when it could easily have been reduced from the very start. This would and could directly influence an ability to develop a sale or determine a source or supplier.

We recommend the following when it comes to purchasing cargo insurance:

1. Control the purchase for the best results in price and coverage. Use Incoterms that afford you that control.
2. Keep relationships strong with insurance brokers and underwriting companies that specialize in cargo insurance.
3. The clear majority of imports and exports require the broadest form of cargo insurance to be acquired: "all risk'"
4. Learn the basics of cargo insurance:
   - Underwriting and brokerage options
   - Underlying terms and conditions
   - Deductibles
   - Geographic scope
   - Exclusions—both explicit and implicit
   - Policy period and products, divisions, entities, etc., covered
5. Cargo insurance management should be proactively thought out and not an afterthought where only reactive behavior comes into play. That is where the costs, hardship, and frustrations will be the greatest.
6. Find a quality marine cargo insurance specialist, such as the Roanoke Companies in the United States, Munich Re in Germany, Watkins in London, and Wells Fargo in the United States, to name a few options.

The cost of a cargo claim can be significant. Make sure you understand the implication of risk and insurance purchase on every Incoterms option and prepare a proactive course of action. It will go a long way in the long term to prevent headache and prove to ultimately make you more competitive.

WAREHOUSING: $

Freight that moves internationally often gets consolidated or deconsolidated or may be held temporarily by decision or by default. When this happens the cost of that storage or related services can add additional cost to the import or export transaction, directly impacting the landed costs.

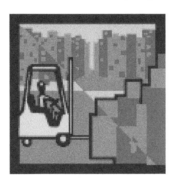

In many instances, management chooses to place warehousing costs onto the domestic side of the balance sheets. The only concern I have when this is done is that if it does not get posted somewhere to the transactional cost of the import or export then the true cost of purchase or sale is not being factored into the decision-making process.

Quality and focused information on landed cost makeup is critical to the sound decision-making process in how we determine competitive and leveraged options in our portfolio. Knowing when to use, when to exercise, and when to implement are decisions best made when costs are clearly and accurately allocated.

In addition, supply chain executives who run "lean" supply chains will always make an attempt in the planning stages to avoid any form of warehousing as it

- Adds cost
- Adds risk
- Adds additional handling and storage can cause claims and exposure to loss and damage
- Causes managing inventory and distribution control to possibly become an issue

Direct shipments are always best and provide the most cost-effective method of international shipping.

When thinking out Incoterms options, it is necessary to review exactly how the freight will transit. The Incoterms choice that best reduces any opportunity for intermediate storage or warehousing (unless absolutely needed) is usually your best option. Warehousing can add cost to an import or export transaction that is typically not planned, budgeted or accounted for until after the fact.

INLAND FREIGHT FROM INBOUND GATEWAY TO THE FINAL DESTINATION: $$$

Depending upon where the final destination is located, this expense could prove to be as large as the international inbound freight cost. In some countries, such as the United States, Russia, Australia, China, Brazil, and Mexico, inland points in some instances could be over 2,000 miles from ocean ports or major city airports. This could add to getting the product to point of use very expensive relative to the total of all the landed costs. The decision on who arranges for and who may control this cost is directly attributed to the Incoterms.

For example, if a company in St. Louis, Missouri, purchases US$100,000 in piece goods from a supplier in Lahore, Pakistan, on a Delivered at Place (DAP) basis, this would entail that the seller or exporter in Pakistan makes the arrangement for the inland freight from the port of entry at Long Beach, California, to the final destination in St. Louis. In this specific example, this importer is a big user of domestic freight services and has some very competitive inland freight and domestic transportation rates. But in this company there is a "disconnect" between the purchasing group arranging for the offshore purchasing and the domestic freight division who manages domestic freight purchasing contracts from large trucking companies.

The distance between St. Louis and Long Beach is approximately 1,975 miles. The cost included in the DAP price from the Pakistani supplier is $1025. As it turns out, this buyer has a contract with a domestic freight company who has a strong capability in bringing freight out of the West Coast ports to the Midwest United States. When the buyer gets the price from the domestic carrier, with its annual volumes, it can arrange for a price from Long Beach to St. Louis for $750, a savings of $275 per shipment.

It imports approximately 50 transactions similar to this from that supplier. Annual savings of over $13,000 are achievable if as the buyer/importer it controls the inland freight from Long Beach to St. Louis. This benefit got lost in the original purchasing decision because the landed cost on a DAP basis was still more competitive than domestic sourcing, even with a high domestic freight cost.

The domestic freight division of this company got connected with the purchasing group and amended the Incoterms to DAT Long Beach. This importer was now in control of the domestic freight from the inbound gateway to the final destination, and savings of over $13,000 on this trade lane was now brought to a lower landed cost and a more competitive price overall.

CUSTOMS CLEARANCE: $$

There are numerous, very detailed, and convoluted factors that influence this inbound cost. To understand this customs clearance process and the costs associated with it, one needs to first look at what *customs* all over the world is all about. Every country around the world has some form of customs that controls people and goods that enter and leave their country. A primary purpose of customs all over the world is to collect duties, taxes, and VAT/GST and related costs. They are also involved in security, trade compliance, and collection of census data.

Similar guidelines are followed everywhere on issues related to harmonized tariff classification, origin issues, and documentation requirements. But as similar as they are, there are some very strong differences as well. Those companies and individuals who operate in supply chain management know from experience that to be successful in dealing with customs in an array of countries, one must

- Have a quality and timely source of information on a local basis
- Partner with string service providers
- Show flexibility, patience, and tolerance in the differences that exist
- Think out of the box and be creative and well prepared for all the challenges one will face when dealing with customs in some countries

One of the most important partners a company can have in its global supply chain is the customs broker it uses to arrange customs clearance on its behalf or on behalf of the supplier or buyer who is party to the sales or purchase agreement. These customs brokers are typically experienced, licensed, and insured service providers with a host of capabilities to manage the clearance process. The management of this process is a "profit center" for these customhouse brokers. They can make a good living providing this service on behalf of principal exporters and importers. Customs brokers typically have a huge laundry list of charges they access for the array of services they provide, such as

- Arrangement of import permits and registrations
- Harmonized tariff review
- Documentation preparation
- Overnight services
- Runner or local delivery services
- Warehousing, storage, and or deconsolidation
- Customs clearance
- Handling
- Security charges (in goods entering the United States—ISF charges)
- Hazardous-material fees
- Overnight services
- U.S. Food and Drug Administration (FDA), agricultural, or equivalent handling charges
- Pedimentos, such as in Mexico for import permit charges
- Fees for laying out duties and taxes

While all customhouse brokers charge for their services, the amount of the fees and how they access the charges could vary dramatically from one company to another.

The choice of the Incoterms will typically determine who is responsible to select the customhouse broker and be liable to pay their fees. This makes the Incoterms choice another variable in the overall incremental cost of landing the goods in a country overseas.

Exporters who handle the customs clearance under DDP terms are engaging customs hundreds if not thousands of miles away, in another time zone and legal system, and should be very careful in selling with this responsibility and choice of the Incoterms DDP. There is so much additional expense they could potentially bear with little local influence or knowledge. When they choose this option, they need to be very careful about whom they select to handle this local clearance overseas as it could greatly impact the landed cost.

The selection of the DDP term for an exporter must be very carefully thought out and entered into only when they have to because of the nature of the sale, client, or nuance of their supply chain. On the other hand, buyers who allow the seller to control the inbound import clearance could be foolish unless specific circumstances warrant that action. Importers who control the inbound clearance process through terms such as FOB, DAP, and CIP typically can control the customs brokers' charges to a more competitive level than the exporter or seller overseas in the country of shipment. Being on the ground locally and having a presence in that market allows for a much greater influence over the process and in turn typically will impact cost more favorably.

Required Documents in Mexico

The following is a list of the documents that typically need to be presented for the imported product to be released from Mexican Customs authorities:

- **Importation Declaration** (*Pedimento de Importación*)
- **Commercial invoice**—must include issue date and place, name and address of the consignee, detailed listing of goods (e.g., quantities, types, identification numbers, unit value), and name and address of supplier
- **Bill of lading** or Airway Bill of lading
- **Sanitary import notice** (to be done on company letterhead, and which should contain the name of the product, quantity, name and address of the producer, name and address of the importer, the port of entry, and the applicable import tariff numbers. The letter should be addressed to the *Secretaria de Salud* [Ministry of Health])
- **NAFTA Certificate of origin** (as applicable), in order to obtain NAFTA tariff benefits
- **Certificate of Free Sale** (U.S. exporters can request these through TTB)

IMPORT LICENSES, PERMITS, AND REGISTRATIONS: $$

In most countries around the world there is an import infrastructure and process that requires an importer to obtain a permit, license, or registration before the goods enter that country. This process will vary greatly in many countries. In the United States as an example, this aspect of the import process is very minimal. In Mexico, Brazil, and the Philippines it could be extensive, adding time, complications, and expense to the import process.

In some countries the fees are flat and simple; in others they are progressive, increasing depending upon commodity, value, and use. Some countries use these fees to make an attempt to discourage importing and to encourage purchasing from local options. They can also be political in nature or impacted by both global and local economic issues. Global supply chain personnel need to know that these add cost to the transportation of goods internationally, and the choice of Incoterms will impact who is responsible to pay these charges.

In many circumstances, the party that controls the import process could favorably and legitimately modify these inbound charges based upon HTS codes, valuations, and documentation. These contributing options need to be carefully analyzed as they impact cost. The wrong choice could increase cost. The right choice could impact lower cost.

In any case, authorities want correct and true information provided, but in all countries there is an interpretative process. In the United States it is called the General Rules of Interpretation (GRI). Parties that know these rules well know how to leverage the interpretative options for landed cost advantage. One cannot be deceptive or take illegal steps, but there is sometimes room for favorable interpretation if one knows how to apply all the options available. Some countries around the world require SGS inspections prior to goods leaving the origin country and before being shipped to them.

BOTTOM OF FORM

Preshipment Inspection

Some of the following countries require preshipment inspection only if the invoice is over a certain value or only on certain types of products. For preshipment inspections, consult with the appropriate company that has contracted with the government of the country to which you are shipping. Phone numbers and websites are listed for inspection companies. This update does not include countries serviced by Control Union Inspection, Inc.

Angola—Société Générale Surveillance, Bureau Veritas

Bangladesh—Bureau Veritas, Intertek Testing, Inspectorate America Corp.

Benin—Bureau Veritas

Bolivia—Inspectorate America Corp., Société Générale Surveillance

Burkina Faso—Société Générale Surveillance

Burundi—Société Générale Surveillance

Cambodia—Société Générale Surveillance

Cameroon—Société Générale Surveillance

Central African Republic—Société Générale Surveillance

Comoros—Cotecna

Congo (Democratic Republic)—Bureau Veritas, Société Générale Surveillance

Cote d'Ivoire—Bureau Veritas, Cotecna

Ecuador—Cotecna, Intertek Testing, Société Générale Surveillance

Ethiopia—Société Générale Surveillance

Ghana—Bureau Veritas, Cotecna

Guinea—Société Générale Surveillance

India—Inspectorate America Corp.

India (Secondary Steel)—Société Générale Surveillance, Inspectorate America Corp.

Indonesia (Waste and Used Equipment)—Société Générale Surveillance

Iran—Bureau Veritas, Intertek Testing, Inspectorate America Corp.

Iran (Voluntary Trade Facilitation Program)—Inspectorate America Corp.

Kenya—Cotecna, Bureau Veritas, Intertek Testing

Kuwait—Intertek Testing

Liberia—Bureau Veritas

Madagascar—Bureau Veritas, Société Générale Surveillance

Malawi—Société Générale Surveillance

Mali—Société Générale Surveillance

Mexico—Bureau Veritas, Intertek Testing, Société Générale Surveillance

Moldova—Société Générale Surveillance

Mauritania—Société Générale Surveillance

Mozambique—Intertek Testing

Niger—Cotecna

Nigeria—Intertek Testing, Cotecna, Société Générale Surveillance

Peru—Bureau Veritas, Cotecna, Société Générale Surveillance

Russia (GOST Certification Services)—Inspectorate America Corp.

Rwanda—Intertek Testing
Saudi Arabia—Intertek Testing
Senegal—Cotecna
Sierra Leone—Bureau Veritas
Tanzania—Cotecna
Togo—Cotecna
Uzbekistan—Intertek Testing, Société Générale Surveillance
Venezuela—Intertek Testing, Société Générale Surveillance
Zanzibar—Société Générale Surveillance

Inspection Companies

Bureau Veritas—(305) 593-7878, http://www.bivac.com
Cotecna—(703) 814-4000, http://www.cotecna.com
Société Générale Surveillance (SGS)—(212) 482-8700, http://www.sgs.com
Intertek Testing Service—(305) 513-3000, http://www.intertek.com
Inspectorate America Corp.—(305) 599-1124, http://www.inspectorate.com
Control Union Inspection Inc.—(504) 227-2025, http://www.controlunion.com

These preshipment inspections add potential time, cost, and risk to a transaction to these countries. Typically the importer unless otherwise agreed would be responsible for these costs. The exporter would have to make the freight available for inspection, but the inspection fees are for the account of the buyer.

Having said that, this could change if the seller was to ship or export on a DDP basis. If you review the previous list, most of these countries are developing nations with typically strict rules on imported freight. One may not be able to sell and ship to these countries on a DDP basis. But if they could then they would most likely take responsibility for the preshipment inspection responsibility, as that would be considered an "import formality."

ANCILLARY FREIGHT CHARGES, DEMURRAGE, ETC.: $

Shippers of cargoes internationally learn quickly the array of additional surcharges that can apply on an ancillary basis that sometimes go way above and beyond what costs were originally anticipated.

Demurrage can be the cost which makes the most unanticipated impact. This cost results from carriers charging fees that grow incrementally when freight is not picked up in the allotted time frame local to the "ordinary and customary" guidelines in that port or country. Demurrage is always a cost which when occurs may not be clear as to who the responsible party is and also how Incoterms might apply.

Many experienced freight personnel budget from 1% to 3% additionally when calculating freight costs in anticipation of unexpected variables. If they don't happen, they're ahead. If they do, they have them covered.

Some of these costs are

- Bunker Fuel Surcharges
- Security Fees
- Container Service Charges
- Terminal Handling Charges
- Demurrage
- Currency Adjustment Factors

Example

An exporter from Germany sells electronic components on a CIF Wellington basis to an importer in Taranga, New Zealand. The goods are shipped by ocean freight through the port of Hamburg.

When the goods arrive and the importer begins the clearance process in New Zealand, they discover that the documents do not meet the documentary guidelines for import in New Zealand.

In Wellington, importers are given 5 days to clear the goods and pick them up from the inbound ocean carrier's facility before penalties (demurrage) are accounted for.

The error in the shipper's export documentation becomes an issue and 9 days expire before the correct documents are provided by the exporter and handed over to New Zealand Customs.

When the importer arranges for pick up from the carrier, they are advised that demurrage penalties will be an additional $850 NZD. In the CIF Incoterms the importer is responsible for clearance, import formalities, and costs. But the exporter is required to provide documentation to the importer enabling them to make the import clearance in their country.

So this case "opens up Pandora's box" and places the situation into a "gray area" of Incoterms global trade management.

Common sense dictates that if the exporter created the problem by sending incorrect documents, they would be responsible for any resulting excess costs. But technically, this is not clear.

A number of issues arise:

- Did the importer in the purchase order advise what documents are required and how they should be constructed?
- Did the exporter ask those questions?
- What role did the export freight forwarder and the import custom-house broker play in the handling of the documentation?
- What role did New Zealand Customs play potentially in an "interpretative" area of import documentary requirements?

DUTIES, TAXES, VAT, OR GST, ETC.: $$$$

Most countries customs authorities' primary reason for existence is for the purpose of collecting duties, taxes, and related costs.

These costs impact the landed costs significantly on most products shipped around the world.

In many countries certain products move across the borders freely, such as, but not limited to, printed matter, personal effects, relief goods, and items sold to government agencies.

Having noted that 99% of goods move under some level of taxation to and from most origins and destinations globally.

It is in that 99% that the decision on the Incoterms will play a large role on what the costs are to each party—the seller and the buyer—and who assumes the risks of managing the customs clearance process in that arriving destination.

In some situations, duties and taxes can amount to as much as 40% of the value of the goods. In many developing nations this is the case as their governments impose stiff taxes in order to "stem" the tide of imports that impact their trade imbalances.

A company in Belgium ships certain machine parts to a customer in Sao Paulo, Brazil. The CIF value heading into Brazil is R$100,000.00 (real/reais).

The duty and tax rate is almost 38%. This brings the landed cost to almost R$140,000; and when you add in import permits, product registrations, warehousing, the clearance process, and inland freight to destination manufacturing point, the costs could increase another R$10,000, making the landed costs very high.

When companies are making choices about Incoterms ... when they take the responsibility for paying duties and taxes they could be assuming a cost which may be half the value of the goods. Treading carefully here is a prudent decision.

Some countries such as Canada, the European Union, Argentina, Australia, and Egypt, among hundreds (complete list in the Appendix), impose a form of VAT or GST taxes on goods imported into that country.

In some countries there is a refund process which enables companies to get back all or part of that tax through a specialized application process.

The United States, along with a few countries like Hong Kong (though now part of China), Saudi Arabia, and Bermuda, do not have any of these forms of value-added taxes (VAT).

VAT is a form of consumption tax. From the perspective of the buyer, it is a tax on the purchase price. From that of the seller, it is a tax only on the "value added" to a product, material, or service, from an accounting point of view, by this stage of its manufacture or distribution. The manufacturer remits to the government the difference between these two amounts, and retains the rest for themselves to offset the taxes they had previously paid on the inputs.

The "value added" to a product by a business is the sale price charged to its customer, minus the cost of materials and other taxable inputs. A VAT is like a sales tax in that ultimately only the end consumer is taxed. It differs from the sales tax in that, with the latter, the tax is collected and remitted to the government only once, at the point of purchase by the end consumer. With the VAT, collections, remittances to the government, and credits for taxes already paid occur each time a business in the supply chain purchases products.

From a historical perspective, Maurice Lauré, joint director of the French Tax Authority, the Direction Générale des Impôts, was first to introduce VAT on April 10, 1954, although German industrialist Dr. Wilhelmvon Siemens proposed the concept in 1918. Initially directed at large businesses, it was extended over time to include all business sectors. In France, it is the most important source of state finance, accounting for nearly 50% of state revenues.

Each country rules this area of tax differently. In general, individual end-consumers of products and services typically cannot recover VAT on purchases, but businesses are able to recover VAT (input tax) on the products and services that they buy in order to produce further goods or services that will be sold to yet another business in the supply chain or directly to a final consumer. In this way, the total tax levied at each stage in the economic chain of supply is a constant fraction of the value added by a business to its products, and most of the cost of collecting the tax is borne by business, rather than by the state. Value-added taxes were introduced in part because they create stronger incentives to collect than a sales tax does. Both types of consumption tax create an incentive by end consumers to avoid or evade the tax, but the sales tax offers the buyer a mechanism to avoid or evade the tax—persuade the seller that he or she (the buyer) is not really an end consumer, and therefore the seller is not legally required to collect it. The burden of determining whether the buyer's motivation is to consume or resell is on the seller, but the seller has no direct economic incentive to collect it. The VAT approach gives sellers a direct financial stake in collecting the tax, and eliminates the problematic decision by the seller about whether the buyer is or is not an end consumer.

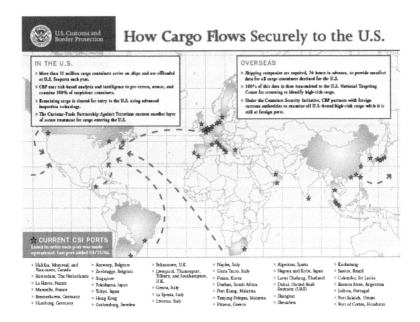

How Cargo Flows Securely to the U.S.

U.S. Customs and Border Protection

IN THE U.S.

» More than 11 million cargo containers arrive on ships and are offloaded at U.S. Seaports each year.

» CBP uses risk-based analysis and intelligence to pre-screen, assess, and examine 100% of suspicious containers.

» Remaining cargo is cleared for entry to the U.S. using advanced inspection technology.

» The Customs-Trade Partnership Against Terrorism ensures another layer of secure treatment for cargo entering the U.S.

OVERSEAS

» Shipping companies are required, 24 hours in advance, to provide manifest data for all cargo containers destined for the U.S.

» 100% of this data is then transmitted to the U.S. National Targeting Center for screening to identify high-risk cargo.

» Under the Container Security Initiative, CBP partners with foreign customs authorities to examine all U.S.-bound high-risk cargo while it is still at foreign ports.

★ CURRENT CSI PORTS
Listed in order each port was made operational. Last port added 01/25/06.

» Halifax, Montreal, and Vancouver, Canada	» Antwerp, Belgium	» Felixstowe, U.K.	» Naples, Italy	» Algeciras, Spain	» Kaohsiung
» Rotterdam, The Netherlands	» Zeebrugge, Belgium	» Liverpool, Thamesport, Tilbury, and Southampton, U.K.	» Gioia Tauro, Italy	» Nagoya and Kobe, Japan	» Santos, Brazil
» Le Havre, France	» Singapore	» Pusan, Korea	» Laem Chabang, Thailand	» Colombo, Sri Lanka
» Marseille, France	» Tokohama, Japan	» Genoa, Italy	» Durban, South Africa	» Dubai, United Arab Emirates (UAE)	» Buenos Aires, Argentina
» Bremerhaven, Germany	» Tokyo, Japan	» La Spezia, Italy	» Port Klang, Malaysia	» Shanghai	» Lisbon, Portugal
» Hamburg, Germany	» Hong Kong	» Livorno, Italy	» Tanjung Pelepas, Malaysia	» Shenzhen	» Port Salalah, Oman
	» Gothenburg, Sweden		» Piraeus, Greece		» Port of Cortes, Honduras

Example: Canada

HOW GST/HST WORKS

The GST (Goods and Services tax) is a tax that applies to the supply of most property and services in Canada. The provinces of Nova Scotia, New Brunswick, and Newfoundland, and Labrador, referred to as the participating provinces, harmonized their provincial sales tax with the GST to create the Harmonized Sales Tax (HST). Generally, the HST applies to the same base of property and services as the GST. In some participating provinces, there are point-of-sale rebates equivalent to the provincial part of the HST on designated items.

As of July 1, 2010, Ontario harmonized its retail sales tax with the GST to implement the HST at the rate of 13% and British Columbia harmonized its provincial sales tax with the GST to implement the HST at the rate of 12%. Also, as of July 1, 2010, Nova Scotia increased its HST rate from 13% to 15%.

Almost everyone has to pay the GST/HST on purchases of taxable supplies of property and services (other than zero-rated supplies). A limited number of sales or supplies are exempt from GST/HST.

Although the consumer pays the tax, businesses are generally responsible for collecting and remitting it to the government. Businesses that are required to have a GST/HST registration number are called registrants.

Registrants collect the GST/HST on most of their sales and pay the GST/HST on most purchases they make to operate their business. They can claim an input tax credit, to recover the GST/HST paid or payable on the purchases they use in their commercial activities.

GST/HST registrants must meet certain responsibilities. Generally, they must file returns on a regular basis, collect the tax on taxable supplies they make in Canada, and remit any resulting net tax owing.

Canada is one of a few countries that allows a foreign entity to become a "registrant" and act as "importer of record" and collect back GST charges.

GOVERNMENT INSPECTION REQUIREMENTS: $

Many government agencies require preshipment inspections, which we outlined in detail earlier in this chapter.

In addition some countries will inspect goods as they come across the border.

A good example of this is when pharmaceuticals come into the United States, which may be subject to FDA guidelines (Food and Drug Administration).

CBP (Customs) may elect to inspect the goods before they are cleared by them as an extension of the authority provided them by the governing agency … the FDA.

They may be concerned about the correct classification, product description, if it is registered, approved, authorized, has prior notice, packing marking and labeling, etc.

CBP will have the freight put aside by the arriving carrier. They will then open the units and inspect. They may have them brought to a laboratory or testing facility away from the gateway for inspection.

While the CBP or FDA does not charge for this service, there could be "handling and service" costs put forward by the carrier or company handling the activity.

If there is a problem with the shipment, there may be fines, penalties, or other consequences applied to the transaction that would have additional financial consequences and costs to the import.

Companies who export should be very wary of taking on an Incoterms DDP transaction when certain goods are involved that are covered by other government agencies, such as but not limited to

- United States Department of Agriculture/USDA or equivalent (US)
- Food and Drug Administration/FDA or equivalent (US)
- Bureau of Alcohol Tobacco and Firearms/BATF or equivalent (US)

- Australian Quarantine and Inspection Service/AQIS or equivalent (Australia)
- State Food and Drug Administration/SFDA or equivalent (CHINA)
- Ministry of Agriculture of the Republic of France/FDA or equivalent (France)
- Environmental Protection Agency/ROMS

The risks and costs could far outweigh the opportunities created by handling shipments on an Incoterms DDP basis. The import process is better left to the importer and their team of local professionals, who may be more familiar with the destination country's regulations.

If an exporter needs to manage the transaction on a DDP basis, then they need to make sure their logistics and forwarding partners in the destination country are strong and capable of handling the "special needs" and protecting their(s) and the importers' import regulatory obligations.

HANDLING AND RELATED SERVICES: $$

When a third party company such as a freight forwarder or customhouse broker handles an export or import, they charge for the array services they provide.

Obviously the principal importer or exporter who is responsible to pay these costs as part of the "overall landed" costs finds value in these services and finds that the expenditure is worth the expense.

Note below the two different sample invoices from a specialized freight forwarder for the services they rendered for an export from the United States.

AMERICAN RIVER LOGISTICS, LTD.
Import/Export Specialists
Licensed Customhouse brokers and Freight Forwarders
1229 OLD WALT WHITMAN ROAD
MELVILLE, NEW YORK 11747
TEL: (631) 396-6800
FAX: (631) 396-6801

INVOICE# I 1108099a
DATE: September 11, 2012

BILL TO: Blue's HOME STORES
1091 Benjamin Avenue
EAST Moriches, NY 11937
ATT: Bob Hawkins

DDP transaction ... Italy to New York, Door to Door, Free Domicile
Italian Specialty Food

PICK UP FROM D & D AND TRANSFER TO PIER	$125.00
ORIGIN HANDLING IN ITALY	$125.00
EXPORT FORMALITIES IN ITALY	$125.00
OCEAN FREIGHT CHARGES FROM ITALY TO NEW YORK	$232.71
WAREHOUSE FEES IN THE USA	$220.00
CUSTOMS CLEARANCE	$135.00
HANDLING FEE	$45.00
MESSENGER FEE	$35.00
DUTY	$155.44
DELIVERY	$475.00
TOTAL	$1673.15

PAYMENT TERMS – NET 30 DAYS   WE THANK YOU FOR THE BUSINESS

Landed Cost Comparison Chart

Packing	Warehouse Fee	Fumigation	Loading & Inland Freight
Insurance	Interest & Banking Fees	Legal/Consularization	Security Surcharge
Messenger Fee	Bunker Fee	Forwarder Handling	AES or Export Fees
Duty	Value Added Tax	Import Service Charge	Container Inspection
Commissions	Delivery	Hazmat Fee	Freight Charges
Packing	Foreign Export Exam Fees	Fumigation	Foreign Inland Freight
Insurance	Port Storage	Specific & Anti-Dumping Duties	Security Surcharge
Messenger Fee	Bunker Fee	Forwarder Handling	AES or Export Fees
Duty	Value Added Tax	Import Service Charge	Container Inspection
Commissions	Delivery	Hazmat Fee	Freight Charges

CASE STUDIES

Landed Duty Paid: Import Case Study 1

Dew Mountain Beverages of Massapequa, New York, purchases 5,000 cases of bottling caps and cases for sparkling water packaging processing from Luigi Mineral Water Machinery, Milan, Italy, for $7,500.00 USD Delivered Duty Paid.

The cost of the international transportation is $900.00 USD. The U.S. inland freight delivery charges are $300.00 USD. The U.S. duties fees and taxes are $700.00 USD.

Upon arrival into the United States, CBP examines the imported articles and determines that the country of origin markings are not sufficient to meet the U.S. country of origin marking requirements enforced by U.S. Customs and Border Protection. It is discovered that the packages are not marked appropriately. A notice of Not Legally Marked Merchandise/ Notice of Redelivery is issued to the Importer of Record, Dew Mountain Beverages of Massapequa, New York.

Dew Mountain is not notified in a timely fashion by the broker of record who was selected by Luigi Mineral Water and received a penalty notice for failure to redeliver the merchandise to CBP custody for marking.

Luigi Mineral Water Machinery is made aware of this issue and refuses to reimburse Dew Mountain for penalty amounts received for Dew Mountain's failure to respond to U.S. CBP requests. Additionally, Luigi states that they are not responsible to meet every request from CBP in the United States on goods that were adequately cleared for export from Italy.

> What Incoterms rules were breached in the above scenario? And how should Dew Mountain use the Incoterms rules to resolve this conflict?

Answer:

Dew Mountain should never have been nominated as the importer of record as the DDP term requires the seller to be responsible for all import customs formalities inclusive of acting as importer of record.

Dew Mountain should refer to A9 of the DDP reference of the *Incoterms 2010* reference and point out to Luigi that as the seller, Luigi did not meet their responsibility to ensure the proper markings were on the packaging performed by Luigi as the seller.

On future purchases Dew Mountain amends the Incoterms to allow them the responsibility for import clearance. Additionally the purchase order outlines packing marking and labeling requirements under both FDA and CBP guidelines.

Landed Cost CIF: Case Study 2

J&J Ltd. of Guangzhou, China, sold solar panel displays to Sunshine Technologies for $300,000 USD CIF. J&J contracted their freight forwarder, Better Freight International Ltd., to move the cargo on a door-to-port basis to the port of Chicago, Illinois.

Better Freight was notified that the shipment would be ready for pick up from J&J on the first of the month. The goods were picked up on time and moved to the port of loading for export loading. The proper Importer Security Filing (ISF) information was filed in a timely manner and the shipping carrier Main Container Line loaded the container accordingly.

While in transit, the container was subject to carriage stress, and movement causing damage to the solar panels resulting in 100% loss of the quality of the goods.

Sunshine, upon investigation, discovered that the freight forwarder Better Freight and the container carrier Main Container Line were notorious for damaged cargo and poor stowage of containers from the Far East. Sunshine filed a claim with J&J for the full value of the cargo plus a 30% profit that was expected after U.S. importation and U.S. resale.

The seller, J&J, upon receipt of notification of the claim for damages refused the claim and informed Sunshine Technologies that they, J&J, were not liable for the loss or damage.

How would you use the Incoterms to assist in the resolution of this dispute?

Answer:

The seller is responsible under CIF to pay the cost to destination and procure insurance on behalf of the buyer; however, the risk of loss or damage to the goods passes from the seller to the buyer as soon as the goods are tendered to the carrier. The claim should be filed by Sunshine with the insurance company and not with J&J.

The other problem associated with this Incoterms utilization is that the insurance company and scope of coverage are not sufficient. The importer has difficulty in submitting the claim, which is denied as the insurance company advises that only major perils were covered and that this loss was not.

Going forward, the importer makes a decision to utilize Incoterms where they control the purchase of the cargo insurance, such as with CFR or CPT terms, so they can make sure the policy conditions are adequate for the risks involved and that they have a relationship with the insurance broker and underwriter who will work on their behalf.

Reducing Costs: Case Study 3

A Dutch company is looking to sell tulip bulbs to Horticulture Company in Cape Town, South Africa. They offer CIP *Incoterms 2010* and plan to ship by airfreight into Cape Town via Lufthansa Airlines originating in Venlo and exported from Amsterdam.

The CIF price, all in, is 23,500 euros. The customer in South Africa advises that the cost is too high. Other suppliers do much better on the airfreight.

The invoice under the CIP sale is as follows:

ExWorks price	20,000 Euros
Inland	500 Euros
Air	2,500 Euros
Insurance	500 Euros
CIP Cape Town	23,500 Euros

Answer:

The customer, unhappy with this price in Cape Town, contacts an airfreight consolidator at Cape Town International Airport, who has an office in Brussels.

This consolidator offers an inbound air freight rate from Brussels to Cape Town for 1,100 euros. The additional cost from originating greenhouse to Brussels is only 150 euros.

The savings is now at a total of 1,250 euros (2,500 minus 1,100 plus 150) per transaction.

The buyer in Cape Town now amends the Incoterms to FCA Brussels and controls the inbound airfreight from Brussels Zaventem Airport.

They arrange their own cargo insurance and the only downside is that as a consolidated shipment it will move on an indirect flight with only two flight options every 2 to 3 days.

They have at least one to two shipments per week for most of the year. This change in the Incoterms and the new logistics will potentially save this importer over 100,000 euros per annum.

Landed cost is an important aspect of global trade which is heavily influenced by the choice of Incoterms.

Global traders need to know the information outlined in this chapter "stone cold" as to be in the best position to make better Incoterms choices that work in favor of lowering landed costs and making their company more competitive.

Small U.S. Exporter, Changing the Incoterms Choice: Case Study 4

A small farmer in Illinois has developed a potential market in Japan for fresh soybeans. The company in Japan is a huge trading company with import and export activity all over the globe. They have a very comprehensive freight and logistics staff in place in their home office in Tokyo.

The Illinois farmer offers a price DAT *Incoterms 2010* Kobe, Japan, to the Tokyo based customer.

> 3000 bushels @ $12.50 USD
> $37,500.00 ExWorks
> $1,100.00 Inland Freight to Long Beach
> $1,950.00 Ocean Freight to Kobe
> $40,550.00 DAT Kobe

The offer is rejected by the Tokyo Company as the DAT price is higher than they pay from other suppliers.

Answer:

In evaluating the situation, the ExWorks price is competitive, but not with all the freight charges added on to ship to Kobe.

The buyer, who has strong freight contracts in place, negotiates a new Incoterms with the Illinois farmer.

The buyer, who has a major contract in place with a favored Japanese Flag Steamship Line—K Line—has an ocean freight price, because of their annualized freight commitment to the carrier, of $1,100.00 USD. They also can improve the inland freight costs because of their existing relationships and tariffs in place with several trucking companies on the West Coast.

The new cost to the Tokyo-based commodity trading company is as follows:

3000 bushels @ $12.50 USD
$37,500.00 ExWorks
$800.00 Inland Freight to Long Beach
$1,100.00 Ocean Freight to Kobe
$39,400.00 DAT Kobe
Savings to the buyer: $1,150.00

As the buyer in Tokyo is planning on several shipments per month over the next 18 months, the overall savings would fall into the over $13,000.00 USD range.

This Incoterms option places the small company in Illinois in a more competitive position in this transaction, when changing the Incoterms options to favor the buyer in Tokyo purchasing prowess on inland and ocean freight contracts, with more favorable pricing.

Both parties win in this Incoterms option and can compete favorably.

Chinese Exports to the United States: Case Study 5

A Chinese chemical manufacturer located just outside of Shanghai is looking to grow sales into the American market, where a number of their products for the cosmetics industry are booming.

They believe in offering DDP Incoterms to their smaller customers who they believe would prefer not to be involved in any customs formalities.

One buyer in Plano, Texas, on their third import from this supplier in Shanghai, is approached by CBP (Customs Border and Protection/ U.S. Customs).

CBP in Dallas is inquiring and looking for forms 7501 and 3461 (U.S. import clearance documents). The buyer advises that while they are the final destination, they are not the importer of record and have no such forms or really anything to do with the import clearance formalities, as they are making the purchases on a DDP Incoterms from the supplier in China.

CBP does the litmus test for ultimate consignees and determines that the import would have never occurred unless for this PO and that the current importer of record showing on this transaction is a disinterested foreign entity who has no interest in this U.S. and delegates the entire customs clearance process to a independent third party.

CBP advises the buyer in Plano that they are not only the ultimate consignee by CBP definition but also the importer of record.

That company in Plano is fined $11,000.00 and is having numerous shipments stopped at the inbound gateway by CBP for inspection.

Soon after this problem arose ... the company in Plano amends the Incoterms to DAP Plano. This requires the Chinese exporter to deliver the goods to Plano but the customs formalities are for the account of the buyer in Plano.

The company in Plano hires a licensed customhouse broker in Dallas who now protects their interests by handling the clearances in their name; they do it correctly and handle all record-keeping requirements.

CBP returns in 6 months and is favorably impressed by how the importer in Plano has acted with due diligence, reasonable care, and supervision and control in the import process.

CBP lessens the inspections and moves ahead favorably with this importer of record.

Trade Compliance Issue: Case Study 6

A U.S. company who manufacturers aviation products that they sell to the military has received an order to supply various aviation spare parts to a government agency in Saudi Arabia destined for their Air Force.

The P.O. states that the buyer wants ExWorks Terms in the contract of sale. The supplier in Kenosha, Wisconsin, has no problem with this term as it takes them out of the loop for export functions.

When the government agency in Saudi contacts their freight forwarder in Jeddah to contact their agent in London to make the freight arrangements out of the United States ... they meet several challenges ... in this customer-routed freight transaction.

The Jeddah's agent in Chicago advises that the nature of the product, the destination, and the intended use all dictate that an export license from the U.S. Department of State maybe required for this export. Also tied into this equation is the Schedule B number, along with DDTC designations.

The first consequence to this circumstance is that the process of the export is delayed due to the potential State Department ITAR protocols: The International Traffic in Arms Regulations of the State Department.

It is finally determined that the exporter has to file for an export license. After a 24-day wait the exporter finally receives the export license.

The license has various stipulations. One of which is that the exporter or the USPPI (U.S. Principal Party in Interest) has to control the outbound export from the United States.

The ExWorks Incoterms does not allow this option in its intent.

The exporter or USPPI (in this case, the supplier in Kenosha) has to make arrangement with a freight forwarder in Chicago to handle this export from the United States.

Concurrently they amend their Incoterms to FCA port of export, in this case Chicago O'Hare Airport, as this is an airfreight shipment.

The FCA O'Hare Incoterms are now secured, allowing the supplier in Kenosha to meet the requirement of the State Department Export License.

While the buyer in Saudi wanted to control the export, they have to compromise their protocols and chose another Incoterm that satisfies the U.S. government so the export can go forward—a compromise that produces favorable results for all the parties in the export transaction—the seller, the buyer, and the U.S. Government!

German Optics Company, the DDP Advantage: Case Study 7

A German optics company located in Berlin has developed multitasking eye care and optical equipment for utilization in optometrists' offices around the globe.

The new equipment will do the work of three pieces of current equipment utilized by eye doctors, saving the eye doctors hundreds of thousands of dollars.

The Berlin company begins to market their products shipped door to door, installed, and upon delivery and installation a company technician will be present to show the technicians and eye doctors how to utilize the new equipment.

In this "turnkey" sale, the eye doctor is only required to pay an advance of 10% upon ordering and pay the balance after the "turnkey" occurs.

In their first few orders they sell with the Incoterms of DAP the doctor's office.

The optics company immediately run into a few problems in some sales into North America, as well as in Southeast Asia. The problems are consistent. Most of the doctors and technicians they are selling to are small operations and lack the resources, contacts, and capabilities to customs clear the goods in their own countries.

The Berlin optical company sees some immediate sales potential begin to dwindle because of this customs clearance dilemma.

Answer:

The Berlin optical company's managing director has a good contact with a freight forwarder in Hamburg who, when advised of the problem, offers a very viable solution.

The forwarder advises that the Incoterms should be amended to DDP and they will handle the entire logistics to destination, inclusive of local customs formalities. This will eliminate the need for the doctors' offices to find local customhouse brokers and deal with the complexities of customs clearance.

Prior to shipment, the forwarder advises what all the landed costs will be—shipping, duties, taxes, fees, etc.—and these costs are built into the sales contract which will be agreed to by the buyer at the time the agreement is finalized and the goods are shipped.

The forwarder, as an option, can also handle the shipment on a collect basis to assure payment takes place when the delivery and the turnkey occur.

In some countries where an exporter can be the importer of record, such as Brazil or Mexico, the forwarder will handle the sale on a DAP basis and their office or agent will step in and represent the buyer's import interests as an extension of the exporter's supply chain.

That forwarders office or agent in that local market will handle the customs formalities on behalf of the doctor's office and make sure the process is minimized for them as much as possible.

In either situation the exporter is providing a door-to-door "white glove" service offered by either:

- Amending the Incoterms utilized or
- Adjusting the role of the freight forwarder's responsibilities upon clearance and delivery at destination

Either scenario allows the Berlin company to be leveraged in their global sales and allows these optometrists' offices easier accesses to equipment that has multi-utilizations and is a better overall spend.

Competitive advantage works to everyone's benefit!

5

Global Regulation and Compliance Management

OVERVIEW

The events of 9/11 in the United States changed how governments regulate import and export trade. Every country in the world was impacted differently, but all have developed greater control over goods passing through their borders. The United States leads most compliance initiatives. Supply chain executives located anywhere on the planet must pay attention to all of these regulatory changes to successfully navigate all the complexities now being initiated to reduce cost and risk. As a result of 9/11, we will look at many of the trade compliance issues facing companies that sell to or buy from the United Sates, which is greatly seen as the entity leading the charge to raise the bar on trade compliance management all over the globe.

Every exporter and importer has to deal with the formalities of the regulatory process to move freight in and out of their origins and destinations in their global supply chains. Never before has trade compliance become a major challenge to shippers, transportation providers, and carriers. Incoterms® greatly impact trade compliance responsibilities and liabilities.

TRADE COMPLIANCE AND REGULATION IMPACT INCOTERMS OPTIONS

Exports

When reading the Incoterms in detail, you will notice that under each term it addresses the party responsible for export formalities. With the exception of ExWorks, the seller is typically that party. This means that the seller is responsible for

- Managing all the paperwork, documentation, and information flow to authorities.
- Understanding the basics of export regulations on goods that ship from that originating country. In many Western countries, such as the United States, Canada, Great Britain, and Germany, these rules are quite extensive. Many companies delegate this formality to a third-party transportation provider, typically a freight forwarder, which acts as the seller's (shipper's) agent for purposes of transferring information to the government and for formalizing documents and communications. In some countries such as the United States, this is accomplished using a power of attorney. In other countries such as France, this is accomplished through posting advices to their customs authorities.
- Arranging for outbound freight options and handling carrier arrangements and bills of lading.
- Paying, where applicable, export charges and duties.

A major concern for exporters, particularly those that ship from Westernized countries such as the United States, Great Britain, Germany, France, and Japan, is to make sure the export process follows the government mandates on export controls. The United States has numerous government agencies who govern the various aspects of export trade compliance, namely, the U.S. Department of State, U.S. Department of Commerce, U.S. Department of the Treasury, U.S. Customs and Border Protection, U.S. Census Bureau, U.S. Department of Agriculture, and U.S. Department of Transportation.

Most companies employ full-time personnel just to handle the export administration responsibilities. When a company purchases goods internationally on an ExWorks basis, the buyer then becomes responsible for export formalities. In some countries this could be a minor administrative process, costing some fees and an extra day or so in the export outbound process. Mexico, Jamaica, South Africa, and China are examples of that scenario. But in countries such as the United States, Japan, Germany, and Great Britain, there is an arduous export administrative process before goods can be sold and exported from their domains.

What follows are a few of the more important issues if a company, because of the Incoterms choice, was to take on the responsibility of the export formalities from the United States.

1. The exporter must make sure that all the entities involved in the transaction—such as the buyer, carriers, transportation providers, foreign intermediaries, warehouses, and any financial institutions involved in the banking—have been screened by the Denied Parties Lists, a group of at least six lists from several government agencies.

2. The exporter must review the transaction to determine if there are any red flags. It is imperative that personnel are trained to identify these and know what to do when they occur, such as not to ship the unit. Examples of red flags are as follows:*

   a. The customer or its address is similar to one of the parties found on the U.S. Commerce Department's Bureau of Industry and Security's list of denied persons.

   b. The customer or purchasing agent is reluctant to offer information about the end use of the item.

   c. The product's capabilities do not fit the buyer's line of business, such as an order for sophisticated computers for a small bakery.

   d. The item ordered is incompatible with the technical level of the country to which it is being shipped, such as semiconductor manufacturing equipment being shipped to a country that has no electronics industry.

   e. The customer is willing to pay cash for a very expensive item when the terms of sale would normally call for financing.

   f. The customer has little or no business background.

   g. The customer is unfamiliar with the product's performance characteristics but still wants the product.

   h. Routine installation, training, or maintenance services are declined by the customer.

   i. Delivery dates are vague, or deliveries are planned for out of the way destinations.

   j. A freight forwarding firm is listed as the product's final destination.

   k. The shipping route is abnormal for the product and destination.

   l. Packaging is inconsistent with the stated method of shipment or destination.

   m. When questioned, the buyer is evasive and especially unclear about whether the purchased product is for domestic use, for export, or for re-export.

3. Determine if the goods being shipped, their quantity or value, the country of destination, the consignee, or the utilization can be

---

* From Helping U.S. Companies Export, http://www.export.gov.

shipped or will require the process of determining if an export license is necessary. Then make those export license arrangements.

4. To manage any of the responsibilities associated with the export license, there could be documentary or logistics specific actions necessary as part of the export license.

5. Handle all documentary requirements, including a record-keeping component. One such documentary requirement is the AES filing.

Filing export information to the U.S. government is a very serious undertaking, particularly when a foreign buyer uses the ExWorks Incoterms. There are some very strict guidelines for companies that control the export process from the United States in what is called a routed freight transaction.* In the Appendix are some guidelines for routed freight transactions.

1. All U.S. Principal Parties in Interest (USPPIs), forwarding agents, carriers or consolidators, etc., using aesdirect.gov to report electronic export information in accordance with 15CFR parts 30.1 through 30.99 must properly register with this site.

2. By submitting a registration to aesdirect.gov, you are hereby certifying that as the registering company, you are and will continue to be in compliance with all applicable laws and regulations. This includes complying with the following security requirements:

   a. Usernames and Passwords are to be kept secure and never be disclosed to any unauthorized user or any persons outside of the registered company.

   b. Registered companies are to take responsibility for those persons having access to a Username, and Password. If a User forgets their Username or Password, they will need to contact their Account Administrator and/or User Managers to ask them to reset their password for them in Account Maintenance. If Users do not know who their Account Administrator or User Managers are they will need to contact Customer Support at 877-715-4433. If an employee with a username and password leaves the company or otherwise is no longer an authorized user, the Account Administrator must immediately disable their account in order to ensure the integrity and confidentiality of Title 13 data. Any

---

* From AES Direct Terms and Conditions, AES Direct, http://www.aesdirect.gov/terms.html.

violation of these security regulations will result in immediate loss of privilege to use AES*Direct* for a period of up to one (1) year.

c. Antivirus software must be installed and set to run automatically on all computers used to access AES*Direct*. All AES*Direct* registered companies will maintain subscriptions with their antivirus software vendor to keep antivirus lists current. Registered companies are responsible for performing full scans of these systems on a regular basis and eliminating any virus contamination. If the registered company is unable to disinfect the system for any reason, that system is not to be utilized for AES*Direct* access until it is virus free. Please contact the antivirus software vendor for instruction. Should a virus be instituted into the AES*Direct* by a registered company, that company will be contacted immediately by Census. The company's AES*Direct* account will be suspended until such time the company can prove their systems used to access AES*Direct* are virus free, and the AES*Direct* is analyzed by AES*Direct* systems administrators and Census security personnel to determine the extent of any related damage.

3. Use of aesdirect.gov is for predeparture and postdeparture export reporting. Predeparture Filing requires that all information be reported prior to tendering the cargo to the exporting carrier. The Postdeparture Filing Program allows companies reporting their Electronic Export Information through AES, to transmit their EEI within 10 calendar days after the date of export. Only USPPIs (exporters, manufacturers, etc.) can be authorized for postdeparture reporting. However, authorized agents may transmit postdeparture shipments on behalf of approved postdeparture USPPIs.

4. Prior to reporting "live" electronic export information through aesdirect.gov, you must successfully pass the online certification quiz.

5. Once reporting "live" electronic export information through aesdirect.gov, you must maintain a 95% error-free rate. This includes reporting the information on a timely basis.

6. As a condition to reporting electronic export information to aesdirect.gov via batch-mode, users must ensure to their Census Representative that all mandatory edits are built into the company software. This application requires all batch transmissions in ANSI X12, set 601 or Customs Proprietary format. For additional information on these mandatory edits, please consult your Census Representative.

7. Limits on reporting through aesdirect.gov: No more than 100 lines per shipment can be reported through interactive keying. No more than 999 lines per shipment can be reported via batch-mode.

8. Users of aesdirect.gov must provide the proper proof of filing citation or AES exemption statement on the bill of lading, air waybill, or other commercial documentation in accordance with Foreign Trade Regulations.

9. Users of aesdirect.gov are required to file corrections, cancellations, or amendments to previously filed electronic export information as soon as the need for such is determined. When a correction, amendment, or cancellation is reported after the required filing time, the user will receive an information message indicating that the shipment was reported late. However, such warning messages will not be counted in determining the 95% error-free rate indicated in 5 above.

10. The electronic export information reported through aesdirect.gov is confidential for use solely for official purposes authorized by the Secretary of Commerce in accordance with 13 U.S.C. Section 301(g). Use for unauthorized purposes is not permitted. The electronic export information may not be disclosed to anyone except the USPPI or their authorized agent (15CFR 30.60). The registered company found violating confidentiality will be liable to a penalty.

11. Electronic export information (except common information) may not be copied to manifests or other shipping documents. USPPIs or their authorized agent may not furnish electronic export information to anyone for unofficial purposes (15CFR30.60).

12. Copies of the electronic export information may be supplied to USPPIs or their agents when such copies are needed to comply with official U.S. government requirements (15CFR30.60).

13. Filing electronic export information for exports constitutes a representation by the USPPI that all statements and information are in accordance with the export control regulations. The commodity described on the declaration is authorized under the particular license as identified on the declaration, all statements conform to the applicable licenses, and all conditions of the export control regulations have been met.

14. It is unlawful to knowingly make false or misleading representation for exportation. This constitutes a violation of the Export Administration Act, 50 U.S.C. App. 2410. It is also a violation of

export control laws and regulations to be connected in any way with altering electronic export information to effect export.

15. Commodities that have been, are being, or for which there is probable cause to believe they are intended to be exported in violation of laws or regulations are subject to seizure, detention, condemnation, or sale under 22 U.S.C. Section 401.
16. To knowingly make false or misleading statements relating to electronic export information is a criminal offense subject to penalties as provided for in 18 U.S.C. Section 1001.
17. Violations of the Foreign Trade Regulations are subject to civil penalties as authorized by 13 U.S.C. Section 305.

U.S. Government Resources for AES

To manage this AES process, foreign buyers using the ExWorks Incoterms need to work directly with the following government agencies:

Census Bureau—Foreign Trade Division (FTD): Provides information on foreign trade statistics, regulations, reference materials, and extensive details on AES.

Customs and Border Protection (CBP): Provides access to the Customs Export section, including information on AES; blocked, denied, and debarred persons lists; and export documents, licenses, and requirements.

Department of Commerce—Bureau of Industry and Security (BIS): Provides information on export control basics, export administration policies and regulations, compliance and enforcement, seminars and training, and links to Export Administration Regulations (EAR), including the Commerce Control List (CCL).

Department of the Treasury—Office of Foreign Assets Control (OFAC): Provides access to specially designated nationals (SDN) and blocked persons lists and sanction programs and country summaries.

Department of State—Directorate of Defense Trade Controls (DDTC): Provides information for registering with the DDTC and applying for a license to ship items on the U.S. Munitions List (USML). Includes a link to the International Traffic in Arms Regulations (ITAR).

Export.gov—U.S. Commercial Service, International Trade Administrations (ITA): Provides access to all export-related assistance and market information offered by the federal government.

Department of Treasury—Internal Revenue Service: Provides detailed information on how to obtain an Employer Identification Number (EIN). Publication 1635, Understanding Your EIN, is posted as a pdf online. This can be accessed to answer FAQs regarding your EIN. Site is also available in Spanish.

18. Supervise the activity of any transportation provider or third party such as but not limited to the freight forwarder and carrier.

North American Free Trade Agreement (NAFTA)[*]

Implementation of the North American Free Trade Agreement (NAFTA) began on January 1, 1994. This agreement will remove most barriers to trade and investment among the United States, Canada, and Mexico.

Under the NAFTA, all non-tariff barriers to agricultural trade between the United States and Mexico were eliminated. In addition, many tariffs were eliminated immediately, with others being phased out over periods of 5 to 15 years. This allowed for an orderly adjustment to free trade with Mexico, with full implementation beginning January 1, 2008, continuing into 2012.

The agricultural provisions of the U.S.–Canada Free Trade Agreement, in effect since 1989, were incorporated into the NAFTA. Under these provisions, all tariffs affecting agricultural trade between the United States and Canada, with a few exceptions for items covered by tariff-rate quotas, were removed by January 1, 1998.

Mexico and Canada reached a separate bilateral NAFTA agreement on market access for agricultural products. The Mexican–Canadian agreement eliminated most tariffs either immediately or over 5, 10, or 15 years. Tariffs

[*] From North American Free Trade Agreement, http://www.fas.usda.gov/itp/policy/nafta/nafta.asp.

between the two countries affecting trade in dairy, poultry, eggs, and sugar are maintained.

For trade between the United States and Canada, any Incoterms choice that benefits the parties engaged in the transaction will work. The relationship and commonality of trade and business relationship between the two countries affords both sellers and buyers with access to all 11 Incoterms. One only needs to analyze the transaction and determine which Incoterms serve best. But shipments in and out of Mexico to either the United States or Canada need to be carefully reviewed before choosing the best Incoterms. For example, a company must be domiciled in Mexico and able to provide a Mexican tax ID to become importer of record. The ability to have a "third party" become importer of record is very complicated and almost impossible compared with accomplishing that in Canada and the United States. That circumstance, with respect to importer of record, would make DDP Incoterms option for U.S. and Canadian exporters not a viable option, as they would have difficulty in becoming the importer of record without having a locally registered company and presence.

The DAP Incoterms provides a better option for a Canadian or U.S. company that wants to deliver goods to an interior place in Mexico, even possibly a final destination, but would not have responsibility for the clearance, pedimentos, or other customs charges.

ACUSE DE RECIBO

ANVERSO
DMD

SAT
Servicio de Administración Tributaria

ANTES DE INICIAR EL LLENADO, LEA LAS INSTRUCCIONES

**DECLARACIÓN DE MERCANCÍAS
DONADAS AL FISCO FEDERAL
CONFORME AL ARTÍCULO 61
FRACCIÓN XVII DE LA LEY
ADUANERA**

NÚMERO DE ACUSE

NÚMERO DE HOJAS QUE
PRESENTA DEL ANEXO 1

1. DATOS DEL DONANTE DE MERCANCÍAS AL FISCO FEDERAL

APELLIDO PATERNO MATERNO Y NOMBRE(S)
DENOMINACIÓN O RAZÓN SOCIAL

CALLE

NO. Y/O
LETRA

DISTRITO O
CIUDAD

CÓDIGO POSTAL
ZONA POSTAL

TELÉFONO

PAÍS

FAX

NÚMERO EN
REGISTRO FISCAL

CORREO
ELECTRÓNICO

NÚMERO DE HOJAS QUE ANEXA A ESTA DECLARACIÓN

2. OBJETO DE LA DONACIÓN

INDIQUE CON UNA "X" EL OBJETO DE LA DONACIÓN

2.1 PARA LA ATENCIÓN DE REQUERIMIENTOS BÁSICOS DE LAS PERSONAS, SECTORES O REGIONES DE ESCASOS RECURSOS — EDUCACIÓN — VIVIENDA — PROTECCIÓN CIVIL — SALUD

2.2 PARA LA ATENCIÓN DE DESASTRE NATURAL — ALIMENTACIÓN — VIVIENDA — VESTIDO — SALUD

2.3 PARA LA ATENCIÓN DE CONDICIONES DE EXTREMA POBREZA — ALIMENTACIÓN — VIVIENDA — VESTIDO — SALUD

3. INDIQUE CON UNA "X" EL DESTINATARIO FINAL DE LA DONACIÓN

FEDERACIÓN — DISTRITO FEDERAL — ESTADO — MUNICIPIO — PERSONA MORAL CON FINES NO LUCRATIVOS

4. PERSONA MORAL AUTORIZADA PARA RECIBIR DONATIVOS DEDUCIBLES DEL IMPUESTO SOBRE LA RENTA, BENEFICIARIA DE LA DONACIÓN

REGISTRO FEDERAL DE CONTRIBUYENTES

DENOMINACIÓN O RAZÓN SOCIAL

CALLE

NO. Y/O LETRA

COLONIA

CIUDAD

CÓDIGO POSTAL ZONA POSTAL

ENTIDAD FEDERATIVA

TELÉFONO

5. REPRESENTANTE LEGAL DE LA PERSONA MORAL BENEFICIARIA DE LA DONACIÓN

REGISTRO FEDERAL DE CONTRIBUYENTES

CLAVE ÚNICA DE REGISTRO DE POBLACIÓN

APELLIDO PATERNO MATERNO Y NOMBRE(S)

CARGO

6. REPRESENTANTE LEGAL AUTORIZADO PARA RECIBIR LA DONACIÓN

REGISTRO FEDERAL DE CONTRIBUYENTES

CLAVE ÚNICA DE REGISTRO DE POBLACIÓN

APELLIDO PATERNO MATERNO Y NOMBRE(S)

DOCUMENTO QUE ACREDITA SU PERSONALIDAD

TELÉFONO

7. NOMBRE COMPLETO Y FIRMA DEL DONANTE

Declaro bajo protesta de decir verdad que cuento con la capacidad legal para disponer de los bienes objeto de la donación.

8. NOMBRE COMPLETO Y FIRMA DEL REPRESENTANTE LEGAL DE LA PERSONA MORAL BENEFICIARIA DE LA DONACIÓN

Acepto subrogarme en las obligaciones derivadas de la importación de las mercancías donadas al fisco federal, conforme a la fracción XVII del artículo 61 de la Ley Aduanera y no destinarlas a propósitos distintos para las cuales es importada.

SE PRESENTA POR CUADRUPLICADO

Pedimento Form

A pedimento is the legal document to import or export from Mexico. There are two main types of pedimentos: definite or temporary.

1. Definite pedimentos are for products that will not be returned to the country of origin. These products are subject to duties and taxes.

2. Temporary pedimentos are for products that will be transformed or be subject of a process and then will be returned to the country of origin. If the products are raw materials they are duty and tax free. Machinery and equipment might be subject to duties and taxes depending on their country of origin.

In Mexico, those customs formalities and responsibilities would be accounted for by the buyer under the DAP option in Incoterms. That understanding makes the statement to U.S. and Canadian exporters who ship to Mexico that the DDP term is a poor choice. All others can be utilized more favorably.

Logistically, trucks move freely between Canada and the United States but not between Mexico and the United States and Canada. It is still highly contested that Mexican trucks have problems crossing U.S. and Canadian borders. This is a political issue with lots of debate that has never been truly resolved. It includes U.S. federal and state concerns tied into "union" issues. Therefore, keep in mind that the best-suited Incoterms are for exports from Mexico where trucks would be used as the main form of carriage on an anticipated "door-to-door" basis. Many carriers will use the same box and chassis, but the cab and driver will change at the border from one of Mexican origin to one of U.S. or Canadian destination.

UNITED STATES FOREIGN TRADE REGULATIONS

Foreign Trade Regulations 15 CFR Part 30, Incoterms, and Routed Transactions

One of the most misunderstood aspects of exporting from the United States is how the Census Bureau of the United States defines a Routed Transaction in the Foreign Trade Regulations (FTR). One very interesting fact is that the Census Bureau completely ignores Incoterms when it comes to Routed Transactions and Incoterms are not mentioned anywhere in the FTR.

So, are these two conflicting sets of regulations: Incoterms and the FTR? The answer is no, Incoterms are not law and they do not automatically apply. An Incoterm is contractually binding only when both parties (seller and buyer) mutually agree in writing to a specific Incoterm. On the other hand, the FTR are law and must be adhered to.

Let's look closely at what the FTR describes a Routed Transaction to be. Section 30.3(e) of the FTR defines it as:

> Responsibilities of parties in a routed export transaction. The Census Bureau recognizes 'routed export transactions' as a subset of export transactions. A routed export transaction is a transaction in which the FPPI (Foreign Principle Party in Interest) authorizes a U.S. agent to facilitate the export of items from the United States *and* to prepare and file EEI 'Electronic Export Information.'

Note the word *and* in the above paragraph. There is a specific reason for it and that is to clearly denote that the FPPI must both control the facilitation (actual movement of the goods) *and* authorize the U.S. agent to file the EEI through AES (Automated Export System) to qualify as an actual "routed transaction."

This is where so much of the confusion comes in. Many exporters believe that if the FPPI selects the carrier and controls the movement of the goods, but they (the exporter) file the EEI as the USPPI it is a routed transaction. That is only partially true, and in the eyes of the Census Bureau, it isn't a routed transaction.

An FPPI has to provide a Power of Attorney (POA) to the U.S. agent authorizing them to file the EEI on their behalf. There is no specific format for such a POA, but it should have wording that clearly specifies that authorization is being granted. The POA should be on company letterhead and signed by an appropriate official of the company. This is the second part of a true, recognized FTR routed transaction.

Here's the part that's a little hard to swallow as a U.S. exporter: In a routed transaction where your customer who is also the FPPI has selected a carrier and provided them authorization to file the EEI, you must provide that agent with 12 data elements so they can file the EEI:

1. Name and address of the USPPI. (Yes, that's you because in the eyes of the FTR you are the beneficiary of the transaction.)
2. USPPI's EIN or DUNS (Now you're getting more nervous.)
3. State of origin (State's name)
4. FTZ, if applicable
5. Commercial description of commodities
6. Origin of goods indicator, Domestic D or Foreign F
7. Schedule B or HTSUSA, Commodity Classification Code
8. Quantities/units of measure

9. Value
10. Export Commodity Control Number (ECCN) or sufficient technical information to determine the ECCN
11. All licensing information necessary to file the EEI for commodities where the Department of State, the Department of Commerce, or other U.S. government agency issues a license for the commodities being exported, or the merchandize being exported under a license exemption or license exception
12. Any information that it knows will affect the determination of license authorization

What makes the "hard to swallow" part is, if the carrier selected is not one you trust or have confidence in to execute the transaction properly, you still have to provide the above data. My advice is to be proactive with your customer and iron out who the carrier will be in advance of the transaction.

The carrier in a routed transaction has no obligation to provide you with any documentation concerning the export which seems contrary to the recordkeeping requirements laid out in the EAR and the ITAR. Their only responsibility is to give back to you what you provided them, i.e., the 12 above-mentioned data elements. You should request the documents from the carrier such as AWB, BOL, and AES submission (with the Internal Transaction Number, ITN) in writing and keep them in your file; that way if the carrier does not give it to you, you have done reasonable due-diligence which will be considered in the event you are ever audited by any government agency. Another piece of advice is to ask your customer to apply a little pressure on the carrier to provide the documents back to you.

Well, what's this got to do with Incoterms?

As mentioned above, Incoterms are not law but are contractually binding when agreed to by both parties and incorporated into the contract or purchase order. Incoterms are an important and vital set of rules that clearly define exactly what each party in a transaction is expected to do. One of the very critical events defined in an Incoterm is who is responsible for the export (as well as the import) clearance.

In both the 13 Incoterms of 2000 and the 11 Incoterms of 2010 the only term that truly allows for the buyer (customer, FPPI) to control the export clearance process is ExWorks. All of the other terms call out for the seller (USPPI) to clear the goods for export. Now comes the tricky part: Does EXW actually fit this particular transaction? I would think in just about every "true" routed transaction the answer is yes. Keep in mind that the delivery point as well as the transfer of risk of loss or damage happens on your dock once you notify the customer that the shipment is ready. Carefully read the guidance notes as well as the 10 seller and 10 buyer obligations before agreeing to an Incoterm. An important note: In the guidance note to EXW for *Incoterms 2010* it is implied that EXW not be used for international transactions.

To summarize:

- Incoterms are not law but the FTR are.
- Unless both actions described under the FTR are in place by the FPPI, i.e., facilitate movement of the goods and authorize a U.S. agent to file EEI, it is not a routed transaction and should not be entered into AES as such.

Hmmm, so if I insist on routed transactions and apply EXW, it gets me off the hook if something goes wrong with the export, right? Don't count on it!

There are quite a few fines and penalties levied on a regular basis due to routed transactions. You might skip by the recordkeeping part if you have a written request to the carrier for it, but the ITAR and the EAR hold us as exporters responsible to know our customer, and in a routed transaction we oftentimes have no clue who the real end user is or what the end use will be. As a matter of fact, there is a lot of talk about banning licensed shipments to move as routed transactions, and there seems to be a lot of support for it not only in government but also in the trade community.

As a trade compliance professional for many years, I would never allow routed transactions for any company I worked or consulted for and advise the same for others; the risk of diversion is too great. We have both a legal and moral obligation to know our customers. Some people will stop at nothing to obtain certain goods, technology, or software, even if it harms others, and that is not something I want on my conscience. Routed transactions provide opportunities to the wrong people: drug smugglers, money launderers, slave traders, makers of weapons of mass destruction, and all kinds of terrorists and other garden-variety bad guys.

One other piece of advice: Carefully read the FTR to fully understand your obligations as an exporter. Next reread the EAR and the ITAR, especially the parts about record-keeping, and know your customer. We have a lot of very important responsibility as U.S. exporters and for good reason.

Bottom line: Avoid routed transactions out of the United States.

ASIA REVIEWED

Asia Pacific trade, exports, and imports are difficult to generalize, as many countries in this region, such as China and North Korea, have separate trade agendas. Asia Pacific has a strong manufacturing market due to the availability of cheap labor.

This translates into manufacturing huge amounts of textiles, electronics, automotive products, heavy equipment, consumer durable goods, and more. China, Japan, and South Korea are major exporters of automobiles, industrial equipment, and heavy machinery. Singapore, China, Japan, South Korea, Taiwan, and Malaysia are major exporters of semiconductors and electronic products. China and Indonesia are leaders in oil and textile exports.

The Asia Pacific region also imports oil and raw materials from Middle East and Latin America. Also, luxury items, cars, and electronics are imported from Europe and the United States. Major import commodities include food, energy products, defense equipment, aviation equipment, heavy vehicles, and raw materials.[*]

It is important to note that Incoterms play a very vital role in Asian trade since price is a major factor in the decision-making process on where Asian companies source.

Since a major import of this market is raw materials such as oil, precious metals, and heavy equipment where all items have high price tags and also are purchased in bulk, the logistics costs play a huge role in determining the overall competitiveness. Changes in small amounts of yen, won, or the yuan in freight costs will significantly impact their competitiveness on the world's stage.

Many Western companies who either manufacture in China or outsource in China from third parties are always very concerned about what their partners or operating divisions are paying for oil and other raw materials that will make up their final manufacturing costs. These companies are always making initiatives to reduce freight costs. One way to reduce freight costs is by using Incoterms, which allow them to leverage freight costs best, and thus to handle the freight costs as part of their responsibilities under their Incoterms option.

As an example, a Chinese manufacturer in Guangzhou wants to import heavy equipment from a supplier in Toledo, Ohio. In evaluating the overall

---

[*] From Economy Watch, http://www.economywatch.com/world-economy/asia-pacific/export-import.html.

trade, it has determined that the supplier is a huge exporter and has some very large freight contracts with some ocean carriers who service the United States-to-China trade lanes.

When the manufacturer compares rates, it determines that it could save as much as 15% off ocean freight costs, so it elects to use Shanghai Incoterms as CIP, which will allow the Ohio supplier to use its ocean freight contract rates for the international leg of the shipment, which bears the largest component of the import logistics costs. Once the Chinese manufacturer makes the CIP Shanghai arrangements, a further investigation of the logistics of moving the goods from the inbound port of Shanghai to the final destination in Guangzhou reveals that the ocean carrier can offer a through bill of lading to the final destination. Therefore, an additional savings of 5% is now available by using one carrier door to door in lieu of two separate carriers. The manufacturer now amends the Incoterms to DAP Guangzhou, which accomplishes a door-to-door delivery but still leaves the import clearance process and duties and taxes for the importer to handle.

At the end of the day, by taking diligent steps in evaluating its shipping costs, the importer changed its intended Incoterms twice to obtain more favorable freight rates, which lowered the freight costs and made the entire transaction more competitive for both the supplier in Ohio and the buyer in Guangzhou. Analysis, comprehension, and actions involving Incoterms can lead to savings. Everyone benefits from this type of behavior, leading to more informed decisions and better choices in Incoterms. This is a perfect example of Incoterms management (ITM).

Importing into China

General Documents

Normally, the Chinese importer (agent, distributor, joint-venture partner, or FIE) will gather the documents necessary for importing goods and provide them to Chinese Customs agents.

Necessary documents vary by product but may include standard documents such as a bill of lading, invoice, shipping list, customs declaration, insurance policy, and sales contract, as well as more specialized documents such as an import quota certificate for general commodities (where applicable), import license (where applicable), inspection certificate issued by the General Administration of the PRC for Quality Supervision, Inspection, and Quarantine (AQSIQ) or its local bureau (where applicable), and other safety and/or quality departments.

Specific Documentary Requirements*

Note: When importing, Chinese state trading enterprises generally require standard contract clauses that go into great detail about shipping documentation, marking, and packaging. All shipments must have the following:

Commercial invoice: The invoice should include a detailed description of the goods, the name and address of the supplier or manufacturer, place and date of shipment, name and address of consignee, gross and net weights, the "real" price of the goods, and insurance fees and other expenses. The invoice also must bear the signature of the consignor, or authorized agent. U.S. exporters should be guided by the Chinese importer for other particulars regarding the format of the invoice, number of copies, and any other information required.

Certificate of origin: May be required by the importer or letter of credit. If requested, two copies of the certificate of origin on the general form sold by commercial printers are required. The certificate of origin must be certified by a recognized chamber of commerce, which usually requires an additional notarized copy for its files.

Packing list: Usually required. The packing list should show the weights in addition to the contents of each shipment.

Bill of lading: There are no special requirements for the bill of lading. A bill of lading customarily shows the name of the shipper, name and address of the consignee, port of destination, description of goods, listing of freight and other charges, number of bills of lading in the full set, and date and signature of the carrier's official acknowledging receipt on-board of the goods for shipment. The information should correspond with that shown on the invoice and packages. The air waybill replaces the bill of lading on air cargo shipments.

U.S. export documents: With few exceptions, the U.S. government requires the submission of information about all shipments from the United States. This information must be submitted electronically through the Automated Export System for all transactions. In addition, a U.S. export license may be required for items subject to U.S. export controls. Additional information about export licenses, the Automated Export System, and other U.S. export controls is available in U.S. Export Regulations and Controls.

---

* From Import Requirements and Documentation in China, Global Trade, http://www.globaltrade. net/f/business/text/china/trade-policy-import-requirements-and-documentation-in-China.html.

Special documents include the following:

Health and sanitary certificates: Imports of animals, plants, and their products may require health or sanitary certificates. For imported feed products made from animal materials, the sanitary certificate must state that the products use animal materials that originated in the country of export, that they do not contain animal materials from a third country, and that none of the products' components has been contaminated by animal material from a third country. The certificate also must indicate the varieties of animals used in making the feed product. Imported products that do not meet these criteria will be treated, re-exported, or destroyed. More information may be obtained from the U.S. Department of Agriculture's Animal and Plant Health Inspection Service http://www.usda/aphis.org. APHIS inspects and certifies that live plants, plant products, and live animals conform to health and sanitary requirements prescribed by the country of destination. Inspections usually are carried out in local offices of APHIS, which are located in major U.S. ports and airports. Export agents or brokers may present products for inspection; inspection of air shipments may be handled through the airlines. Although information on documents required for the importation of agricultural products (including food items), plants, and animals is available from the U.S. Department of Agriculture, U.S. exporters also should obtain information directly from the importer prior to shipment because of the complexity of sanitary and health regulations. Information also can be obtained from the appropriate ministry of the Chinese government.

Wholesomeness certificate: Fresh and frozen meat and poultry products require a Meat and Poultry Certificate of Wholesomeness for Export to the People's Republic of China (FSIS form 9295-1). The certificate is issued by the U.S. Department of Agriculture's Food Safety and Inspection Service and requires a number of special statements concerning the product. China's State Administration for Quality Supervision and Inspection and Quarantine (AQSIQ) requires advance e-mail notification of all scheduled shipments. As of Oct. 15, 2009, the e-mail must be addressed to ChinaCertificates@fsis.usda.gov and must include the following information in the subject line: "CHINA CERTIFICATE [enter unique MPH or MPG six-digit export certificate number] FOR ESTABLISHMENT NUMBER [enter establishment number where the product was certified for export]." Each e-mail must include only one PDF-formatted attachment of the FSIS 9060-5 export certificate, which must be named "China Certificate Number, FSIS Form 9060-5 MPH or MPG-XXXXXX [six-digit export certificate number].pdf." The Meat and Poultry Export Certificate of Wholesomeness for Export to the People's Republic of China (FSIS form 9295-1), if applicable, must be included in the PDF document file. Additional information about meat and poultry certification is available from the U.S. Food Safety and Inspection.

Quarantine certificate: A quarantine certificate issued by the official institution in the country of export may be required to support the importer's application for inspection and quarantine for meat products intended for human consumption; goods in transit that contain genetically modified organisms; animals, including those in transit; plants subject to review and approval and their products; aquatic products; and containers and packaging materials for these products. Quarantine certificates for aquatic products must specify, in Chinese and English, variety name and official name of the product; place of origin; catch area; production area; names and registration numbers of the manufacturer and processor; processing method; production date; means of transportation, including name of the carrier, number, and container number; seal number; names of the consignee and the consignor; quantity; weight; the destination, which should be stated as the People's Republic of China; and name of the department issuing the certificate. In addition, the certificate must state the following information: the fishery products come from a processing plant approved by a competent authority; the products were produced, packed, stored, and transported under sanitary conditions approved by a competent authority; the products were inspected and quarantined by a competent authority, and no pathogenic bacteria or foreign or harmful substances regulated in China were found; and the products meet veterinary requirements to be fit for human consumption. Certificates cannot be altered and must bear an official stamp and the inspector's signature. Each batch of aquatic products must be covered by an original certificate. More information may be obtained from APHIS.

Certificate of free sale: Drugs and medical devices require a certificate of free sale. The certificate for medical devices may be obtained from the U.S. Food and Drug Administration's Center for Devices and Radiological Health. The certificate of free sale for drugs is available from the U.S. Food and Drug Administration's Center for Drug Evaluation and Research. A certificate of free sale also is required for products containing genetically modified organisms, including pesticides and fertilizers, seeds, and veterinary medicines. The certificate of free sale for pesticides and fertilizers is available from the Environmental Protection Agency, Office of Pesticide Programs, Registration Division, 1200 Pennsylvania Ave. N.W., MC 7505C, Washington, D.C. 20460; (703) 305-5447; fax: (703) 305-6920. Information about the certificate for seeds and plant products is available from the U.S. Food and Drug Administration's Center for Food Safety and Applied Nutrition, Office of Food Safety; the certificate of free sale for veterinary medicines is available from the U.S. Food and Drug Administration's Center for Veterinary Medicine.

Product registration: Numerous products must be registered in China by the relevant government agency. The application for registration usually is submitted by the importer and may require from the exporter or manufacturer any number of documents concerning product safety, production methods, scientific analysis, environmental impact, etc. Exporters are urged to consult with their customers in China regarding requirements for specific products. See also Standards, Labeling, and Packing for additional information.

Solid wood packing materials: Packing materials from the United States containing solid wood must conform to the International Plant Protection Convention's International Standards for Phytosanitary Measures concerning solid wood packing materials (ISPM 15). ERM 35:42. Shipping restrictions include the following. Insurance generally is handled by the People's Insurance Company of China, the state-owned insurance company, which underwrites marine, land, and air transportation, postal shipments, ships' hulls, machinery insurance, and reinsurance. Effective April 1, 2010, plant propagation materials, including seeds, seedlings, cuttings, and rootstock, must enter China through designated ports only. The list of ports is extensive; exporters are urged to consult with their customers in China to determine which port is acceptable for their shipments.

Companies who ship into China on a DDP Incoterms basis need to heed all the regulatory requirements, which are comprehensive, convoluted, and arduous. It may be prudent to sell with Incoterms that do not include the import formalities that literally would be all the others.

AUSTRALIA

As a modern trading nation, Australia is a diversified and reliable supplier of high-quality goods and services to over 200 countries and a sophisticated import market for products from all over the world. Australia's seaports and airports are dynamic and efficient. The ports of Sydney and Melbourne on the east coast of Australia are the major trading centers for manufactured goods. Coal, iron ore, and an array of other natural resources and commodities such as liquefied natural gas (LNG), various minerals, and wheat are also shipped from major facilities around the nation's extensive coastline.

Australia has a long history of trading with the world. One of the earliest exports was wool, from which the expression "Australia riding on the sheep's back" was born. Today, a more diverse export industry has grown incorporating manufacturing products, services such as education and tourism, and high-quality food and wine.

As of 2007, Australia's largest export markets were Japan, China, the United States, Republic of Korea, and New Zealand.

Australia is a strong advocate of trade liberalization, and consistently supports trade liberalization in the World Trade Organization (WTO). In 1948, Australia was one of the inaugural 23 signatories to the General Agreement on Tariffs and Trade (GATT)—the precursor to the WTO—and has played an active role in global trade talks.

One of Australia's initiatives was bringing together the Cairns Group, a coalition of 19 agricultural exporting nations, which has become an influential voice for the liberalization of agricultural trade. It met for the first time in the Far North Queensland city of Cairns in 1986.

Australia has also played an activist role in forming regional trade and economic groupings, such as the Asia-Pacific Economic Cooperation (APEC) which was launched in Canberra in 1989. It has since become the premier forum for economic growth, cooperation, trade, and investment in the Asia-Pacific region—the fastest-growing economic region of the world.

Trade has always been a vital component in Australia's economic prosperity. The hallmarks of its trading success have been strong infrastructure and stable institutions, a flexible and skilled workforce, and a rich resource and agricultural base.*

Incoterms options can be quite varied for companies who both buy and sell to and from Australia. They have a quality transportation infrastructure,

---

* From Green Earth Systems (GES) Commodities, Sydney, Australia, http://www.gescommodity.com/pages-L2/gesaust.html.

stable insurance, and banking capability, and their laws are traditional to Western culture as a society and in their legal profile. This allows companies to look at all options when negotiating sales and purchase orders and leveraging the Incoterms without fear of negative consequence.

As a comparison, if we look at Russia, we would be very concerned about a choice of Incoterms that had a foreign company involved with domestic trucking, warehousing, clearance, or any activities inside of their borders. These internal affairs for global trade are so disconnected from the rest of the world—graft, corruption, gratuities, military involvement (both former and current), and lack of consistent performing infrastructure—that one would choose only an Incoterms that keeps the foreign entity any from any of this internal issues they would have to deal with. As Russia progresses in global trade, many of these infrastructure issues will go away. Russia's role in the world economy is too important for it to act as a developing nation, and it will move into more Westernized business processes in the future.

Australia, on the other hand, would present no serious issue in any of these areas, allowing a foreign entity to buy or sell on any Incoterms where it can obtain leverage.

SOUTH KOREA

South Korea is an export-orientated country, with a total trade volume of 884.2 billion in 2010. This figure also makes them the 7th largest exporter and 10th largest importer in the world. Since 2003, South Korea has established its network of free trade agreements to boost trade and economic ties with other countries.

Currently, South Korea has 5 FTAs in effect, 3 FTAs which have concluded discussions, and 19 FTAs under negotiation and consideration. So far, the biggest FTA of South Korea is the Korea-U.S. Free Trade Agreement (KORUS FTA) signed in 2007. This free trade agreement plans to liberate 95% of the trade tariffs between the two countries. It is also the first U.S. free trade agreement with a major Asian economy and biggest deal since the North America Free Trade Agreement (NAFTA) signed with Japan in 1993.

With a lack of natural resources, South Korea has a high dependence on import of capital goods, raw materials, and industrial supplies. The country is also the 5th largest importer of oil in the world, with 3.074 million barrels imported per day.

Korea's free trade agreements are as follows:

Korea-US FTA
Korea-EU FTA
Korea-Peru FTA
Korea-Chile FTA
Korea-Singapore FTA
Korea-India CEPA FTA
Korea-ASEAN FTA
Korea-EFTA (European Free Trade Area)*

The newest trade agreement with the United States promises to provide a platform for substantial activity between the two countries that already have large activity in their import and export business. Most companies who export to South Korea should be reluctant to enter into any choice such as DDP where they are responsible for the clearance process.

Customs clearance in Korea is complicated and fraught with exposures—both from a compliance standpoint and from a fiscal risk. Companies who buy from Korea will do so typically on terms such as FOB and FCA, where the supplier will deliver the goods to the outbound gateway. ExWorks would not be a good option, but all other choices would work.

EUROPE

France

France's trade is one of the largest in the world. France exports and imports various raw materials, automobiles, and electronic products. The

---

country ranks sixth in the world in terms of export volumes and fifth when it comes to imports.

In 2010, France's exports totaled $456.8 billion including:

- Machinery and transportation equipment and aircraft
- Plastics, chemicals, and pharmaceutical products
- Iron and steel
- Beverages

to export trading partners Germany (14.3%), Italy (8.7%), Spain (8.3%), United Kingdom (7.8%), Belgium (7.6%), United States (5.8%), Netherlands (4.2%) Germany (14.9%), Spain (9.3%), Italy (8.9%), UK (8.1%), Belgium (7.3%), United States (6.1%), and Netherlands (4.1%).

France's imports totaled up to $532.2 billion in 2010 declining from $692 billion in 2008. France's main import commodities are

- Machinery and equipment
- Vehicles and aircraft
- Crude oil
- Plastics and chemicals

to main import partners Germany (17.9%), Belgium (11.7%), Italy (8.3%), Spain (6.9%), Netherlands (6.8%), United Kingdom (5.1%), United States (4.3%).

Besides French trade, tourism is also a big contributor to the national GDP. France rules the tourism industry with over 82 million tourists visiting the country for its rich heritage and culture.

Agriculture is also another strong point for France's economy, with almost 25 percent of the EU's total agricultural products being produced in France. The government provides subsidies to the agricultural sector and the development of this sector is likely to give export activities a further boost.

France is a comprehensive and sophisticated global market with capabilities in import and export trade that are among the best in the world. This affords the use of any Incoterms that works to the advantage of the seller or buyer. In some regions and countries around the world, as outlined in this section, we point to some very specific Incoterms that sellers and buyers need to keep away from or gravitate toward based upon the local nuances that impact cost and risk in their transaction.

We have no concerns with any Incoterms use for goods being sold to from or within France because the market's sophistication, like many other European countries, affords the use of any Incoterms that works best.

France has many laws regarding legal, tax, accounting, title, and revenue recognition that all can be impacted by the choice of Incoterms, so one must be prudent about the Incoterms choice to make sure all interests involved in cost and risk are protected. But France, like Germany, the United Kingdom, Spain, and the Netherlands, is an example for which any Incoterms options can work and provide benefit, thus providing the importer and exporter or even the domestic shipper with all 11 Incoterms options to choose from.

EXAMPLES OF VALUE-ADDED TAXES

A company engaged in global trade needs to understand what the VAT and related tax issues are as goods pass through international borders. They have a direct impact on cost and risk and become part of the overall obligations of the seller or buyer or both, depending upon the following:

- Choice of Incoterms
- Trade compliance regulations in that country
- Contractual arrangements in the sales or purchase order

Companies can impact their landed costs not only by choice of Incoterms but also by understanding how these VAT taxes apply and how they can or should be used for leverage.

An example relates to certain countries like Great Britain where VAT monies paid can be refunded under certain sets of circumstances by host companies that know how to manage the recovery process.

Some companies have specific staff assignments in-house or have outsourced capabilities managing VAT and GST refund programs. Knowing how these work and then choosing the right Incoterms to make these happen can produce substantial cash flow back to certain parties in the international transaction, making it profitable or enhancing overall financial picture. This is usually a role for senior management in their ITM lead program.

Canada

The Canadian Goods and Services Tax (GST) (French: *Taxe sur les produits et services*, TPS) is a multilevel value-added tax introduced in Canada on January 1, 1991, by Prime Minister Brian Mulroney and finance minister Michael Wilson. The GST replaced a hidden 13.5% Manufacturers' Sales Tax (MST) because it hurt the manufacturing sector's ability to export. The introduction of the GST was very controversial. As of January 1, 2008, the GST stood at 5%.

As of July 1, 2010, the federal GST and the regional Provincial Sales Tax (PST) were combined into a single value-added sales tax, called the Harmonized Sales Tax (HST). The HST is in effect in 5 of the 10 Canadian provinces: British Columbia, Ontario, New Brunswick, Newfoundland and Labrador, and Nova Scotia.

United Kingdom

The third largest source of government revenues is value-added tax (VAT), charged at the standard rate of 20% on supplies of goods and services. It is therefore a tax on consumer expenditure. Certain goods and services are exempt from VAT, and others are subject to VAT at a lower rate of 5% (the reduced rate) or 0% ("zero-rated").

Australia

The Goods and Services Tax is a value-added tax of 10% on most goods and services sold in Australia.

It was introduced by the Howard Government on July 1, 2000, replacing the previous federal wholesale sales tax system and designed to phase out the various state and territory taxes such as banking taxes, stamp duty and land value tax. While this was the stated intent at the time, the States still charge duty on a various transactions, including but not limited to vehicle transfers and land transfers, insurance contracts and agreements for the sale of land. Many States, such as Western Australia, have made recent amendments to duties laws to phase out particular duties and clarify existing ones.

New Zealand

The Goods and Services Tax (GST) is a value-added tax of 12.5% on most goods and services sold in New Zealand.

It was introduced by the Fourth Labour Government on October 1, 1986, at a rate of 10%. This was increased to 12.5% on July 1, 1989, and 15% on October 1, 2010.

Europe

A common VAT system is compulsory for member states of the European Union. The EU VAT system is imposed by a series of European Union directives, the most important of which is the Sixth VAT Directive (Directive 77/388/EC). Nevertheless, some member states have negotiated variable rates (Madeira in Portugal) or VAT exemption for regions or territories. The regions below fall out of the scope of EU VAT:

- Åland Islands (Finland)
- Heligoland island, Büsingen territory (Germany)
- Guadeloupe, Martinique, French Guiana, Réunion (France)
- Mount Athos (Greece)
- Ceuta, Melilla, The Canary Islands (Spain)
- Livigno, Campione d'Italia, Lake Lugano (Italy)
- Gibraltar, The Channel Islands (United Kingdom)

Under the EU system of VAT, where a person carrying on an economic activity supplies goods and services to another person, and the value of the supplies passes financial limits, the supplier is required to register with the local taxation authorities and charge its customers, and account to the local taxation authority for VAT (although the price may be *inclusive* of

VAT, so VAT is included as part of the agreed price, or *exclusive* of VAT, so VAT is payable in addition to the agreed price).

VAT that is charged by a business and paid by its customers is known as *output* VAT (that is, VAT on its output supplies). VAT that is paid by a business to other businesses on the supplies that it receives is known as *input* VAT (that is, VAT on its input supplies). A business is generally able to recover input VAT to the extent that the input VAT is attributable to (that is, used to make) its taxable outputs. Input VAT is recovered by setting it against the output VAT for which the business is required to account to the government, or, if there is an excess, by claiming a repayment from the government.

Different rates of VAT apply in different EU member states. The minimum standard rate of VAT throughout the EU is 15%, although reduced rates of VAT, as low as 5%, are applied in various states on various sorts of supply (for example, domestic fuel and power in the UK). The maximum rate in the EU is 25%.

The Sixth VAT Directive requires certain goods and services to be exempt from VAT (for example, postal services, medical care, lending, insurance, betting), and certain other goods and services to be exempt from VAT but subject to the ability of an EU member state to opt to charge VAT on those supplies (such as land and certain financial services). Input VAT that is attributable to exempt supplies is not recoverable; although a business can increase its prices so the customer effectively bears the cost of the "sticking" VAT (the effective rate will be lower than the headline rate and depend on the balance between previously taxed input and labor at the exempt stage).

Finally, some goods and services are "zero-rated." The zero-rate is a positive rate of tax calculated at 0%. Supplies subject to the zero-rate are still "taxable supplies," i.e., they have VAT charged on them. In the UK, examples include most food, books, drugs, and certain kinds of transport. The zero-rate is not featured in the EU Sixth Directive as it was intended that the minimum VAT rate throughout Europe would be 5%. However, zero-rating remains in some Member States, most notably the UK, as a legacy of pre-EU legislation. These Member States have been granted a derogation to continue existing zero-rating but cannot add new goods or services. The UK also exempts or lowers the rate on some products depending on situation; for example milk products are exempt from VAT, but if you go into a restaurant and drink a milk drink it is VAT-able. Some products such as feminine hygiene products and baby products (nappies, etc.) are charged at 5% VAT along with domestic fuel.

When goods are imported into the EU from other states, VAT is generally charged at the border, at the same time as customs duty. *Acquisition* VAT is payable when goods are acquired in one EU member state from another EU member state (this is done not at the border but through an accounting mechanism). EU businesses are often required to charge themselves VAT under the *reverse charge* mechanism where services are received from another member state or from outside of the EU.

Businesses can be required to register for VAT in EU member states, other than the one in which they are based, if they supply goods via mail order to those states, over a certain threshold. Businesses that are established in one member state but which receive supplies in another member state may be able to reclaim VAT charged in the second state under the provisions of the Eighth VAT Directive (Directive 79/1072/EC). To do so, businesses have a value added tax identification number. A similar directive, the Thirteenth VAT Directive (Directive 86/560/EC), also allows businesses established outside the EU to recover VAT in certain circumstances.

Following changes introduced on July 1, 2003 (under Directive 2002/38/EC), non-EU businesses providing digital electronic commerce and entertainment products and services to EU countries are also required to register with the tax authorities in the relevant EU member state, and to collect VAT on their sales at the appropriate rate, according to the location of the purchaser. Alternatively, under a special scheme, non-EU businesses may register and account for VAT on only one EU member state. This produces distortions as the rate of VAT is that of the member state of registration, not where the customer is located, and an alternative approach is therefore under negotiation, whereby VAT is charged at the rate of the member state where the purchaser is located.

The differences between different rates of VAT were often originally justified by certain products being "luxuries" and thus bearing high rates of VAT, whereas other items were deemed to be "essentials" and thus bearing lower rates of VAT. However, often high rates persisted long after the argument was no longer valid. For instance, France taxed cars as a luxury product (33%) up into the 1980s, when most of the French households owned one or more cars. Similarly, in the UK, clothing for children is "zero rated" whereas clothing for adults is subject to VAT at the standard rate of 20%.

GERMAN EXPORT CONTROL

The United States is not the only country with strong export controls. Another country with strong export controls is Germany. Please find some basic information in summary from the Federal Republic of Germany export control arm, BAFA.

BAFA as a central licensing authority is responsible for the administrative implementation of the federal government's export control policy. Together with the monitoring and investigating authorities, especially the different customs offices, it is involved in a complex export control system.

Objectives of Export Control[*]

The foreign trade with commodities of strategic importance, mainly weapons, armaments, and dual-use items, is subject to control. Dual-use items are goods, software, and technology that may be used for civil and military purposes. A milling machine, for example, may be used for processing components for civil as well as military products.

Within the framework of its legal and international commitments, the export control policy of the federal government is oriented to the security need and foreign political interests of the Federal Republic of Germany. Particularly its security must not be threatened by conventional armaments and weapons of mass destruction. German exports should neither intensify conflicts nor contribute to internal repression or other severe human rights violations in crisis areas. Its international involvement obliges the Federal Republic of Germany not to burden its foreign relations by critical exports.

With the increasing globalization, efficient export controls are only possible on the basis of an intensified international and European

---

[*] From Federal Office of Economics and Export Control (BAFA), Export Control, accessed from http://www.bafa.de/bafa/en/export_control.

co-operation. The Federal Republic of Germany is a member of numerous international treaties and export control regimes aiming at the harmonization of export control regulations and licensing policies. Of special importance are the lists of items established by the international regimes; these lists are technically updated in regular periods.

International Export Control Bodies

There are four international export control bodies:

- MTCR (Missile Technology Control Regime)—for items relevant for missile systems
- Australia Group—for dual-use items relevant for chemical and biological weapons
- NSG (Nuclear Suppliers Group)—for items in the nuclear area
- Wassenaar Arrangement—for armaments and dual-use items related to the area of conventional armaments

The export of dual-use items from the European Union has been harmonized to a large extent. It is subject to European law.

BAFA regularly sends its experts to the meetings of the control bodies and the EU-work groups.

Licensing Procedure

One of BAFA's main tasks is to check whether the export of a commodity is subject to licensing and if a license may be granted.

An export license is always required if the commodity is mentioned in the European or national list of items. Items covered by the lists range from weapons, ammunition and related production facilities via material, plants and equipment for nuclear purposes, high-grade materials, specific machine tools, electronic equipment, computers, telecommunications up to specific chemical units and chemicals. In addition to the licensing requirements for listed items, there are European and national licensing requirements depending on the use of the items. This "catch-all" clause normally applies to sensitive countries only. In case of certain countries, technical support, as well as brokering activities, are subject to additional controls.

An export license may be granted if the export does not impair the foreign policy and security interests of the Federal Republic of Germany.

The legal and administrative problems are very complex when looking at the licensing procedure of dual-use items. Although the majority of them serve civil purposes, they can also be used in the military sector. Dual-use items make up the highest percentage of the millions of exports crossing the borders every year; normally their intended use is not directly visible. BAFA decides on granting or refusing an authorization after taking into consideration all the available information about the intended use. In a number of cases BAFA takes such a decision only after political consultations with the Federal Ministry of Economics and Technology and the Federal Foreign Office. The granting of a license is also made dependent on the exporter's reliability. In this connection, BAFA may request the nomination of a person responsible for exports on the level of the management.

DEVELOPING NATION: IMPORTING INTO NIGERIA

In pursuit of government decision to abolish the Pre-Shipment Inspection Scheme for imports to Nigeria and the introduction of the Destination Inspection Scheme for imports with effect from January 1, 2006, the following guidelines, procedures, and documentation requirements shall apply in respect of import transactions with effect from that date.

Import Guidelines*

1. Any person intending to import physical goods into Nigeria shall in the first instance process Form M through any Authorized dealer bank irrespective of the value and whether or not payment is involved;
2. The Form M shall have a validity period of six months for all imports except Plants and Machinery which shall have a validity period of one year. Requests for subsequent revalidation thereafter should be directed to the Director of Trade and Exchange Department at the Central Bank of Nigeria.
3. Supporting documents shall be clearly marked "Valid for Forex/Not Valid for Forex" as appropriate, i.e., depending on whether or not foreign exchange remittance would be involved.
4. All applications for goods subject to Destination Inspection shall carry the "BA" code, while those exempted shall include "CB" in the

---

* From Destination Inspection, Nigeria Customs Service (NCS), https://www.customs.gov.ng/Guidelines/Destination_Inspection.

prefix of the numbering system of the Form M. Payments for goods exempted from Destination Inspection under the Scheme, would not be carried out in the Foreign Exchange Market, without a prior approval from the Central Bank of Nigeria. The list of goods exempted from Destination Inspection shall be as approved by the Honourable Minister of Finance and the approval shall be a pre-condition for the completion of Form M exempted from Destination Inspection.

5. The Form M and the relevant pro-forma invoice (which shall have a validity period of 3 months) shall carry a proper description of the goods to be imported to facilitate price verification viz;
   - Generic product name, i.e., product type, category
   - Mark or brand name of the product where applicable
   - Model name and or model or reference number, where applicable
   - Description of the quality, grade, specification, capacity, size, performance, etc.
   - Quantity and packaging and/or packing

6. Form M shall be valid for importation only after acceptance by the relevant Scanning/Risk Management Provider. Consequently, Authorized Dealers are to confirm acceptance of the Form M before proceeding with other import processes.

7. Documents in respect of each import transaction shall carry the name of the product, country of origin, specifications, date of manufacture, batch or lot number, Standards to which the goods have been produced (e.g., NIS, British Standards—PD, ISO, IES, DIN, etc).

8. All goods to be imported into the country shall be labeled in English in addition to any other language of transaction; otherwise the goods shall be confiscated.

9. Where import items such as food, drinks, cosmetics, drugs, medical devices, chemicals, etc., are regulated for health or environmental reasons, they shall carry expiry dates or the shelf life and specify the active ingredients, where applicable.

10. Electrical appliances (fluorescent lamps, electric bulbs, electric irons and ties, etc) shall carry information on life performance while cables shall carry information on the ratings.

11. All electronic equipment and instruments shall carry:
    - Instruction manual
    - Safety information and/or safety signs
    - A guarantee/warranty of at least 6 months

12. All computer hardware, software, operating and embedded system shall continue to be year 2000 compliant.

13. Any wrong or fraudulent misrepresentation of facts will result in delays and/or impoundment/seizures.

14. Importation of Blank products and/or without valid Form M shall automatically qualify for seizure and destruction without warning, and subject to prosecution.

15. All imports into the country shall be accompanied by the following documents:
    - Combined Certificate of Value and Origin (CCVO), and contain the following details in addition to those on the pro-forma invoice:
        1. Form M no.
        2. Adequate description of goods
        3. Port of destination (the actual port shall be specified, e.g., Tin Can, Apapa, Kano, Onne, etc.)
        4. Shipment identification, date of shipment, Country of Origin, Country of supply
    - Packing list
    - Shipped/Clean on Board Bill of Lading/Airway bill/Way bill/ Road Way bill
    - Manufacturer's Certificate of production which shall state standards and where it is not applicable, the Phytosanitary Certificate or Chemical Analysis Report should be made available.
    - Laboratory test certificates for chemicals, foods, beverages, pharmaceuticals, electrical appliances and other regulated products, where applicable.

16. The following procedure shall be adopted for payments for
    - Letters of credit transactions: where the transactions involve issuance of Certificate of Capital Importation (CCI) and or supplier's credit, all negotiating documents and or shipping documents (as may be applicable), must be routed from the Beneficiary/Supplier through his/her bank to the correspondence bank of the issuing bank and thereafter to the issuing bank. For the avoidance of doubt, on no account must banks endorse or pay on documents which do not comply with the routing outlined above.
    - For Bills for Collection transactions and Unconfirmed Letters of Credit, documents must come to the issuing bank either directly from the supplier's bank or through the offshore correspondent of the issuing bank.

- For Not Valid for foreign exchange transactions (which do not require foreign exchange transfer), the supplier should forward the documents directly to the bank that opened the Form M. In addition, applicable returns on non-submission of shipping documents after 90 days in respect of such transactions must henceforth be rendered.

In the case of personal effects, the relevant documents should be forwarded to the appropriate Service Provider. However, where dutiable goods are found to be in excess of the approved passenger concession, they shall be liable to the clearance procedure applicable to commercial goods and accordingly all import documentation requirements must be complied with, failing which they shall be liable to seizure.

17. For transactions with Post Landing charges, a retention fee of 5%–15% of the project cost as agreed between the importer and the overseas supplier shall be indicated on both the Contract Agreement and the Pro-forma invoice which shall form part of the supporting documents for the registration of relevant Form M. In addition,
    - The stated fee shall not be remitted until a satisfactory evaluation of the project has been undertaken by the Industrial Inspectorate Department of the Federal Ministry of Industry.
    - The Scanning Company shall forward to the Federal Ministry of Industry (Industrial Inspectorate Department) and the Central Bank of Nigeria, Trade and Exchange Department copies of the Contract Agreement and Pro-forma invoice of such projects for monitoring purposes.
    - During Destination Inspection, the Nigeria Customs Service shall take cognizance of the value of shipment and Post Landing charges as would have been indicated on the Risk Assessment Report (RAR).
    - The Industrial Inspectorate Department, Federal Ministry of Industry shall thereafter carry out an evaluation of the project and advise the Central Bank of Nigeria accordingly.
    - On receipt of the report of the evaluation from the Federal Ministry of Industry (Industrial Inspectorate Department), the Central Bank of Nigeria shall advise the respective scanning company on the issuance of the RAR in respect of the retained value and the Authorized Dealer advised to remit same to the beneficiary.

LATIN AMERICA

Brazil[*]

The economy of Brazil is the world's seventh largest by nominal GDP and eighth largest by purchasing power parity.

Brazil has moderately free markets and an inward-oriented economy. Its economy is the largest in Latin American nations and the second largest in the Western Hemisphere.

Brazil is one of the fastest-growing major economies in the world with an average annual GDP growth rate of over 5%. In Brazilian real (currency), its GDP was estimated at R$ 3.143 trillion in 2009. The Brazilian economy has been predicted to become one of the five largest economies in the world in the decades to come.

Brazil is a member of diverse economic organizations, such as Mercosul, Unasul, G8+5, G20, WTO, and the Cairns Group. Its trade partners number in the hundreds, with 60 percent of exports mostly of manufactured or semimanufactured goods. Brazil's main trade partners in 2008 were Mercosul and Latin America (25.9% of trade), EU (23.4%), Asia (18.9%), the United States (14.0%), and others (17.8%).

According to the World Economic Forum, Brazil was the top country in upward evolution of competitiveness in 2011, gaining eight positions among other countries, overcoming Russia for the first time, and partially closing the competitiveness gap with India and China among the BRIC economies. Important steps taken since the 1990s toward fiscal sustainability, as well as measures taken to liberalize and open the economy, have significantly boosted the country's competitiveness fundamentals, providing a better environment for private-sector development.

The owner of a sophisticated technological sector, Brazil develops projects that range from submarines to aircraft and is involved in space research: the country possesses a satellite launching center and was the only country in the Southern Hemisphere to integrate the team responsible for the construction of the International Space Station (ISS). It is also a pioneer in many fields, including ethanol production.

Brazil, together with Mexico, has been at the forefront of the Latin American multinationals phenomenon by which, thanks to superior

---

[*] From Bloomberg BNA, http://www.bna.com, and Helping U.S. Companies Export, http://www.export.gov.

technology and organization, local companies have successfully turned global. These multinationals have made this transition notably by investing massively abroad, in the region and beyond, and thus realizing an increasing portion of their revenues internationally.

Brazil is also a pioneer in the fields of deep water oil research from where 73% of its reserves are extracted. According to government statistics, Brazil was the first capitalist country to bring together the 10 largest car assembly companies inside its national territory.

The annual Brazil Investment Summit takes place in São Paulo and is the largest gathering in Brazil of international investment experts covering opportunities in alternative vehicles, infrastructure, and advanced trading strategies.

With still high levels of inequality, though it has diminished in the last years, the Brazilian economy has become one of the major economies of the world. According to Forbes 2011, Brazil has the eighth largest number of billionaires in the world, a number much larger than what is found in other Latin American countries, and ahead of even Japan. By the end of 2011, Brazil's economy had become the world's sixth largest.

Exporting to Brazil can be a complicated matter. What we can give is a overview of how the process is to export a generic product to Brazil:

1. Verify that your product can legally be exported to Brazil.
2. Before shipment, a proforma invoice must be sent to the Brazilian importer.
3. The Brazilian importer has to request an Import License (LI) from Integrated Foreign Trade System (Siscomex).
4. The exporter must send the Brazilian importer all necessary documents following embarkation. This includes:
   • Shipping information
   • Commercial invoice
   • Certificate of origin
   • Other certificates if required
5. The Import Duty and the Tax on Industrial Products (IPI) will have to be paid.
6. When goods arrive to Brazil, the importer must prepare the Import Declaration (DI).
7. All documents including the Import Declaration, a receipt generated by the Siscomex and ICMS payment receipt (or waiver) must be presented to the Secretariat of Federal revenue (SRF).

When completing these steps the clearance process is finished and the product can be traded in Brazil.

Remember that in addition to Import Duty, IPI, and ICMS, you will also have to pay the PIS and COFINS taxes on the imported product.

This is only a generic overview and some products will need product registration in Brazil before embarkation.

Many companies and trade professionals who are experienced exporters would clearly identify Brazil as a difficult country for export. Their government has a regular practice of making the import process a difficult one.

This places a significant burden on the exporter to Brazil to comply with certain business processes as identified already.

Therefore we do not want to export to Brazil where the Incoterms places any burden of clearance or on forwarding point past the inbound gateway, such as with DAT, DAP, or DDP. When we purchase goods from Brazil we don't want to be involved with export formalities and just take delivery once goods are loaded outbound, such as with a FOB or FCA option.

Mexico[*]

Mexico's trade regime is built upon 13 trade agreements with 44 countries, including the United States, Canada, and the European Union. In 2010 it exported nearly $300 billion of goods, led by electronic and other machinery (38% of total), road vehicles and transportation equipment (17.8%), and mining and crude oil (14.6%). Mexico relies heavily on supplying the U.S. market but has also sought to diversify its export destinations. Eighty percent of Mexico's exports went to the United States in 2010, down from a high of nearly 90% in 2001.

The United States exported $163 billion of goods to Mexico in 2010. Mexico is the United States' second-largest export market (after Canada) and third-largest trading partner (after Canada and China). Two-way trade (exports plus imports) reached nearly $400 billion in 2010, more than quadruple what it was 20 years ago. Top U.S. exports to Mexico include electronic equipment, motor vehicle parts, and chemicals. Trade matters are generally settled through direct negotiations between the two countries or addressed via World Trade Organization (WTO) or North American Free Trade Agreement (NAFTA) formal dispute settlement procedures. Mexico

---

[*] From Mexico Export, Import, and Trade, Economy Watch, http://www.economywatch.com/world_economy/mexico/export-import.html.

is an active and constructive member of the World Trade Organization, the G-20, and the Organization for Economic Cooperation and Development.

Mexico is making progress in its intellectual property rights enforcement efforts, although piracy and counterfeiting rates remain high. Mexico appeared on the Watch List in the 2011 Special 301 report. The United States continues to work with the Mexican government to implement its commitment to improving intellectual property protection.*

As an export orientated country, Mexico is the 15th largest exporter in the world. They are also the United States' second largest export market, making about 12.21 percent of U.S. total exports in 2009. With the signing of the North American Free Trade Agreement (NAFTA) in 1994 with the United States, Mexico's trade economy is heavily linked to the United States', with as high as 80.5% for Mexico's exports going to the United States.

As a result, Mexico's economy suffered greatly during the 2008 global financial crisis and U.S. economic downturn, due to a drop in U.S. demand of exports. Mexico's exports to United States fell from US$234.6 billion in 2008 to $184.9 billion in 2009. GDP (PPP) of Mexico also posted a negative 5.25 percent growth in 2009, a drop from US$1.553 trillion in 2008 to US$1.471 trillion in 2009.

Mexico has also built an extensive network of free trade agreements with over 40 countries, such as the European Union, Japan, Israel, and countries in South and Central America. These agreements liberalize the trade tariffs between countries and regions, and have made Mexico one of the

---

* From U.S. Department of State, http://www.state.gov/outofdate/bgn/mexico/191338.htm.

most open countries to trade. The United States and Canada are the two biggest importers of Mexico's goods. Following is a list of Mexico's FTAs:

North American Free Trade Agreement
Costa Rica–Mexico FTA
Nicaragua–Mexico FTA
Chile–Mexico FTA
European Union–Mexico FTA
Israel–Mexico FTA
El Salvador–Mexico FTA
Guatemala–Mexico FTA
Honduras–Mexico
Japan–Mexico FTA
EFTA–Mexico
(EFTA includes Iceland, Liechtenstein, Norway, and Switzerland)

Argentina*

Argentina has risen to be a major economy in the Latin American market with a significant growing international presence. Latin America's number three economy, it grew at one of the region's fastest rates in 2011, although some economists say widely questioned official data overstates growth. With the exception of 0.9% growth in 2009, Argentina has posted strong annual growth since Nestor Kirchner, Fernandez's late husband and predecessor as president, took office in 2003 following the 2001–2002 economic crisis.

An agricultural powerhouse, Argentina is the world's top supplier of soy oil and soy meal, and the number two exporter of corn. Soy exports rose to nearly $20 billion last year, representing more than a quarter of total export earnings.

The auto industry has driven surging factory output in recent years and car production surged 41% in 2010, according to trade industry association data.

Argentina's free trade agreements include the following:

---

* From Argentina's Economy and Risks, Reuters, March 28, 2011, http://www.reuters.com/article/2011/03/28/us-latam-summit-argentina-idUSTRE72R1XD20110328.

- MERCOSUR, ALADI, UNASUR, SELA. Andean Community (associate).
- CEPAL, BID, FEALAC, ASPA, OEA.
- Free Trade Agreements (FTAs) of Argentina (MERCOSUR member): Chile, Mexico, Peru, India, Egypt, Israel, Andean Community, and European Union

These FTAs place Argentina in a competitive position in Latin America and in a growth posture for import and export trade. Argentine products are in demand in world markets, and that export growth is helping its balance of trade.

Incoterms options for sales to Argentina are those that bring the goods to their border but do not impact customs clearance or on forwarding to final destinations. ExWorks, FOB, FCA, CIF, and CIP are all good options on sales top Argentine customers. For exports out of Argentina it is best to allow the supplier to minimally get the goods to the outbound gateway and take responsibility for any export formalities. ExWorks should not be an option for Argentine exports. Allow the supplier to move the goods to the outbound gateway and take responsibility in dealing with the Argentine exodus process.

IMPORTS

Importers need to pay attention to the Incoterms as they impact the costs and risks in their purchase order.

Read each Incoterm in detail, and you will observe that it addresses who is responsible for import clearance and formalities, payment of duties, taxes, and VAT. The only term where this responsibility is the seller's is the Delivered Duty Paid (DDP). Most other terms are silent or, like DAP and CIP, specifically say it is for the account of the buyer or the importer and the exporter/seller.

The DDP terms are the most engaging for the seller as they undertake delivery all the way to a final destination and handle the import process and lay out all costs. This could add greatly to transactional values and costs for the seller. If they depend upon a freight forwarder to manage the DDP process, they better get a good one because the quality of that partner will determine the outcome of the transaction from being profitable to being a loss.

Almost every country's primary responsibility of customs is to collect duties and taxes, which in most countries is a significant source of revenue. In many countries customs takes on additional responsibilities such as the following:

- Trade compliance
- Trade security
- Trade audits
- Police and crime investigation
- Trade statistics
- Intellectual property rights protection (IPR)

Importing into the United States

Most companies around the world who sell products into the United States complain about all the complications of U.S. import regulations, protocol, and business processes.

Basic Guidelines for Importing into the United States

1. An individual may make his own customs clearance of goods imported for personal use or business.
2. The U.S. Customs Service does not require an importer to have a license or permit. Other agencies may require a permit, license, or other certification, depending on the commodity.
3. All merchandise coming into the United States must clear customs and is subject to a customs duty unless specifically exempted from this duty by law. Clearance involves a number of steps—entry, inspection, appraisal, classification, liquidation.

4. Customs duties are, generally, an *ad valorem* rate (a percentage) which is applied to the dutiable value of the imported goods. Some articles, however, are dutiable at a *specific* rate of duty (so much per piece, liter, kilo, etc.); others at a compound rate of duty (combination of both *ad valorem* and specific rates).

5. The dutiable value of merchandise is determined by Customs. Several appraisal methods are used to arrive at this value. Generally, the transaction value of the merchandise serves as the basis of appraisement. Transaction value is the price the buyer actually pays the seller for the goods being imported.

6. The Harmonized Tariff Schedule of the United States (HTSUS), issued by the International Trade Commission, prescribes the rates of duty and classification of merchandise by type of product; e.g., animal and vegetable products, textile fibers and textile products.

7. The tariff schedule provides several rates of duty for each item: "general" rates for most-favored nations; "special" rates for special trade programs (free, or lower than the rates currently accorded most-favored nations); and "column 2" rates for imports not eligible for either general or special rates.

8. Processing fees may also apply.

Arrival of Goods

Imported goods may not be entered legally until the shipment has arrived within the limits of the port of entry and delivery of the merchandise has been authorized by Customs. This is normally accomplished by filing the appropriate documents, either by you as the importer or by your agent/Licensed Customs Broker. Customs entry papers may usually be presented, however, before the merchandise arrives. ISF now affords earlier clearances in certain sets of import circumstances.

The Customs Service does not notify you of the arrival of your shipment. Notification is usually made by the carrier of the goods. You should make your own arrangements to be sure you or your agent is informed immediately so that the entry can be filed and delays in obtaining your goods avoided.

Imported merchandise not entered through Customs in a timely manner (up to 30 days) is sent by Customs to a general order warehouse to be held as unclaimed. The importer is responsible for storage charges which are incurred while unclaimed merchandise is held at the warehouse. If it remains unclaimed at the end of six months, the merchandise is sold at auction.

You must make whatever entry is required at the first port of arrival. If you are unable to be there to prepare and file your entry, commercial brokers, known as customs brokers and licensed by the Customs Service, may act as your agent. Such brokers charge a fee for their services. A list of customs brokers may be obtained from your local Customs office or classified telephone directory.

In the case of a single noncommercial shipment, you may appoint a relative or other individual to act as your agent for customs purposes. This person must have knowledge of the facts pertaining to your shipment and must be authorized in writing to act for you.

Customs (CBP) employees are prohibited by law from performing these tasks for the importing public. They will advise and give information to importers about Customs (CBP) requirements, however.

Entry of Goods

To make or file a customs entry, the following documents are generally required:

1. A bill of lading, airway bill, or carrier's certificate (naming the consignee for customs purposes) as evidence of the consignee's right to make entry.
2. A commercial invoice, obtained from the seller, which shows the value and description of the merchandise.

3. Entry manifest (CBP 7533) or Entry/Immediate Delivery (CBP 3461).
4. Packing lists, if appropriate and other documents necessary to determine whether the merchandise may be admitted.

When the entry is filed, the importer indicates the tariff classification and pays any estimated duty and processing fee. A surety bond containing various conditions, including a provision for paying any increased duty that may be later found to be due, may also be required.

Other Types of Entry

Imported goods may be sent in-bond from the first port of arrival to another Customs port. Arrangements for in-bond shipments should be made before the goods leave the country of export. In-bond entries postpone final customs formalities, including payment of duty and processing fee, until the goods arrive at the final port.

Imported merchandise may also be sent to a bonded warehouse under a warehouse entry. Duties and processing fees are not paid on warehoused merchandise until the goods are withdrawn for consumption. Storage fees are paid to the warehouse proprietor by the importer.

Customs (CBP) Examination of Goods

In simple cases involving small shipments or certain classes of goods such as bulk shipments, examination may usually be made on the docks, at container stations, cargo terminals, or the importer's premises. The goods are then released to the importer. In other shipments, representative packages of the merchandise may be retained by Customs (CBP) for appraisal or classification purposes and the remainder of the shipment released. These packages will also be released to the importer after examination has been completed.

Examination of goods is necessary to determine:

1. The value of the goods for customs purposes and their dutiable status.
2. Whether the goods must be marked with the country of their origin or with special marking or labeling. If so, whether they are marked in the manner required. Generally, imported merchandise must be legibly marked in a conspicuous place and in a manner to indicate the English

name of the country of origin to the ultimate purchaser in the United States. Certain specific articles are exempt from this requirement.

3. Whether the goods have been correctly invoiced.
4. Whether the shipment contains prohibited articles.
5. Whether requirements of other federal agencies have been met.
6. Whether goods in excess of the invoiced quantities are present or a shortage of goods exists.

If necessary, goods may be analyzed by a Customs (CBP) laboratory to determine proper classification and appraisal.

When examination or appraisal of the goods by Customs (CBP) reveals differences from the entered descriptions in terms of characteristics, quantity or value, or when Customs finds that a different rate of duty than the one indicated by the importer applies, an increase in duties may be assessed.

When all the information has been acquired, including the report of the Customs import specialist as to the customs value of the goods, and the laboratory report, if required, a final determination of duty is made. This is known as *liquidation* of the entry. At this time, any overpayment of duty is returned or underpayments billed.

Importing into the United States requires:

- Due diligence
- Reasonable care
- Supervision and control
- Proactive engagement

These government standards are set to outline what their expectations are of companies operating in the global supply chain for products and services moved to and from the United States.

Trade compliance is governed in the United States by developing internal protocols and standards that mean those four basic government standards. It is not an easy proposition to manage these responsibilities, and sellers to the United States need to be cautious about the use of Incoterms that place import formality on their plate. This would typically be DDP. An exporter to the United States might consider this option as an accommodation to the buyer or as a means to be more competitive. But doing so creates risk that unless the exporter has control over this process done well it could be looking at fines, penalties, and loss of import privileges.

Importer's Security Filing and Incoterms in the United States

The *Incoterms 2010* changes have received much acclaim for including new criteria that results in a more efficient and manageable supply chain process such as the inclusion of two new rules and acknowledge of U.S. domestic application in addition to the international applications in use since their creation.

The *Incoterms 2010* changes deserve additional applause for the compliance assistance provided within the context that involves global security management, specifically related to the Importers Security Filing program (ISF) formerly known as 10+2.

Many U.S. importers continue to struggle to implement a process of compliance management related to the ISF regulation for many reasons. Some include the inability to get timely information from foreign sellers to include in a proactive filing 24 hours to the scheduled loading of an ocean container onto a vessel.

It is an issue that has resulted in fines and penalties structured at $5,000 per container. Compliance personnel around the globe are taking advantage of the delayed enforcement period to work out the glitches in their process, however note it remains a task to get cooperation from foreign sellers who are not used to providing required information to buyers that far in advance of the shipment loading process. Reluctance and push back is common to many who seek advance information from sellers.

The *Incoterms 2010* provides a compliment to this effort to obtain security related information from sellers. The new rules specifically place the responsibility on the seller to provide security-related information to the buyer, which the buyer will need to obtain import clearance in the destination country. This is a new element of the Incoterms that many procurement, logistics, compliance, and operations personnel are not familiar with unless they have undergone specific training on the new *Incoterms 2010*.

This responsibility of the seller is documented in the *Incoterms 2010* reference and is being utilized as a world-class practice of compliance management to ensure cooperation and adherence to buyers' request for advanced information to assist them in meeting strict advance manifest filing guidelines.

A review of your supply chain practices related to ISF management is recommended to identify if your organization is also dealing with push back from foreign sellers related to providing security information.

If this is the case, you may use the *Incoterms 2010* as your point of reference in the event that your purchases have been made consistent with the new *Incoterms 2010*. It is recommended that all companies familiarize themselves with education and training on the new *Incoterms 2010* changes to compliment this and additional areas of their supply chain process.

Powers of Attorney and Incoterms

Every country in the world has some sort of regulatory process or procedure that principal exporters and importers use to authorize transportation service providers to complete work on their behalf and act as an interface for dealing with export control agencies or their customs equivalents. Transportation providers such as 3PLs, freight forwarders, and customhouse brokers will typically require these powers of attorney to execute logistics on behalf of that corporation or individual. This is typically a government requirement that protects both the principal importer and exporter and the transportation provider.

The choice of Incoterms will determine which party is responsible for handling export or import formalities. For example, when we ship FOB, the exporter is responsible for export formalities. When we ship DDP, the exporter is responsible for both export and import formalities. When we ship CIP, the exporter is responsible for export formalities and the importer is responsible for import formalities. Thus, the Incoterms choice impacts these regulatory requirements, which will have legal implications for the company taking on this responsibility. It impacts the exporter, importer, and the service providers supporting the shipping and logistics. The choice of Incoterms could impact the responsibilities both favorably and unfavorably as follows:

- Potential errors and omissions issues for the transportation service providers
- Legal implications if export and import regulations are not adhered to
- Additional exposure for fines and penalties, seizures, and loss of import and export privileges
- Detentions, delays, and freight disruption
- Being red flagged to authorities on future shipment activity

In the United States, import regulations state the following.

Customs Powers of Attorney

1. Importer of record: A person or party who is responsible for duties, fees, taxes, and penalties as a result of imported goods entering the United States.
2. Customs broker: A person or party who is licensed by the Department of Treasury/Homeland Security to conduct customs business on behalf of an importer of record.
3. Customs and Border Protection: The enforcement agency that administers the laws governing importation of merchandise, baggage, and collection of duties thereon.

All customs brokers must have a valid power of attorney to conduct customs business on behalf of an importer of record. The penalty for conducting customs business on behalf of an importer without a valid power of attorney is an amount of up to the value of the merchandise for each transaction and or loss of broker's license. The power of attorney extends the authority to a broker to become an extension of the traffic department of the importer. Exercise caution when executing a power of attorney.

Revocation of a Power of Attorney

Expiration date: All powers of attorney should be dated with a date of expiration as a supervision and control issue.

Letter of revocation: A letter to the Port Director of Customs stating an importer's request to revoke a previously issued POA will be in effect on the date that CBP receives the request.

Keep in mind that each country's powers of attorney differ and have varied applications in the import and export process.

Customs Bonds

As with powers of attorney, most countries globally have some process for arranging security on goods that pass through their borders. This is typically involved with imports where a customhouse bond is posted as collateral for the payment of duties, taxes, VAT, GST, or other import charges. The choice of Incoterms would decide who would be responsible for the posting of these bonds, which adds cost and risk to any import transaction for either the exporter or importer, depending upon the Incoterms chosen.

For example, an importer in the United States that purchases goods from China on a CIP basis will have the responsibility of handling the import formality, which includes the posting of a customs bond upon entry. That U.S. importer would arrange that bond directly with a surety company either on a transaction or annualized basis or would use the services of its customhouse broker's bonding capability—as an extension of that service provider's value-added capabilities.

In the United States, bond regulations are stated as follows. A customs bond is a contract that obligates the importer to perform certain functions in the importing process, including:

1. The obligation to pay duties and related charges on a timely basis
2. To pay as demanded by CBP, all additional duties, taxes and charges subsequently found due
3. To file complete entries
4. To produce documents where CBP releases merchandise conditionally
5. To hold the merchandise at the place of examination until the merchandise is properly released
6. To, in a timely fashion, redeliver merchandise to CBP custody

For example, where the merchandise is inadmissable (e.g., product of convict labor, noncompliance automobile) or more commonly, where it does not comply with the country of origin marking rules.

The requirement for a bond is found in 19USC1623. This section of the United States Code gives the Secretary of the Treasury the authority to allow CBP to take bonds or other security (other security meaning cash deposits, U.S. bonds except savings bonds, treasury notes, or treasury bills) in an amount equal to the amount of the bond.

- Principal (Importer)
- Surety (Insurance Company)
- Beneficiary (Bureau of Customs and Border Protection)

A bond is not designed or intended to protect the importer (rather it protects the government of the United States), nor does it relieve the importer of any of their obligations.

The surety company, by bonding the importer, assumes the same duties and responsibilities of the importer. If an importer fails to honor any condition of the bond, surety can be compelled to do so in their place.

Types of Bonds

- Single Transaction—covers a particular entry (declaration) at a particular port
- Continuous—covers all entries (declarations) at all ports in the United States.

Amount of Bond

- Single Transaction Bond
  - Unrestricted Merchandise—entered value, plus all duties, taxes, and fees
  - Restricted Merchandise—entered value x 3
- Continuous Bond
  - Ten (10) percent of all duties, taxes, and fees paid in the preceding calendar year.
  - If no duties, taxes, and fees were paid in the preceding calendar year, then ten (10) percent of all duties, taxes, and fees, estimated to be paid in the current calendar year.

Breach of Bond

For failure to comply with bond conditions the importer will be assessed liquidated damages in the following amounts:

- Unrestricted merchandise—entered value, plus all duties, taxes, and fees
- Restricted merchandise—three (3) times the entered value

The choice of Incoterms impacts the party responsible for import formalities and as in the United States and most countries there is likely a form of security required, many times referred to as a "bond."

Parties to the PO or sales contract need to know their obligations for bonds and what the costs and risks are to assure these are part of the landed costs and that steps are taken to mitigate risk.

MANAGING INCOTERMS TRADE COMPLIANCE ISSUES: USPPI AND ULTIMATE CONSIGNEE

USPPI: United States Principal Party in Interest

Companies who purchase from or ship from the United States must be sensitive to and act with prudence because of changes made after the events of 9/11. Trade compliance, as we previously discussed, is a component of what would be responsibilities outlined in the Incoterms.

But having said that, the three government agencies in the United States that participate in governing export activity are the Census, CBP, and DOC/BIS. They have rules in effect via the USPPI that impact trade compliance and the choice of the Incoterms.

In effect is the concept that U.S. regulations regarding the reporting of the export, referred to as EEI, Electronic Export Information filed via AES (Automated Export System) require that, irrespective of the Incoterms, the party who receives the primary financial benefit for the transaction be identified as the USPPI and be responsible for the export formalities of the transaction.

If a U.S.-based manufacturer was to sell ExWorks, the wording under this term would point to the importer in the country of taking on that responsibility; in most places around the world that would be true, but not in the United States. In the United States, the USPPI takes on that responsibility whether they sell ExWorks, CIP, or DDP.

An importer overseas who purchases ExWorks and makes arrangements with a local freight forwarder to handle that shipment on their behalf is typically referred to as a *routed export transaction*. There are specialized provisions in U.S. export regulations that require that foreign party to follow in tandem with the originator of the freight (the USPPI) to follow that places the onus on the USPPI to take responsibility of all export compliance protocols and also onus on that freight forwarder. This calls for cooperation in data collection, transfer, and documentation. This places burden on all parties involved in the handling of the transaction to ship the goods from the United States. This strict guideline is not found in too many countries that export and is a direct result of the events of

9/11, where the United Sates significantly enhanced the security procedures on all export as well as import business.

Exporter of Record Replaced by U.S. Principal in Interest (USPPI)

The U.S. Principal Party in Interest: The person in the United States who receives the primary benefit monetary or otherwise of the export transaction.

Generally that person can be the

- U.S. seller (wholesaler/distributor) of the merchandise for export.
- U.S. manufacturer if selling the merchandise for export.
- U.S. order party: Party who directly negotiated between the U.S. seller and foreign buyer and received the order for the export of the merchandise.
- Foreign Entity, if in the United States when items are purchased or obtained for export.

Responsibility of USPPI and Forwarding Agent in a Normal Export Transaction[*]

- USPPI
  - Prepare the EEI *or* authorize a forwarding or other agent to prepare and file the EEI, with a power of attorney or written authorization.
  - If authorizing forwarding or other agent, provide information to such agent for completing the EEI.

---

[*] From AES Direct, http://www.aesdirect.gov.

- Maintain documentation to support the information reported on the EEI.
- Forwarding Agent
  - Prepare the EEI based on information received from the USPPI or other parties to the transaction.
  - Obtain a power of attorney or written authorization from a principal party in interest.
  - Provide the USPPI with a copy of the export information in a manner prescribed by the USPPI.
  - Maintain documentation to support information reported on the EEI.

Responsibility of USPPI and Forwarding Agent in a Routed Export Transaction

- USPPI
  - Provide basic commodity information to the forwarding or other agent for completing the EEI, including name, EIN, Schedule B no., and value, excluding ultimate consignee.
  - Maintain documentation to support information provided to the forwarding or other agent. (Note: In a routed export transaction, the U.S. Principal Party in Interest is not required to provide the forwarding or other agent with a power of attorney or written authorization.)
- Forwarding Agent
  - Prepare, sign, and file the EEI based on information obtained from the USPPI and/or other parties to the transaction.
  - Obtain a power of attorney or written authorization from the foreign principal party in interest to act on its behalf in the export transaction.
  - Maintain documentation to support information reported on the EEI.
  - Upon request, provide the U.S. Principal Party in Interest with documentation that the information provided by the U.S. Principal Party in Interest was accurately reported on the EEI.

The USPPI interest is a government compliance issue that overrides the responsibilities outlined in various Incoterms, which is unique to shipments being exported from the United States.

Ultimate Consignee

Another issue that surfaces in the United States for inbound shipments is the ultimate consignee regulations with U.S. Customs/CBP.

The events of 9/11 increased import security for goods entering the United States. Both exporters to the United States and importers in the United States need to be concerned about how CBP views importers of record and ultimate consignee issues. Many circumstances exist where there is an importer of record on an inbound cargo shipment, which is a different party from the ultimate consignee. The ultimate consignee may inadvertently believe it is out of the loop of import compliance responsibilities, by design, default, or the Incoterms definitions that are used. CBP may view a situation and hold the ultimate consignee to some or all of the same standards as the importer of record.

Since 9/11, the U.S. government has been trying to identify who is getting what for import and export. One of the gray areas has been when an importer brings in goods from foreign origin and automatically drops the freight at its customers' door or another company location (the ultimate consignee). During the entry process the broker is required to input the importer of record, name, address, and Internal Revenue Service (IRS) number. This tells customs who is taking responsibility of the import. If the freight being imported is going to a different address from what is listed as the importer of record, customs requests the name, address, and IRS number of the ultimate consignee. This way CBP can track shipments to the actual company or warehouse receiving the freight.

Therefore, if you are importing goods that are going to be "drop-shipped" to your customer, it is best if you can provide the IRS number of the ultimate consignee to your broker prior to the shipment being cleared through customs. There are many variations on how the information can be presented, but the bottom line is that CBP wants the name, address, and IRS number of the company receiving the freight.

If the product is going to be delivered to the importer of record, then the broker will input the importer of record a second time as the ultimate consignee. At this point the transaction for the import has been completed, and no new information needs to be provide to customs. However, if you are having the carrier or broker deliver directly to your customer or a different company location, the IRS number and information should be provided at the time of entry. (CBP does allow a broker, trucker, or carrier of any type to be listed as an ultimate consignee of import shipments.)

As per customs: "In cases where the filer fails to provide, or supplies an identification (IRS) number for the ultimate consignee which is inconsistent with the provisions of this pipeline, the Importer of Record and Filer will be referred to the Enforcement Evaluation Team or Broker Compliance Office for appropriate informed or enforced compliance action." Thus when importing goods that you know are going to a separate location than your importer of record address, you should provide a full name, address and IRS number to your broker.

Incoterms defines who the responsible party for import formalities is, but this may be overridden by local laws, such as this ultimate consignee provision in U.S. import regulations. This brings "trade compliance" into supply chain management and the various options we have available to choose for Incoterms. In a situation where the U.S. company purchases on a DDP basis from a foreign supplier, it may want to scrutinize how CBP may look at this circumstance and choose another Incoterms where it would be in charge of the clearance process, such as DAP. The theory behind this decision is that if CBP is potentially going to hold the ultimate consignee responsible for import compliance, then it may as well take charge from a purchase and contractual basis so it is absolutely clear who would be responsible to CPB and all import regulations.

This is an example of exercising due diligence in carefully thinking through the business process of how the supply chain is managed to reduce risk, penalties, and unforeseen issues with customs.

Customs working with a vessels captain in controlling shipping activity.

REFERRED WEBSITES FOR MANAGING COMPLIANCE

The United States Council for International Business, http://www.uscib.org.
The United States Council for International Business promotes openmarkets, competitiveness and innovation, sustainable development and corporate responsibility, supported by international engagement and prudent regulation. USCIB's vision and strength are provided by an active membership of leading corporations and organizations, while our unique global network helps turn the vision into reality. USCIB also provides a range of business services, including the ATA Carnet for temporary exports, to facilitate overseas trade and investment.

The World Academy, http://www.theworldacademy.com
The World Academy provides training programs and seminars for

> Trade Associations
> Global Trade Organizations
> In Association with Pre-existing Teaching Centers
> Public Seminars
> Customized In-house Training Programs
> Specially Designed and Tailored Training Activities

Topics covered in classes and workshops include all phases of Import/Export logistics and compliance including hazardous materials (HAZMAT), letters of credit, harmonized tariff schedules, Incoterms, and other topics needed to compete in today's global trade arena, such as sales and sales management classes.

The American Management Association (AMA), http://www.amanet.org

Seminars

Sharpen skills and stay ahead of the competition with AMA's leading-edge seminars in 21 distinct subject areas. With over 140 workshops to choose from in 40 cities across the country, AMA offers training to meet every individual's needs.

Professional Association of Import/Export Compliance Managers (PACMAN), http://www.compliancemaven.com

About PACMAN

Our Mission Statement:
To provide a formal structure of corporate executives engaged in import and export compliance management for mutual solution development, more compliant and secure global supply chain management and career advancement opportunities.

Deliverables:
- To develop a free exchange of ideas in import/export compliance management
- To provide a testing and certification capability for all professional members
- To develop a database of resources, such as websites, literature, and regulations for all members
- To provide a lobbying presence in Washington

- To provide a medium to gain access to senior government officials in the BIS, U.S. Customs, DOT and State Departments, ITAR, CDC, USDA/FDA, etc.
- To provide web-based and telephone "help-lines" for questions and inquiries
- To provide a forum for research, education, and training on import/export compliance management
- To grow the membership and overall forum, to be a positive advocate in overall global trade and international business
- Career development opportunities
- Compliance technology capability
- Develop dialogue with carriers for more compliant and secure transportation services
- Develop better trade relations with various government agencies
- Develop in-house capability for establishing SOP's on compliance management
- In-house education and training systems

The International Trade Administration (ITA), http://www.trade.gov
ITA strengthens the competitiveness of U.S. industry, promotes trade and investment, and ensures fair trade through the rigorous enforcement of our trade laws and agreements. ITA works to improve the global business environment and helps U.S. organizations compete at home and abroad. ITA supports President Obama's recovery agenda and the National Export Initiative to sustain economic growth and support American jobs.

ITA is organized into four distinct but complementary business units:

U.S. and Foreign Commercial Service—Promotes U.S. exports, particularly by small and medium-sized enterprises, and provides commercial diplomacy support for U.S. business interests around the world.

Manufacturing and Services—Strengthens U.S. competitiveness abroad by helping shape industry-specific trade policy.

Market Access and Compliance—Assists U.S. companies and helps create trade opportunities through the removal of market access barriers.

Import Administration—Enforces U.S. trade laws and agreements to prevent unfairly traded imports and to safeguard the competitive strength of U.S. businesses.

International Chamber of Commerce, http://www.iccwbo.org
ICC is the voice of world business championing the global economy as a force for economic growth, job creation, and prosperity.

Because national economies are now so closely interwoven, government decisions have far stronger international repercussions than in the past.

- ICC—the world's only truly global business organization responds by being more assertive in expressing business views.
- ICC activities cover a broad spectrum, from arbitration and dispute resolution to making the case for open trade and the market economy system, business self-regulation, fighting corruption or combating commercial crime.
- ICC has direct access to national governments all over the world through its national committees. The organization's Paris-based international secretariat feeds business views into intergovernmental organizations on issues that directly affect business operations.

The world business organization
Paris: Home of the ICC and Incoterms

The world's most influential business lobby group.

—Financial Times, **2008**

Networking

Networking has to be a consistent commitment by the supply chain executive. A portion of time anywhere from 3 to as much as 10 per cent of one's time can be structured into creating networking opportunities.

Networking creates:

- Camaraderie
- Information flow
- Benchmarking
- Resource development

All these create an environment to learn, to grow and positively act for mutual benefit to the company and the executive.

Develop Resources

No matter how experienced an individual is in supply chain management there is just too much information that one needs to process everyday to successfully operate in global business.

The key element to one's success is to develop resources from numerous areas so that when circumstances come up they have variable option(s) to find out what their solutions are.

Resource development is considered by many to be their "gateway" to managing all their responsibilities successfully. The old adage about you are as good as who you associate with … could easily be amended to say … you are as good in business as your contacts and resources!

Key U.S. and Globally Based Associations

- **Professional Association of Import/Export Compliance Managers (PACMAN)**—Elizabeth, NJ; http://www.compliancemaven.com
- **Transportation Intermediaries Association (TIA)**—Alexandria, VA; http://www.tianet.org
- The **National Customs Brokers & Forwarders Association of America (NCBFAA)**—Washington, DC 20036; http://www.ncbfaa.org
- The National Industrial Transportation League (**NITL**)—Arlington, VA; http://www.nitl.org
- **American Management Association (AMA)**—New York, NY; http://www.amanet.org
- The **United States Council for International Business (USCIB)**—New York, NY; http://www.uscib.org
- The **Institute for Supply Management (ISM)**—Tempe, AZ; http://www.ism.ws
- **Council of Supply Chain Management Professionals (CSCMP)**—Lombard, IL; http://www.cscmp.org

Global Examples

- Federation of International Trade Associations (FITA), Washington, DC, http://www.fita.org
- Casa Eagle Pass de Mexico, A.C. Piedras Negras, Coahuila, Mexico
- North American International Trade Corridor Partnership, San Nicolas de los Garza, Nuevo Leon, Mexico
- REPEX—Regroupement Des Professionnels De L Exportation, Montreal, Quebec, Canada
- The European Free Trade Association, Brussels, Belgium, http://www.efta.int/about-efta/the-european-free-trade-association.aspx
- Asian Food Trade Association, China and California, http://www.asianfoodtrade.org

Key Periodicals

One must develop a number of resources that provide timely information on competitors, vendors, service providers, governmental issues, and industry trends. The author reads over 60 magazines, newsletters, and periodicals every month. Below is a recommended sampling that is useful for import and export supply chain executives.

- The Export Practitioner—Telephone: (202) 463-1250; website: http://www.exportprac.com
- The Exporter—Telephone: (212) 269-2016; website: http://www.exporter.com
- Export America—Telephone: (866) 512-1800; website: http://www.exportamerica.doc.gov
- Logistics Management—Telephone: (847) 390-2377; website: http://www.Logisticsmgmt.com
- American Shipper—Telephone: (212) 233-3589; website: http://www.americanshipper.com
- Global Logistics & Supply Chain Strategies—Telephone: (516) 829-9210; website: http://www.glscs.com
- Inbound Logistics—Telephone: 212-629-1560; website: http://www.inboundlogistics.com
- The Journal of Commerce—Telephone: (888) 215-6084: website: http://www.joc.com
- Traffic World—Telephone: (888) 215-6084; website: http://www.trafficworld.com

- Air Cargo World—Telephone: (202) 661-3387; website: http://www.aircargo.com
- AFSM International—Telephone: (239) 275-7887; website: http://www.afsmi.org
- Shipping Digest—Telephone: (888) 215-6084; website: http://www.shippingdigest.com
- Managing Imports and Exports (MIE)—Telephone: (800) 524-2493; website: http://www.theworldacademy.com

There are an array of other quality options that might fit your specific needs better. In our Internet listing on the following page, a number of other options are identified.

Recommended Schools in Import/Export Supply Chain Management

- The World Academy—Telephone: (800) 524-2493; website: http://www.theworldacademy.com
- PACMAN Association—Telephone: (631) 396-6800; website: http://www.compliancemaven.com
- World Trade Institute—Telephone: (888) PACE-WTI; website: http://www.wti.pace.edu
- American Management Association—Telephone: (212) 586-8100; website: http://www.amanet.org
- Global Training Center—Telephone: (800) 860-5030; website: http://www.xportnow@aol.com
- Farmingdale State University—Telephone: (631) 420-2246; website: http://www.farmingdale.edu
- Global Maritime and Transportation School—Telephone: (516) 773-5161; website: http://www.usmma.edu/gmats

Key International Websites

1travel.com: http://www.onetravel.com

A UK service for small businesses that provides preliminary information on trade: http://www.dti.uk/ots/explorer/rade.html

ACW (Air Cargo Week): http://www.aircagoweek.com

Addresses & Salutations: http://www.bspage.com

AES Direct (Automated Export System): http://www.aesdirect.gov

Africa Online: http://www.africaonline.com

AgExporter: http://www.fas.usda.gov

Air Cargo World: http://www.aircargoworld.com

AIRCARGO News: http://www.air-cargo-news.com

Airforwarders Association: http://www.airforwarders.org

Airline Toll-Free Numbers and website: http://www.princeton.edu/Main/air800.html

American Association of Port Authorities (AAPA): http://www.aapa-ports.org

American Computer Resources, Inc.: http://www.the-acr.com

American Countertrade Association (ACA): http://www.countertrade.org

American Institute for Shippers' Associations (AISA): http://www.shippers.org

American Journal of Transportation (AJOT): http://www.ajot.com

American River International: http://www.worldest.com

American Shipper: http://www.americanshipper.com

American Short Line and Regional Railroad Association (ASLRRA): http://www.aslrra.org

American Stock Exchange: http://www.amex.com

American Trucking Association (ATA): http://www.trucking.org

ASXTraders: http://www.ASX.com

ATA Carnet (Merchandise Password): http://www.uscib.org

ATMs Around the World: http://www.fita.org/marketplace/travel.html#atm

Aviation Consumer Action Project: http://www.acap1971.org

Aviation Week: http://www.aviationnow.com

Bureau of Industry and Security (BIS): http://www.bis.doc.gov

Bureau of National Affairs, Int'l Trade Reporter Export Reference Manual: http://www.bna.com

Business Advisor: http://www.business.gov

Business Traveler Info Network: http://www.business-trip.com

Career China: http://www.dragonsurf.com

Cargo Systems: http://www.cargosystems.net

Cargovision: http://www.editorial@cargovision.org

Census Bureau, Foreign Trade Division: http://www.census.gov/foreigntrade/www

Central Europe Online: http://www.centraleurope.com

Chicago Stock Exchange: http://www.chicagostockex.com

Chinese News (in English): http://www.einnews.com/china

Classification Schedules: http://www.census.gov/ftp/pub/foreign-trade/www/schedules.html

Commerce Business Daily: http://www.cbdnet.gpo.gov

Commercial Carrier Journal (CCJ): http://www.etrucking.com

Commercial Encryption Export Controls: http://www.bxa.doc.gov/Encryption/Default.htm

Compliance Consulting of Importers/Exporters: http://www.compliancemaven.com

Correct Way to Fill Out the Shipper's Export Declaration: http://www.census.gov/ftp/pub/foreign-trade/www/correct.way.html

Country Risk Forecast: http://www.controlrisks.com/html/index.php

Create Your Own Newspapers: http://www.crayon.com

Culture and Travel: http://www.ciber.bus.msu.edu/busres/static/culture-travel-language.htm

Currency: http://www.oanda.com

Daily Intelligence Summary: http://www.dtic.mil/doctrine/jel/doddoct/data/d

Database at the UN World Bank: http://www.worldbank.org/data/onlinedatabases/onlinedatabases

Department of Transportation: http://www.dot.gov

Diverse languages of the modern world: http://www.unicode.org

DOT's Office of Inspector General: http://www.oig.dot.gov

Dr. Leonard's Healthcare Catalog: http://www.drleonards.com

Dun & Bradstreet: http://www.dnb.com

Economic Times (India): http://www.economictimes.com

Economist: http://www.economist.com

Electronic Embassy: http://www.embassy.org

Embassies & Consulates: http://www.embassyworld.com

Embassy Web: http://www.embassy.com

European Union (EU): http://www.europa.eu.int

Excite Travel: http://www.excite.com/travel

Export Administration Regulations (EAR): http://www.ntis.gov/products/type/database/export-regulations.asp

Export Assistant: http://www.cob.ohio-state.edu

Export Hotline: http://www.exporthotline.com

Export-Import Bank of the United States (Ex-Im Bank): http://www.exim.gov

Export Legal Assistance Network (ELAN): http://www.fita.org/elan

Export Practitioner (Export Regulations): http://www.exportprac.com

Far Eastern Economic Review: http://www.feer.com

Federal Register Notice on the Status of AES and AERP: http://www.access.gpo.gov

Federation of International Trade Associations (FITA): http://www.fita.org

Financial Times: http://www.ft.com

For female travelers: http://www.journeywoman.com

Global Business: http://www.gbn.org

Global Business Information Network: http://www.bus.indiana.edu

Global Information Network for Small and Medium Enterprises: http://www.gin.sme.ne.jp/intro.html

Global Law & Business: http://www.law.com

Glossary of Internalization and Localization terms: http://www.bowneglobal.com/bowne.asp?page=9&language=1

Glossary of Ocean Cargo Insurance Terms: http://www.tsbic.com/cargo/glossary.htm

Government Resources: http://www.ciber.bus.msu.edu/busres/govrnmnt.htm

Hong Kong Trade Development Counsel (TDC): http://www.tdctrade.com

iAgora Work Abroad: http://www.iagora.com/pages/html/work/index.html

IMEX Exchange: http://www.imex.com

Import Export Bulletin Board: http://www.iebb.com

Inbound Logistics: http://www.inboundlogistics.com

Incoterms 2000: http://www.iccwbo.org/home/menu_incoterms.asp

Independent Accountants International: http://www.accountants.org

Information on Diseases Abroad: http://www.cdc.gov

Inside China Today: http://www.einnews.com

Intellicast Weather (4-day forecast): http://www.intellicast.com/LocalWeather/World

Intermodal Association of North America (IANA): http://www.intermodal.org

International Air Transport Association (IATA): http://www.iata.org

International Association for Medical Assistance to Travelers (IAMAT): http://www.iamat.org

International Business: Strategies for the Global Marketplace Magazine: http://www.internationalbusiness.com

International Chamber of Commerce (ICC): http://www.iccwbo.org

International Commercial Law Monitor: http://www.lexmercatoria.org

International Economics and Business: http://dylee.keel.econ.ship.edu/econ/index.html

International Executive Service Corps (IESC): http://www.iesc.org

International Freight Association (IFA): http://www.ifa-online.com

International Law Check: http://www.law.comindex.shtml

International Maritime Organization (IMO): http://www.imo.org

International Monetary Fund (IMF): http://www.imf.org

International Society of Logistics (SOLE): http://www.sole.org

International Trade Administration (ITA): http://www.ita.doc.gov

International Trade Shows and Business Events: http://www.ciber.bus.msu.edu/busre

International Trade/Import-Export Jobs: http://www.internationaltrade.org/jobs.html

International Trade/Import-Export Portal: http://www.imakenews.com

Intershipper: http://www.intershipper.com

IWLA: http://www.warehouselogistics.org

Journal of Commerce Online: http://www.joc.com

Latin Trade: http://www.latintrade.com

Libraries: http://www.libraryspot.com/librariesonline.htm

Library of Congress: http://www.loc.gov

Local Times Around the World: http://www.times.clari.net.au

Logistics Management & Distribution Report: http://www.manufacturing.net/magazine/logistic

London Stock Exchange: http://www.londonstockexchange.com

Mailing Lists: http://www.ciber.bus.msu.edu/busres/maillist.htm

Marine Digest: http://www.marinedigest.com

Market Research: http://www.imakenews.com

Matchmaker site: http://www.ita.doc.gov/efm

Medical Conditions Around the World: http://www.cdc.gov/travel/blusheet.htm

More Trade Leads: http://www.ibrc.bschool.ukans.edu

NAFTA Customs: http://nafta-customs.org

National Association of Foreign Trade Zones: http://www.NAFTZ.org

National Association of Purchasing Management (NAPM): http://www.napm.org

National Association of Rail Shippers (NARS): http://www.railshippers.com

National Business Travel Association: http://www.biztraveler.org

National Customs Brokers & Forwarders Association of America (NCBFAA): http://www.ncbfaa.org

National Institute of Standards and Technology (NIST): http://www.nist.gov

National Law Center For Inter-American Free Trade: http://www.natlaw.com

National Motor Freight Traffic Association (NMFTA): http://www.nmfta.org

New Records Formats for Commodity Filing and Transportation Filing: http://www.customs.ustreas.gov

New York Times: http://www.nytimes.com

North American Industry Classification System (NAICS): http://www.census.gov/epcd/www/naics.html

Office of Anti-Boycott Compliance: http://www.bxa.doc.gov/AntiboycottCompliance

Online Chambers of Commerce: http://www.online-chamber.com

Online Newspapers: http://www.onlinenewspapers.com

Original Notice/Bureau of Census re: a classification of the definition of the exporter of record for SED rep. Purp.: http://www.access.gpo.gov

Overseas Private Investment Corp. (OPIC): http://www.opic.gov

Pacific Dictionary of International Trade and Business: http://www.pacific.commerce.ubc.ca/ditb/search.html

PACMAN: http://www.compliancemaven.com

Passenger Rights: http://www.passengerrights.com

PIERS (Port Import/Export Reporting Service): http://www.PIERS.com

Ports and Maritime Service Directory: http://www.seaportsinfo.com

Professional Association of Import/Export Compliance Managers: http://www.compliancemaven.com

Resources for International Job Opportunities: http://www.dbm.com/jobguide/internat.html

Reuters: http://www.reuters.com

Russia Today: http://www.russiatoday.com

SBA: http://www.sbaonline.com

SBA Office of International Trade: http://www.sba.gov/oit

SBA Offices and Services: http://www.sba.gov/services

Schedule B Export Codes: http://www.census.gov/foreign-trade/schedules/b

Search Engine: http://www.google.com

Service Corps of Retired Executives (SCORE): http://www.score.org

Shipping International: http://www.aajs.com/shipint

Shipping Times (Singapore): http://www.business-times.asia1.com.sg/shippingtimes

SIC Codes: http://www.trading.wmw.com/codes/sic.html

Small Business Administration (SBA): http://www.sba.gov

Small Business Association: http://www.sbaonline.gov

Small Business Development Centers (SBDC): http://www.sba.gov/sbdc

Statistical Data Sources: http://www.ciber.bus.msu.edu/busres/statinfo.htm

STAT-USA & NTDB: http://www.stat-usa.gov

Telephone Directories on the Web: http://www.teldir.com

The Expeditor: http://www.theexpeditor.com

The Exporter: http://www.exporter.com

The Global Business Forum: http://www.gbfvisa.com

The Import-Export Bulletin Board: http://www.iebb.com/sell.html

The International Air Cargo Association (TIACA): http://www.tiaca.org

The Times: http://www.londontimes.com

The Trading Floor: http://www.trading/wmw.com

The World Academy: http://www.TheWorldAcademy.com

Tokyo Stock Exchange: http://www.tse.or.jp

Trade and Development Agency (TDA): http://www.tda.gov

Trade Compass: http://www.tradecompass.com

Trade Information Center (TIC): http://www.ita.doc.gov/td/tic

Trade Law Web site: http://www.hg.org/trade.html

Trade Net: http://www.tradenet.gov

Trade Point USA: http://www.tradepoint.org

Trade Statistics: http://www.ita.doc.gov/media

Trading Floor Harmonized Code Search Engine: http://www.trading.wmw.com

Traffic World: http://www.trafficworld.com

Transportation Intermediaries Association (TIA): http://www.tianet.org

Transportation Jobs & Personnel: http://www.quotations.com/trans.htm

Travlang: http://www.travlang.com

UN Conference on Trade and Development: http://www.uncad-trains.org

UN International Trade Center (ITC): http://www.intracen.org

Unibex: http://www.unibex.com

United Nations (UN): http://www.un.org

United States-Mexico Chamber of Commerce: http://www.usmcoc.org/nafta.html

Universal Travel Protection Insurance (UTPI): http://www.utravelpro.com

U.S. Business Advisor: http://www.business.gov

U.S. Census Bureau: http://www.census.gov

U.S. Census Bureau Economic Indicators: http://www.census.gov/econ/www

U.S. Census Bureau Foreign Trade Division Harmonized Tariff Classification Schedule: http://www.census.gov/foreign-trade/www/schedules.html

U.S. Council for International Business (USCIB): http://www.uscib.org

U.S. Customs Services: http://www.cbp.gov

U.S. Department of Commerce (DOC): http://www.doc.gov

U.S. Department of Commerce Commercial Service: http://www.export.gov/com_svc/

U.S. Department of Commerce International Trade Administration: http://www.ita.doc.gov

U.S. Export Assistance Centers (USEAC): http://www.export.gov/eac.html

U.S. Export Portal: http://www.export.gov

U.S. Federal Maritime Commission (FMC): http://www.fmc.gov

U.S. Foreign Trade Zones: http://www.ia.ita.doc.gov/ftzpage

U.S. Government Glossary and Acronym of International Trade Terms: http://www.joc.com/handbook/glossaryofterms.shtml

U.S. Patent and Trademark Office (USPTO): http://www.uspto.gov

U.S. State Department Travel Advisory: http://www.travel.state.gov

U.S. Trade Representative (USTR): http://www.ustr.gov

USA/Internet: http://www.stat-usa.gov

USDA Foreign Agricultural Service (FAS): http://www.fas.usda.gov

USDA Shipper and Export Assistance (SEA): http://www.ams.usda.gov/tmd/tsd

USDOC Trade Information Center: http://www.trade.gov/td/tic

Various Utilities and Useful Information: http://www.ciber.bus.msu.edu/busres/statics/online-tools-utilities.htm

Wall Street Journal: http://www.wsj.com

Wells Fargo: http://www.wellsfargo.com

World Academy: http://www.theworldacademy.com

World Bank Group: http://www.worldbank.org

World Chambers of Commerce Network: http://www.worldchambers.com

World Customs Organization (WCO): http://www.wcoomd.org

World Factbook: http://www.odci.gov/cia/publications/factbook/index.html

World Intellectual Property Organization (WIPO): http://www.wipo.int

World Newspapers On-line: http://www.virtourist.com/newspaper
World Trade Analyzer: http://www.tradecompass.com
World Trade Centers Association (WTCA): http://www.iserve.wtca.org
World Trade Magazine: http://www.worldtrademag.com
World Trade Organization (WTO): http://www.wto.org
World Wide Shipping: http://www.ship.com
WorldPages: http://www.worldpages.com

Developing resources that provide timely updates not found in printed material is a key component of Incoterms management (ITM).

An example of information is from U.S. Customs ... CBP on the costs involved in fees for imported merchandise into the United States.

One such fee—MPF is profiled below, as this information taken off of the CBP website outlines above (http://www.cbp.gov)—which adds cost to the import process or increases landed cost spend.

U.S. Merchandise Processing Fee Increase

(10/26/2011) Recent trade legislation, H.R. 2832, was signed into law on October 21, 2011, changing the merchandise processing fee (MPF) rate for formal entries from 0.21% (.0021) to 0.3464% (.003464), effective October 1, 2011. The minimum and maximum fees, $25 and $485 respectively, did not change. CBP is currently in the process of modifying our automated systems to accept the new MPF rate of 0.3464%. We do not have an estimated completion date at this time; however, we will notify the trade as soon as possible via the Cargo Systems Messaging Service, when filers may begin transmitting entry summary information with the new MPF rate.

For entries filed on or after October 1, 2011, until the CBP system changes take effect with the 0.3464% rate, CBP will bill the importer for the increase in MPF. CBP will disregard differences of less than $20.

The only sure method of timely information is from sources that update daily. This makes websites like cbp.gov and all the others listed excellent "go to" locations for the most up to date and critical information for making the best decisions for the responsibilities of exercising "best practices and leveraging risks and costs.

Incoterms are a choice best made with timely and comprehensive information.

6

Education, Training, and Skill Set Development

Personnel engaged in global trade typically lack the skill sets necessary to manage their supply chain responsibilities. Internal training programs offer an excellent option in raising the bar for international business skill sets and understanding of all the issues that impact import and export sales and purchases.

Training is the single most important aspect of managing the entire subject of global trade, supply chain management, freight, and logistics inclusive of Incoterms®. Each person who is engaged in the global supply chain has a responsibility that collides and intersects with Incoterms. The better he or she understands, the better he or she can leverage.

Training in global trade and the relationship to Incoterms is usually the responsibility of all parties in the supply chain, but managers must take the lead in these initiatives to assure that all personnel completely comprehend and know how to best leverage sales and purchases operate with sales and purchase agreements that contain various supply chain issues including Incoterms.

INTERNAL TRAINING OPTIONS: CONNECTIVITY IN YOUR COMPANY

No matter what a company does to create standard operating procedures (SOPs), protocols, and business processes to the global supply chain in Incoterms management, if the personnel are not trained in Incoterms all is for naught. Training is a cornerstone and foundation for making a company raise the bar of performance.

Incoterms are not a subject any of us really learn in school—certainly not in detail anyway. Most of us learn while on the job, by experience, and through sweat equity.

Training needs to be formalized by every company and indoctrinated into the corporate culture. For Incoterms, this may require use of external resources with firms engaged in this form of training. Three companies that do this work come highly recommended:

International Chamber of Commerce (ICC), Paris, France: http://www. iccwbo.org

United States Council for International Business (USCIB), New York, New York, USA: http://www.uscib.org

World Academy, Woodbridge, New Jersey, USA: http://www. theworldacademy.com

Some companies may want to send their Incoterms guru designees to both intermediate and advanced Incoterms training boot camps that train them to be corporate trainers.

The World Academy has a specific training program called Train the Trainer, which was set up 18 years ago just for that purpose. It has trained over 500 executives in companies worldwide so they can do the training independently.

When companies structure SOPs and protocols into business units they must train the personnel on all the nuances of how they make those procedures work and function. Training becomes the conduit or thread in a company that allows established business processes to function with the personnel executing actions.

Training can be accomplished individually or in groups. Each situation has its own merits in considering the best options.

When we discuss issues in the global supply chain with subjects such as free trade agreements, Sarbanes–Oxley (SOX), the Foreign Corrupt Practices Act (FCPA), and trade compliance and then bring Incoterms management into the equations, without proper and comprehensive training there would be no real way of assuring compliant behavior by supply chain operatives.

Training becomes that critical component that government agencies that watchdog these programs and how corporations behave within the appropriate regulatory environment. Training is what mitigates the government's scrutiny. If government authorities see expansive and comprehensive training initiatives in a corporation, that corporation would have already mitigated any issues they may have with that government agency. Proactive behavior and training go hand in hand. Monies spent on training programs always come back to benefit that company.

For Incoterms we recommend that training be separated into three potential areas first:

- Senior management overview
- Middle management oversight
- Operational level functionality

SENIOR MANAGEMENT OVERVIEW

Senior management needs to know only why Incoterms are important. SOPs have to be developed and personnel trained. They must understand the benefits of proper initiatives and consequences of inaction. They also need to know allocated spend and infrastructure issues and personnel deployment.

Middle Management Oversight

Middle managers need to know what senior management is being made aware of, as already outlined. They also have to obtain a working knowledge of Incoterms options. They will be involved in setting up the SOPs that manage Incoterms in their organization.

Middle managers should at least have taken a half-day Incoterms class with updates every two to three years. Middle managers also need to understand how Incoterms risk, cost, and competitiveness.

Middle managers will

- Also take ownership of corporate training overall
- Develop outsourced options in training
- Assure corporate compliance of agreed Incoterms SOPs and protocols through training, education, and information flow
- Appoint point personnel, Incoterms gurus, and committee members

Middle managers will also require training in related areas to Incoterms such as title transfer, revenue recognition, intellectual property rights (IPRs), and contractual dispute matters.

Operational Level Functionality

Personnel in operations, such as

- Warehousing
- Traffic
- Logistics
- Manufacturing
- Distribution
- Customer service
- Import and export
- Accounting clerks

These personnel need to understand Incoterms at a very functional level. They will be involved in such operational details as

- Processing orders
- Dealing with customers and suppliers
- Handling vendors and service providers

- Managing forwarder and carrier relationships
- Packing, marking, labeling and shipping processes
- Making payments or collecting funds

Choice of Incoterms impacts all these areas, and those operational personnel need to understand at a very functional level in what way that will impact affect landed costs. Landed costs, as outlined in Chapter 2, are extremely important because they will determine whether you are competitive on export sales or that sourcing options for imports are competitive options.

Responsibility in most corporations and supply chains rolls downhill, which is why these operational personnel need to be heavily trained in Incoterms. For example, they would need to understand the 11 Incoterms options and where risks and costs begin and end. They need to know what responsibilities the company is undertaking with each option and what exposures might exist when these choices are exercised. Incoterms basic and advanced training should be part of their training regimen. They also typically will be at the front line in working with both customers and suppliers in also understanding their costs and risks.

Cargo insurance is typically arranged at this level, which is both an Incoterms and a payment issue. So these operational personnel need to be trained in marine insurance and claims handling. At this operational level they will also be arranging for transportation in the export or import and therefore need to be trained to master international logistics. They are also involved in the basics of packing, marking, and labeling and have to be trained in resource development to know what they have to deal with from a security, regulatory, and ease of shipping perspective.

Training Skill Set Agenda

Each company and the unique footprint of its supply chain will have various training needs. But a laundry list of skill sets can easily be identified that each company irrespective of its global presence will need to be trained on the following:

1. The 11 Incoterms in *Incoterms 2010*
2. Incoterms that are best suited for that company's various supply chains
3. Landed cost issues for that company for both export and import concerns

4. Trade compliance implications
5. Lines of connectivity, accountability, and responsibility within that company's supply chain
6. Resource options
7. Technology options
8. Gray areas of risk and cost under current set of Incoterms use
9. When delivery occurs in their transactions
10. When title transfers
11. When and how payment is made or received (receivable concerns)
12. Documentation requirements
13. Managing service providers, carriers, and third-party companies
14. Government and regulatory concerns
15. Marine insurance and cargo claims handling
16. Potential IPR-related issues and concerns

What each company needs to do is to assure that all these topics are part of a structured training program tailored and customized to that company's supply chain. Approximately 70%–75% of Incoterms material would be the same from one company to the next. The critical part is the 25%–30% that is unique to that company's global supply chain. This would then include an in-depth analysis of a company's supply chain before creating an Incoterms training program that addresses both industry and market conditions along with all the proprietary details that are part of that company's profile.

Incoterms training should have both a generalized aspect and an individualized and customized aspect. Quality training programs address both areas in-depth, comprehensively and contemporarily. Training becomes the "cornerstone" of how a company assures that Incoterms are managed correctly and to the best advantage of that company's global operations.

7

Risk Management and Insurance Controls

A central subject of this book is to mitigate risk and maximize profit. This is detailed in this chapter, so the global supply chain executive can rest easy and be assured that the risks in doing business internationally are brought to manageable levels.

Choosing the correct Incoterms® is both an art and a science. It is a skill set that can be developed. When it is developed well, the global supply chain benefits by reducing the risks that impact global trade and at the same time increasing the opportunities for better profits and more competitive operating profile.

RISK MANAGEMENT IN THE GLOBAL SUPPLY CHAIN: A 10-STEP PRIMER

Overview

Import, export, and other executives engaged in managing various aspects of the global supply chain, such as risk, purchasing, sales, customer service, legal, finance, and manufacturing are now paying much more attention to how they need to manage their global supply chain responsibilities with the purpose of reducing risk. Conversely, the immediate benefit is that while we reduce risk we are setting the best opportunity to assure and grow profits.

For public companies, Sarbanes–Oxley, and private enterprise, best practices mandate risk reduction as part of any comprehensive business strategy. The global supply chain presents its own unique set of challenges:

- Many personnel who are involved in the international arena lack both the experience and skill sets necessary to operate successfully or certainly at the highest level of capabilities.
- The complexities of international business—politics, economics, geographic distances, diverse cultures, currencies, trade compliance issues, foreign logistics, customs authorities, political risks, weather, war, and indifference—all pose a unique and complex set of obstacles that challenge executives who operate globally. And making this even more difficult, it is a moving target that changes daily and sometimes with great immensity and variance.
- The pressures mandated by short-term results often cause careless practices, shortcuts, and lack of prudent decision-making. This creates issues, risks, and unnecessary exposures to a company's business model.

And often executives are faced with making decisions totally based on price, which creates added pressures in the arena of performance. This all creates risk.

Outlined is a tried and proven 10-step process that can be used as a business model in global supply chains to reduce risk and provide the best opportunity for success.

1. Ensure senior management commitment.
2. Establish a risk management focus.
3. Complete a global risk management assessment and benchmarking.
4. Identify the three key risk providers.
5. Profile the major areas of risk and establish risk strategies.
6. Decide risk retentions and transference policies.
7. Identify the benefits of loss control management.
8. Establish trade compliance protocols.
9. Use technology in risk mitigation.
10. Recognize that training is a work-in-process.

Ensure Senior Management Commitment

The processes of reducing loss and mitigating risk to the global supply chain will always begin with senior management support. It is often a step in the process that staff and middle managers avoid for fear of intimidation, scrutiny, and career exposures. Our experience tells us that none of those concerns are real and become reactive rationalizations to avoid the process.

The risk management process in any corporation will require funding, infrastructure change, re-personnel deployment, creation of standard operating procedures (SOPs), and a coordination and initiative expanding profit and cost centers. If senior management is not involved in these initiatives, the chance of success in any risk management program is severely minimized.

Our experience in creating risk management programs in companies all over the world has demonstrated to us over time that when senior management is on-board, committed, and shows genuine leadership, any risk management initiative will have its best opportunity for success.

Senior management:

- Encourages risk mitigation
- Allocates funds and leads budgeting for risk management to occur
- Brings down internal resistance, manages fiefdom barriers and forces reluctant campers to go along
- Creates proper incentives to do the right thing—guides and encourages positive change
- Fosters internal connectivity to make sure everyone is on the same page

It has been our experience that senior managers will always take steps to reduce risk when the benefits are clearly identified and achievable. The key issues here are "identified and achievable." Typically, middle management or operational staff will take the initiative to study risk exposures in a corporation along with a reasonable strategy that can be accomplished to achieve desired results, betterments, and risk mitigation. These need to be presented to senior management with a plan that clearly outlines the risks and benefits with achievable bullet points or targets demonstrating that any spend or action will have financial benefit by the end of the day.

Obtaining senior management support is and will always be a proposition showing the consequences of bad or no action and the focus on action and benefit or risk–cost–action–risk mitigation.

Establish a Risk Management Focus

Reducing risk has the inverse effect of increasing profit. Corporation executives who find that theme is valid then create a mind-set that risk management will pay off in spades at some point both in the short- and long-term.

Monies spent on risk reduction steps will eventually reward the company in reduced costs and potentially greater profits. This theory, proven successful across thousands of corporations when put into a "focused" action plan, will prove to benefit a company's operation and more particularly in the management of the global supply chain where risk abounds. Senior management will generally provide the "leadership and drive" to bring risk management into a primary focus for all managers and employees to engage in. It then becomes a "cultural icon" for the company in every step, action, and direction they choose.

A perfect example of this in action would be the decision-making processor reducing cost in the supply chain. Every company will have that as a desired goal. Obtaining cheap quotes is easy. There is always some carrier that will do it not only for less but also dirt-cheap. Prudent managers know that the "cheapest" comes with risk. Typically, that risk will come in the names of security, safety, or transit time. And usually when a risk management approach is used it would not be a favored choice.

A risk-prudent supply chain manager will weigh the risks and rewards and look for a more balanced approach in purchasing freight—one that offers a reasonable compromise with price and the other considerations and eliminates the "cheapest" from any option that company would favor.

Complete a Global Risk Management Assessment and Benchmarking

Companies that compete in global trade have to be at the top of their game. Errors in judgment are costly and sometimes without recovery opportunity. So how does a company know where it stands? Success, growth, and profits are certain benchmarks, but could the company do better? Is it "lucky" or "good"? Does it know what risks loom around the corner, and is it prepared to deal with them when they happen? Could those risks be avoided altogether? Can the risks be mitigated?

These are all very reasonable questions, but can a company across its global supply chain really answer them?

Identify the Three Key Risk Providers

The most important risk providers fall into three categories: supply chain risk consultants, international-oriented insurance brokers, and specialized underwriting facilities. All three assist a company in determining what risks exist in their global supply chain and provide basically three options:

- Assumption of risk
- Mitigation of risk
- Transfer of risk

They provide an assessment capability that then matches which option works best. It may be a single option or a hybrid form where more than one is used.

When choosing these providers, choose wisely.

- Determine their specific expertise in your area of need
- Clearly identify deliverables and expectations
- Develop a trust so intimate information, which will give them the necessary information in full scope, can pass easily and they can better assist.
- Obtain fair and competitive pricing
- Look to a long-term relationship; it will pay back in spades in the long run.

Profile the Major Areas of Risk and Establish Risk Strategies

We recommend that you create an outline or agenda of the major areas of risk in your global supply chain. Categories might include the following:

- Risk of loss or damage in storage or in transit
- Payment/receivable issues
- Force majeure concerns
- Economic
- Political
- Supplier/customer
- Vendors/service providers/carriers
- Regulatory
- Trade compliance
- Contractual
- Production/manufacturing/distribution
- Costing
- Currency

Decide Risk Retentions and Transference Policies

Every company engaged in managing their global supply chain will need to determine what levels of risk it can assume and what levels it must transfer to a third party. Tied into this decision-making process are loss control and mitigation options that may impact the decision on risk retention levels.

Identify the Benefits of Loss Control Management

Loss prevention pays back in spades. Historical insurance industry data, when analyzed, always points to favorable benefits in the supply chain.

Companies can gain great strides in reducing the opportunity for loss, damage, and financial consequence when steps are taken proactively. Some of these steps are

- Risk assessment and benchmarking
- Actions taken to avoid and mitigate risk opportunity
- Training of personnel in risk avoidance protocols
- Bringing insurance management principals into the global supply chain operations

Establish Trade Compliance Protocols

This book has focused a great deal on trade compliance management. In itself, trade compliance is like loss control for regulatory consequence. Action steps in trade compliance will mitigate and prevent future financial consequence for companies that import and export as the concerns with regulation will be handled within all the SOPs and protocols established to provide the framework for employees on how to operate successfully even with regulatory challenge.

Use Technology in Risk Mitigation

Technology can play a great role in mitigating risk in a number of ways:

- Improved communications will avoid risk.
- More comprehensive information flow will provide loss control actions.
- Eliminate human error opportunity on all areas involved in detailed activity: denied party checking, documentation, ECCN review.

- Efficient methods for freight and logistics can produce better outturns.
- Certain software is available to be used in evaluating risk and providing tools to avoid, mitigate, or transfer.
- Information technology connections can be made between companies operating in the global market and their insurance brokers and underwriting facilities for information exchange and in the overall management of their risks and insurance policies, particularly in the marine cargo insurance world.

Training Is a Work-in-Process

When people say they have had all the training they need, they are for sure a fool. Training is a work-in-process in international business mainly because the world is a huge place with a lot of convolutions, nuances, and peculiarities. It changes every day. It is not a snapshot but is a moving and living organism that one must be ahead of in the curve through training to avoid negative consequences.

RISK MANAGEMENT CASE STUDY

To open this section in the book on risk management, let us view an example where a "glitch" becomes developed in an export sale on goods originating in Brazil being exported to a buyer in Paris, France. This demonstrates the exposure that exists in the choice of Incoterms, not related to the choice but rather in how the company has agreed to be paid in the transaction.

Terms of Sale versus Terms of Payment

Incoterms impact cost and risk. Many believe that they are a defined guide on when a seller or buyer needs to purchase cargo insurance for their transaction. While it is a guide, it is not an end-all, mainly because depending on how a company gets paid will potentially and significantly impact risk, which may influence the purchasing of cargo insurance.

Let's look at an example of how the Incoterms and how a company gets paid influence risk and financial exposure. In our consulting practice, cases are frequently referred to us that end up as commercial disputes that attorneys and the legal profession have difficulty litigating. In our example, we have a meat packing company based in Sao Paulo, Brazil, that sells a 40-foot container load of beef valued at US$67,500 FOB Recife, Brazil, to a first-time buyer in Paris, France.

After the Incoterms are agreed upon, the salesperson, Janos, negotiates with the buyer, Henri, for a 60-day site draft payment term. So we end up with an FOB, site draft sale:

Origin: Sao Paulo
Destination: Paris
Export Gateway: Recife
Import Gateway: Le Havre
Term of Sale: FOB Recife
Term of Payment: Site Draft 60 Days
Origin
Port of Loading
Port of Discharge
Destination
Sao Paulo
Recife
Le Havre
Paris

The graphic shows the outline of this transaction. The responsibility and the liability for this transaction for the seller ends once the goods are successfully loaded on the vessel, according to *Incoterms 2010*. Conversely, the responsibility and liability for the transaction is now assumed by the buyer once the goods are loaded on-board. If a loss or damage occurred prior to loading, it would be for the risk and account of the seller. After the goods are on-board, risk of loss or damage passes to the buyer. In this specific transaction, the goods are successfully shipped from origin to the port of export and are successfully loaded on-board.

Understanding how freight actually transits in international business is another critical element of global trade management. Because Recife is the last port of call and Le Havre is the first port of call, this will impact how and where this container gets stowed on the ocean-going vessel. Steamship lines always want to run their loading and unloading operations in port as efficiently as possible. We all benefit from that with lower ocean freight rates. So the carriers employ professionals who work on cargo stowage and load planning to maximize port time efficiency.

In this case, the container carrying the beef is loaded on deck in the very top stow in the front of the vessel, so when the vessel arrives in Le Havre it will be the first to come off, maximizing port unloading and then loading efficiency. Port rotation greatly impacts cargo stowage. This vessel sails from Recife on December 15 and is scheduled in Le Havre on January 10. On December 31, the vessel encounters some very heavy weather in the North Atlantic. The vessel loses four containers overboard, one of which is the shipment of beef to the exporter's new customer in Paris.

The captain of the ship alerts his vessel agent in Recife, who puts on notice the actual shipper in Sao Paulo. Janos the salesperson is now so advised. He now has to alert the new customer, Henri, in Paris, of this issue. He also has to collect US$67,500. When he speaks with Henri, he meets several levels of resistance, as Henri is quite unhappy that this first shipment is not coming. The buyer will now have ingredient and processing issues at its plant in Paris; it had planned for this product's arrival for use in its meat processing facility. Payment on that first shipment also will become a potential problem since the consignee, Henri, though obligated to pay contractually, may drag his feet when payment is due. Collection is now a principal concern of the Brazilian company.

In this case study, though risk transfer was accomplished according to the FOB choice of Incoterms, once the goods were loaded on-board the exporter in Brazil still has risk from loss or damage until the point that it gets paid. This problem could have been resolved proactively in two ways:

1. The seller has affirmation in writing from the buyer that the buyer has cargo insurance to cover its exposure and names the seller in that cargo policy to protect its interest.
2. The seller procures cargo "unpaid vendor" or "contingency" insurance to protect their interest.

This case study demonstrates the delicate line between the intent of Incoterms to structure cost and risk in an international transaction that gets "disturbed" because the payment term now presents a different dynamic in the transaction that adds risk well beyond the intention of the Incoterms used. In this case, the FOB term works against a payment obligation after delivery has occurred.

If payment had been received prior to the shipment, this matter would not have been an issue for the exporter but only for the importer. This example clearly makes the case that choice of Incoterms has a huge impact on all aspects of an international transaction and must be factored in when determining cost and risk and what other factors in their transaction that will impact cost and risk, when used in tandem with certain Incoterms options such as freight, insurance, and payment.

MARINE CARGO INSURANCE AND INCOTERMS

Incoterms, as outlined in all previous chapters of this book, deal with cost and risk. Risk is discussed with each Incoterm as a point in time when the risk of loss or damage is passed from the seller to the buyer. This identifies the party that has financial exposure should something happen to the cargo during transit. This would then identify the party that would either assume the risk or transfer the risk to a third party through the purchase of marine cargo insurance.

Marine cargo insurance covers all freight transiting all modes of transit, not just marine, as outlined in the policy terms and conditions. Cargo insurance began in the 1600s when ocean freight was the primary mode of transportation for international freight, so the term *marine* is attached. However, today when we have air, rail, and truck as everyday options the underwriters that issue marine cargo policies cover all modes of transport.

Incoterms 2010 has better defined risk and the application for the purchase of cargo insurance. Two Incoterms—CIF and CIP—are the only ones that clearly outline a seller's or exporter's responsibility to procure cargo insurance.

There are three basic forms of cargo insurances, though there is an ability to totally customize coverage terms and conditions for the basic and variable needs of all global supply chains.

Lloyd's of London (http://www.lloyds.com), which is a leader in cargo insurance, reference these three basic cargo insurances as Institute Cargo

Clauses A, B, and C. Clause A is the broadest form, with all-risk protection. Clause B is middle-of-the-road coverage. Clause C is the least amount of coverage, with average terms.

The following sections present strict guidance on these three options.

1/1/09

INSTITUTE CARGO CLAUSES (A)
RISKS COVERED
Risks

1. This insurance covers all risks of loss of or damage to the subject-matter insured except as excluded by the provisions of Clauses 4, 5, 6, and 7 below.

General Average

2. This insurance covers general average and salvage charges, adjusted or determined according to the contract of carriage and/or the governing law and practice, incurred to avoid or in connection with the avoidance of loss from any cause except those excluded in Clauses 4, 5, 6, and 7 below.

"Both to Blame Collision Clause"

3. This insurance indemnifies the Assured, in respect of any risk insured herein, against liability incurred under any Both to Blame Collision Clause in the contract of carriage. In the event of any claim by carriers under the said Clause, the Assured agree to notify the Insurers who shall have the right, at their own cost and expense, to defend the Assured against such claim.

EXCLUSIONS

4. In no case shall this insurance cover
    4.1 loss damage or expense attributable to wilful misconduct of the Assured
    4.2 ordinary leakage, ordinary loss in weight or volume, or ordinary wear and tear of the subject-matter insured
    4.3 loss damage or expense caused by insufficiency or unsuitability of packing or preparation of the subject-matter insured to withstand the ordinary incidents of the insured transit where

such packing or preparation is carried out by the Assured or their employees or prior to the attachment of this insurance (for the purpose of these Clauses "packing" shall be deemed to include stowage in a container and "employees" shall not include independent contractors)

4.4 loss damage or expense caused by inherent vice or nature of the subject-matter insured

4.5 loss damage or expense caused by delay, even though the delay be caused by a risk insured against (except expenses payable under Clause 2 above)

4.6 loss damage or expense caused by insolvency or financial default of the owners managers charterers or operators of the vessel where, at the time of loading of the subject-matter insured on board the vessel, the Assured are aware, or in the ordinary course of business should be aware, that such insolvency or financial default could prevent the normal prosecution of the voyage

This exclusion shall not apply where the contract of insurance has been assigned to the party claiming hereunder who has bought or agreed to buy the subject-matter insured in good faith under a binding contract

4.7 loss damage or expense directly or indirectly caused by or arising from the use of any weapon or device employing atomic or nuclear fission and/or fusion or other like reaction or radioactive force or matter.

5.

5.1 In no case shall this insurance cover loss damage or expense arising from

   5.1.1 unseaworthiness of vessel or craft or unfitness of vessel or craft for the safe carriage of the subject-matter insured, where the Assured are privy to such unseaworthiness or unfitness, at the time the subject-matter insured is loaded therein

   5.1.2 unfitness of container or conveyance for the safe carriage of the subject-matter insured, where loading therein or thereon is carried out prior to attachment of this insurance or by the Assured or their employees and they are privy to such unfitness at the time of loading.

5.2 Exclusion 5.1.1 above shall not apply where the contract of insurance has been assigned to the party claiming hereunder who has bought or agreed to buy the subject-matter insured in good faith under a binding contract.

5.3 The Insurers waive any breach of the implied warranties of seaworthiness of the ship and fitness of the ship to carry the subject-matter insured to destination.

6. In no case shall this insurance cover loss damage or expense caused by

6.1 war, civil war, revolution, rebellion, insurrection, or civil strife arising therefrom, or any hostile act by or against a belligerent power

6.2 capture, seizure, arrest, restraint, or detainment (piracy excepted), and the consequences thereof or any attempt thereat

6.3 derelict mines, torpedoes, bombs, or other derelict weapons of war.

7. In no case shall this insurance cover loss damage or expense

7.1 caused by strikers, locked-out workmen, or persons taking part in labour disturbances, riots, or civil commotions

7.2 resulting from strikes, lock-outs, labour disturbances, riots, or civil commotions

7.3 caused by any act of terrorism being an act of any person acting on behalf of, or in connection with, any organisation which carries out activities directed towards the overthrowing or influencing, by force or violence, of any government whether or not legally constituted

7.4 caused by any person acting from a political, ideological, or religious motive.

DURATION

Transit Clause

8.

8.1 Subject to Clause 11 below, this insurance attaches from the time the subject-matter insured is first moved in the warehouse or at the place of storage (at the place named in the contract of insurance) for the purpose of the immediate loading into or onto the carrying vehicle or other conveyance for the commencement of transit, continues during the ordinary course of transit and terminates either

8.1.1 on completion of unloading from the carrying vehicle or other conveyance in or at the final warehouse or place of storage at the destination named in the contract of insurance,

8.1.2 on completion of unloading from the carrying vehicle or other conveyance in or at any other warehouse or place of storage, whether prior to or at the destination named in the contract of insurance, which the Assured or their employees elect to use either for storage other than in the ordinary course of transit or for allocation or distribution, or

8.1.3 when the Assured or their employees elect to use any carrying vehicle or other conveyance or any container for storage other than in the ordinary course of transit or

8.1.4 on the expiry of 60 days after completion of discharge overside of the subject-matter insured from the oversea vessel at the final port of discharge, whichever shall first occur.

8.2 If, after discharge overside from the oversea vessel at the final port of discharge, but prior to termination of this insurance, the subject-matter insured is to be forwarded to a destination other than that to which it is insured, this insurance, whilst remaining subject to termination as provided in Clauses 8.1.1 to 8.1.4, shall not extend beyond the time the subject-matter insured is first moved for the purpose of the commencement of transit to such other destination.

8.3 This insurance shall remain in force (subject to termination as provided for in Clauses 8.1.1 to 8.1.4 above and to the provisions of Clause 9 below) during delay beyond the control of the Assured, any deviation, forced discharge, reshipment or transshipment and during any variation of the adventure arising from the exercise of a liberty granted to carriers under the contract of carriage.

TERMINATION OF CONTRACT OF CARRIAGE

9. If owing to circumstances beyond the control of the Assured either the contract of carriage is terminated at a port or place other than the destination named therein or the transit is otherwise terminated before unloading of the subject-matter insured as provided for in Clause 8 above, then this insurance shall also terminate *unless prompt notice is given to the Insurers and continuation of cover is requested when this insurance shall remain in force, subject to an additional premium if required by the Insurers,* either

9.1 until the subject-matter insured is sold and delivered at such port or place, or, unless otherwise specially agreed, until the expiry of

60 days after arrival of the subject-matter insured at such port or place, whichever shall first occur, or

9.2 if the subject-matter insured is forwarded within the said period of 60 days (or any agreed extension thereof) to the destination named in the contract of insurance or to any other destination, until terminated in accordance with the provisions of Clause 8 above.

CHANGE OF VOYAGE

10.

10.1 Where, after attachment of this insurance, the destination is changed by the Assured, *this must be* notified promptly to Insurers for rates and terms to be agreed. Should a loss occur prior to such agreement being obtained cover may be provided but only if cover would have been available at a reasonable commercial market rate on reasonable market terms.

10.2 Where the subject-matter insured commences the transit contemplated by this insurance (in accordance with Clause 8.1), but, without the knowledge of the Assured or their employees the ship sails for another destination, this insurance will nevertheless be deemed to have attached at commencement of such transit.

CLAIMS

INSURABLE INTEREST

11.

11.1 In order to recover under this insurance the Assured must have an insurable interest in the subject-matter insured at the time of the loss.

11.2 Subject to Clause 11.1 above, the Assured shall be entitled to recover for insured loss occurring during the period covered by this insurance, notwithstanding that the loss occurred before the contract of insurance was concluded, unless the Assured were aware of the loss and the Insurers were not.

FORWARDING CHARGES

12. Where, as a result of the operation of a risk covered by this insurance, the insured transit is terminated at a port or place other than that to which the subject-matter insured is covered under this insurance, the

Insurers will reimburse the Assured for any extra charges properly and reasonably incurred in unloading storing and forwarding the subject-matter insured to the destination to which it is insured. This Clause 12, which does not apply to general average or salvage charges, shall be subject to the exclusions contained in Clauses 4, 5, 6, and 7 above, and shall not include charges arising from the fault negligence insolvency or financial default of the Assured or their employees.

Constructive Total Loss

13. No claim for Constructive Total Loss shall be recoverable hereunder unless the subject-matter insured is reasonably abandoned either on account of its actual total loss appearing to be unavoidable or because the cost of recovering, reconditioning, and forwarding the subject-matter insured to the destination to which it is insured would exceed its value on arrival.

Increased Value

14.

14.1 If any Increased Value insurance is effected by the Assured on the subject-matter insured under this insurance the agreed value of the subject-matter insured shall be deemed to be increased to the total amount insured under this insurance and all Increased Value insurances covering the loss, and liability under this insurance shall be in such proportion as the sum insured under this insurance bears to such total amount insured. In the event of claim the Assured shall provide the Insurers with evidence of the amounts insured under all other insurances.

14.2 **Where this insurance is on Increased Value the following clause shall apply:** The agreed value of the subject-matter insured shall be deemed to be equal to the total amount insured under the primary insurance and all Increased Value insurances covering the loss and effected on the subject-matter insured by the Assured, and liability under this insurance shall be in such proportion as the sum insured under this insurance bears to such total amount insured.

In the event of claim the Assured shall provide the Insurers with evidence of the amounts insured under all other insurances.

BENEFIT OF INSURANCE

15. This insurance

15.1 covers the Assured which includes the person claiming indemnity either as the person by or on whose behalf the contract of insurance was effected or as an assignee,

15.2 shall not extend to or otherwise benefit the carrier or other bailee.

MINIMISING LOSSES

Duty of Assured

16. It is the duty of the Assured and their employees and agents in respect of loss recoverable hereunder

16.1 to take such measures as may be reasonable for the purpose of averting or minimising such loss, and

16.2 to ensure that all rights against carriers, bailees, or other third parties are properly preserved and exercised and the Insurers will, in addition to any loss recoverable hereunder, reimburse the Assured for any charges properly and reasonably incurred in pursuance of these duties.

Waiver

17. Measures taken by the Assured or the Insurers with the object of saving, protecting, or recovering the subject- matter insured shall not be considered as a waiver or acceptance of abandonment or otherwise prejudice the rights of either party.

AVOIDANCE OF DELAY

18. It is a condition of this insurance that the Assured shall act with reasonable despatch in all circumstances within their control.

LAW AND PRACTICE

19. This insurance is subject to English law and practice.

Note: Where a continuation of cover is requested under Clause 9, or a change of destination is notified under Clause 10, there is an obligation to give prompt notice to the Insurers and the right to such cover is dependent upon compliance with this obligation.

CL382

01/01/2009

1/1/82

INSTITUTE CARGO CLAUSES (B)
RISKS COVERED

1. This insurance covers, except as provided in Clauses 4, 5, 6, and 7 below,

    1.1 loss of or damage to the subject-matter insured reasonably attributable to

        1.1.1 fire or explosion

        1.1.2 vessel or craft being stranded, grounded, sunk, or capsized

        1.1.3 overturning or derailment of land conveyance

        1.1.4 collision or contact of vessel craft or conveyance with any external object other than water

        1.1.5 discharge of cargo at a port of distress,

    1.2 loss of or damage to the subject-matter insured caused by

        1.2.1 general average sacrifice

        1.2.2 jettison or washing overboard

        1.2.3 entry of sea lake or river water into vessel, craft, hold, conveyance container, liftvan, or place of storage,

    1.3 total loss of any package lost overboard or dropped whilst loading on to, or unloading from, vessel or craft.

2. This insurance covers general average and salvage charges, adjusted or determined according to the contract of affreightment and/or the governing law and practice, incurred to avoid or in connection with the avoidance of loss from any cause except those excluded in Clauses 4, 5, 6, and 7 or elsewhere in this insurance.

3. This insurance is extended to indemnify the Assured against such proportion of liability under the contract of affreightment "Both to Blame Collision" Clause as is in respect of a loss recoverable hereunder. In the event of any claim by shipowners under the said Clause the Assured agree to notify the Underwriters who shall have the right, at their own cost and expense, to defend the Assured against such claim.

EXCLUSIONS

4. In no case shall this insurance cover

4.1 loss, damage, or expense attributable to wilful misconduct of the Assured

4.2 ordinary leakage, ordinary loss in weight or volume, or ordinary wear and tear of the subject-matter insured

4.3 loss, damage, or expense caused by insufficiency or unsuitability of packing or preparation of the subject-matter insured (for the purpose of this Clause 4.3 "packing" shall be deemed to include stowage in a container or liftvan but only when such stowage is carried out prior to attachment of this insurance or by the Assured or their servants)

4.4 loss, damage, or expense caused by inherent vice or nature of the subject-matter insured

4.5 loss, damage, or expense proximately caused by delay, even though the delay be caused by a risk insured against (except expenses payable under Clause 2 above)

4.6 loss, damage, or expense arising from insolvency or financial default of the owners, managers, charterers, or operators of the vessel

4.7 deliberate damage to or deliberate destruction of the subject-matter insured or any part thereof by the wrongful act of any person or persons

4.8 loss, damage, or expense arising from the use of any weapon of war employing atomic or nuclear fission and/or fusion or other like reaction or radioactive force or matter.

5.

5.1 In no case shall this insurance cover loss damage or expense arising from unseaworthiness of vessel or craft, unfitness of vessel craft conveyance container or liftvan for the safe carriage of the subject-matter insured, where the Assured or their servants are privy to such unseaworthiness or unfitness, at the time the subject-matter insured is loaded therein.

5.2 The Underwriters waive any breach of the implied warranties of seaworthiness of the ship and fitness of the ship to carry the subject-matter insured to destination, unless the Assured or their servants are privy to such unseaworthiness or unfitness.

6. In no case shall this insurance cover loss damage or expense caused by

6.1 war civil war revolution rebellion insurrection, or civil strife arising therefrom, or any hostile act by or against a belligerent power

6.2 capture seizure arrest restraint or detainment (piracy excepted), and the consequences thereof or any attempt thereat

6.3 derelict mines torpedoes bombs or other derelict weapons of war.

7. In no case shall this insurance cover loss damage or expense

7.1 caused by strikers, locked-out workmen, or persons taking part in labour disturbances, riots, or civil commotions

7.2 resulting from strikes, lock-outs, labour disturbances, riots, or civil commotions

7.3 caused by any terrorist or any person acting from a political motive.

DURATION

8.

8.1 This insurance attaches from the time the goods leave the warehouse or place of storage at the place named herein for the commencement of the transit, continues during the ordinary course of transit and terminates either

8.1.1 on delivery to the Consignees' or other final warehouse or place of storage at the destination named herein,

8.1.2.1 for storage other than in the ordinary course of transit or

8.1.2.2 for allocation or distribution, or

8.1.3 on the expiry of 60 days after completion of discharge overside of the goods hereby insured from the oversea vessel at the final port of discharge, whichever shall first occur.

8.2 If, after discharge overside from the oversea vessel at the final port of discharge, but prior to termination of this insurance, the goods are to be forwarded to a destination other than that to which they are insured hereunder, this insurance, whilst remaining subject to termination as provided for above, shall not extend beyond the commencement of transit to such other destination.

8.3 This insurance shall remain in force (subject to termination as provided for above and to the provisions of Clause 9 below) during delay beyond the control of the Assured, any deviation, forced discharge, reshipment or transshipment and during any variation of the adventure arising from the exercise of a liberty granted to shipowners or charterers under the contract of affreightment

9. If owing to circumstances beyond the control of the Assured either the contract of carriage is terminated at a port or place other than the destination named therein or the transit is otherwise terminated before delivery of the goods as provided for in Clause 8 above, then this insurance shall also terminate *unless prompt notice is given to the Underwriters and continuation of cover is requested when the insurance shall remain in force, subject to an additional premium if required by the Underwriters, either*

   9.1 until the goods are sold and delivered at such port or place, or, unless otherwise specially agreed, until the expiry of 60 days after arrival of the goods hereby insured at such port or place, whichever shall first occur, or

   9.2 if the goods are forwarded within the said period of 60 days (or any agreed extension thereof) to the destination named herein or to any other destination, until terminated in accordance with the provisions of Clause 8 above.

10. Where, after attachment of this insurance, the destination is changed by the Assured, held covered at a premium and on conditions to be arranged subject to prompt notice being given to the Underwriters.

CLAIMS

11.

   11.1 In order to recover under this insurance the Assured must have an insurable interest in the subject-matter insured at the time of the loss.

   11.2 Subject to 11.1 above, the Assured shall be entitled to recover for insured loss occurring during the period covered by this insurance, notwithstanding that the loss occurred before the contract of insurance was concluded, unless the Assured were aware of the loss and the Underwriters were not.

12. Where, as a result of the operation of a risk covered by this insurance the insured transit is terminated at a port or place other than that to which the subject-matter is covered under this insurance, the Underwriters will reimburse the Assured for any extra charges properly and reasonably incurred in unloading storing and forwarding the subject-matter to the destination to which it is

insured hereunder. This Clause 12, which does not apply to general average or salvage charges, shall be subject to the exclusions contained in Clauses 4, 5, 6, and 7 above, and shall not include charges arising from the fault negligence insolvency or financial default of the Assured or their servants.

13. No claim for Constructive Total Loss shall be recoverable hereunder unless the subject-matter insured is reasonably abandoned either on account of its actual total loss appearing to be unavoidable or because the cost of recovering, reconditioning, and forwarding the subject-matter to the destination to which it is insured would exceed its value on arrival.

14.

14.1 If any Increased Value insurance is effected by the Assured on the cargo insured herein the agreed value of the cargo shall be deemed to be increased to the total amount insured under this insurance and all Increased Value insurances covering the loss, and liability under this insurance shall be in such proportion as the sum insured herein bears to such total amount insured.

In the event of claim the Assured shall provide the Underwriters with evidence of the amounts insured under all other insurances.

14.2 Where this insurance is on Increased Value the following clause shall apply:

The agreed value of the cargo shall be deemed to be equal to the total amount insured under the primary insurance and all Increased Value insurances covering the loss and effected on the cargo by the Assured, and liability under this insurance shall be in such proportion as the sum insured herein bears to such total amount insured.

In the event of claim the Assured shall provide the Underwriters with evidence of the amounts insured under all other insurances.

BENEFIT OF INSURANCE

15. This insurance shall not inure to the benefit of the carrier or other bailee.

MINIMIZING LOSSES

16. It is the duty of the Assured and their servants and agents in respect of loss recoverable hereunder

16.1 to take such measures as may be reasonable for the purpose of averting or minimizing such loss, and

16.2 to ensure that all rights against carriers, bailees, or other third parties are properly preserved and exercised and the Underwriters will, in addition to any loss recoverable hereunder, reimburse the Assured for any charges properly and reasonably incurred in pursuance of these duties.

17. Measures taken by the Assured or the Underwriters with the object of saving, protecting, or recovering the subject-matter insured shall not be considered as a waiver or acceptance of abandonment or otherwise prejudice the rights of either party.

AVOIDANCE OF DELAY

18. It is a condition of this insurance that the Assured shall act with reasonable despatch in all circumstances within their control.

LAW AND PRACTICE

19. This insurance is subject to English law and practice.

Note: It is necessary for the Assured when they become aware of an event which is "held covered" under this insurance to give prompt notice to the Underwriters and the right to such cover is dependent upon compliance with this obligation.

INSTITUTE CARGO CLAUSES (C)
RISKS COVERED

1. This insurance covers, except as provided in Clauses 4, 5, 6, and 7 below

   1.1 loss or damage to the subject-matter insured reasonably attributable to

      1.1.1 fire or explosion

      1.1.2 vessel or craft being stranded, grounded, sunk, or capsized

      1.1.3 overturning or derailment of land conveyance

      1.1.4 collision or contact of vessel, craft, or conveyance with any external object other than water

      1.1.5 discharge of cargo at a port of distress

   1.2 loss of or damage to the subject-matter insured caused by

      1.2.1 general average sacrifice

      1.2.2 jettison

2. This insurance covers general average and salvage charges, adjusted or determined according to the contract of affreightment and/or the governing law and practice, incurred to avoid or in connection with the avoidance of loss from any cause except those excluded in Clauses 4, 5, 6, and 7 or elsewhere in this insurance.

3. This insurance is extended to indemnify the Assured against such proportion of liability under the contract of affreightment "Both to Blame Collision" Clause as is in respect of a loss recoverable hereunder. In the event of any claim by shipowners under the said Clause the Assured agree to notify the Underwriters who shall have the right, at their own cost and expense, to defend the Assured against such claim.

EXCLUSIONS

4. In no case shall this insurance cover:

   4.1 loss, damage, or expense attributable to willful misconduct of the Assured

   4.2 ordinary leakage, ordinary loss in weight or volume, or ordinary wear and tear of the subject-matter insured

   4.3 loss, damage, or expense caused by insufficiently or unsuitability of packing or preparation of the subject-matter insurance (for the purpose of this Clause 4.3 "packing" shall be deemed to include stowage in a container or liftvan but only when such stowage is carried out prior to attachment of this insurance or by the Assured or their servants)

   4.4 loss, damage, or expense caused by inherent vice or nature of the subject-matter insured

   4.5 loss, damage, or expense proximately caused by delay, even though the delay be caused by a risk insured against (except expenses payable under Clause 2 above)

   4.6 loss, damage, or expense arising from insolvency or financial default of the owners managers charterers or operators of the vessel

   4.7 deliberate damage to or deliberate destruction of the subject-matter insured or any part thereof the wrongful act of any person or persons

   4.8 loss, damage, or expense arising from the use of any weapon of war employing atomic or nuclear fission and/or fusion or other like reaction or radioactive force or matter.

5.

5.1 In no case shall this insurance cover loss, damage, or expense arising from Unseaworthiness of vessel or craft, unfitness of vessel, craft, conveyance container, or liftvan for the safe carriage of the subject-matter insured, where the Assured or their servants are privy to such unseaworthiness or unfitness, at the time the subject-matter insured is loaded therein

5.2 The Underwriters waive any breach of the implied warranties or seaworthiness of the ship and fitness of the ship to carry the subject-matter insured to destination, unless the Assured or their servants are privy to such Unseaworthiness or unfitness.

6. In no case shall this insurance cover loss damage or expense caused by

6.1 war, civil war, revolution, rebellion, insurrection, or civil strife arising therefrom, or any hostile act by or against a belligerent power

6.2 capture, seizure, arrest, restraint, or detainment, and the consequences thereof or any attempt thereat

6.3 derelict mines, torpedoes, bombs, or other derelict weapons of war.

7. In no case shall this insurance cover loss, damage, or expense

7.1 caused by strikers, locked-out workmen, or person taking part in labour disturbances, riots, or civil commotions

7.2 resulting from strikes, lock-outs, labour disturbances, riots, or civil commotions

7.3 caused by any terrorist or any person acting from a political motive.

DURATION

8.

8.1 This insurance attaches from the time the goods leave the warehouse or place of storage at the place named herein for the commencement of the transit, continues during the ordinary course of transit, and terminates either

8.1.1 on delivery to the Consignees' or other final warehouse or place of storage at the destination named herein,

8.1.2 on delivery to any other warehouse or place of storage, whether prior to or at the destination named therein, which the Assured elect to use either

       8.1.2.1 for storage other than in the ordinary course of transit or

       8.1.2.2 for allocation or distribution, or

    8.1.3 on the expiry of 60 days after completion of discharge overside of the goods hereby insured from the oversea vessel at the final port of discharge.

Which ever shall first occur.

8.2 If, after discharge overside from the oversea vessel at the final port of discharge, but prior to termination of this insurance, the goods are to be forwarded to a destination other than that to which they are insured hereunder, this insurance, whilst remaining subject to termination as provided for above, shall not extend beyond the commencement of transit to such other destination.

8.3 This insurance shall remain in force (subject to termination as provided for above and to the provisions of Clause 9 below) during delay beyond the control of the Assured, and deviation, forced discharge, reshipment, or transshipment and during any variation of the adventure arising from the exercise of a liberty granted to shipowners or charterers under the contract of affreightment.

9. If owing to circumstances beyond the control of the Assured either the contract of carriage is terminated at a port or place other than the destination named therein or the transit is otherwise terminated before delivery of the goods as provided for in Clause 8 above, then this insurance shall also terminate *unless prompt notice is given to the Underwriters and continuation of cover is requested when the insurance shall remain in force, subject to an additional premium if required by the Underwriters,* either

9.1 until the goods are sold and delivered at such port or place, unless otherwise specially agreed, until the expiry of 60 days after arrival of the goods hereby insured at such port or place, whichever shall first occur, or

9.2 if the goods are forwarded within the said period of 60 days (or any agreed extension thereof) to the destination named herein or to any other destination, until terminated in accordance with the provisions of Clause 8 above.

10. Where, after attachment of this insurance, the destination is changed by the Assured, held covered at a premium and on conditions to be arranged subject to prompt notice being given to the Underwriters.

CLAIMS

11.

11.1 In order to recover under this insurance the Assured must have an insurable interest in the subject-matter insured at the time of the loss.

11.2 Subject to 11.1 above, the Assured shall be entitled to recover for insured loss occurring during the period covered by this insurance, notwithstanding that the loss occurred before the contract of insurance was concluded, unless the Assured were aware of the loss and the Underwriters were not.

12. Where, as a result of the operation of a risk covered by this insurance, the insured transit is terminated at a port or place other than that to which the subject-matter is covered under this insurance, the Underwriters will reimburse the Assured for any extra charges properly and reasonably incurred in unloading storing and forwarding the subject-matter to the destination to which it is insured hereunder.

This Clause 12, which does not apply to general average or salvage charges, shall be subject to the exclusions contained in Clauses 4, 5, 6, and, 7 above, and shall not include charges arising from the fault negligence insolvency or financial default of the Assured or their servants.

13. No claim for Constructive Total Loss shall be recoverable hereunder unless the subject-matter insured is reasonably abandoned either on account of its actual total loss appearing to be unavoidable or because the cost of recovering, reconditioning, and forwarding the subject-matter to the destination to which it is insured would exceed its value on arrival.

14.

14.1 If any Increased Value insurance is effected by the Assured on the cargo insured herein the agreed value of the cargo shall be deemed to the total amount insured under this insurance and all Increased Value insurances covering the loss, and liability under this insurance shall be in such proportion as the sum insured herein bears to such total amount insured.

In the event of claim the Assured shall provide the Underwriters with evidence of the amounts insured under all other insurance.

14.2 Where this insurance is on Increased Value the following clause shall apply:

The agreed value of the cargo shall be deemed to be equal to the total amount insured under the primary insurance and all Increased Value insurances covering the loss and effected on the cargo by the Assured, and liability under this insurance shall be in such proportion as the sum insured herein bears to such total amount insured.

BENEFIT OF INSURANCE

15. This insurance shall not inure to the benefit of the carrier or other bailee.

MINIMIZING LOSSES

It is the duty of the Assured and their servants and agents in respect of loss recoverable hereunder

15.1 to take such measures as may be reasonable for the purpose of averting or minimizing such loss, and

15.2 to ensure that all rights against carriers, bailees, or other third parties are properly preserved and exercised and the Underwriters will, in additional to any loss recoverable hereunder, reimburse the Assured for any charges properly and reasonably incurred in pursuance of there duties

It is the duty of the Assured and their servants and agents in respect of loss recoverable hereunder

16.1 to take such measures as may be reasonable for the purpose of averting or minimizing such loss, and

16.2 to ensure that all rights against carriers, bailees or other third parties are properly preserved and exercised and the Underwriters will, in addition to any loss recoverable hereunder, reimburse the Assured for any charges properly and reasonably incurred in pursuance of these duties.

17. Measures taken by the Assured or the Underwriters with the object of saving, protecting, or recovering the subject-matter insured shall not be considered as a waiver or acceptance of abandonment or otherwise prejudice the rights of either party.

AVOIDANCE OF DELAY

18. It is a condition of this insurance that the Assured shall act with reasonable dispatch in all circumstances within their control.

LAW AND PRACTICE

19. This insurance is subject to English law and practice.

Note: It is necessary for the Assured when they become aware of an event which is "held covered" under this insurance to give prompt notice to the Underwriters and the right to such cover is dependent upon compliance with the obligation.

Cargo insurance is often misunderstood by executives operating in import and export trade ... till there is a claim, loss, or damage.[*]

Import and export operators handling cargo insurance needs are best to

- Learn the basics of risk in their operations
- Learn how marine insurance as an option can be utilized to transfer risk
- Learn how to leverage marine insurance
- Learn how to identify and manage both brokers and underwriters who specialize in cargo insurance
- Learn how to price out the coverage to make the most cost effective purchases
- Learn the basic underwriting terms and conditions and how best to tailor and customize coverage for the nuances of their global supply chain

TRANSFER OF TITLE AND REVENUE RECOGNITION

Transfer of Title or Ownership

Incoterms do not address the subject of ownership transfer or what many refer to as title.

Incoterms 2010, page 6, 2nd paragraph, outlines as follows:

4. Remember the Incoterms rules do not give you a complete contract of sale ...

---

[*] From Lloyd's Market Association (LMA), http://www.lmalloyds.com.

Incoterms rules *do* say which party to the sale contract has the obligation to make carriage or insurance arrangements, when the seller delivers the goods to the buyer, and which costs each party is responsible for. Incoterms rules, however, say nothing about the price to be paid or the method of its payment. Neither do they deal with the transfer of ownership of the goods, or the consequences of a breach of contract. These matters are normally dealt with through express terms in the contract of sale or in the law governing that contract. The parties should be aware that mandatory local law may override any aspect of the sale contract, including the chosen Incoterms rule.

One of the most misunderstood aspects of Incoterms is this issue of title. In my practice and for over 30 years of international trade experience, it still amazes me that many finance, legal, and supply chain professionals believe that when delivery occurs in an international transaction, so does title transfer. They tie this into the Incoterms option. By reading the previous excerpt, it is clear that Incoterms do not address title.

Title is supposed to be addressed elsewhere in a sales contract or a purchase agreement, by stating at what point ownership or title is transferred between a seller and a buyer or an exporter and an importer. This does not mean that in an agreement that Incoterms cannot be used at that point in time and trade when ownership is indeed transferred. This means that a seller can place in the commercial invoice or the sales contract that title does transfer when delivery has occurred, as identified by the Incoterms.

For example, an Indian exporter/seller that creates a transaction on FOB Mumbai terms with a buyer in London places wording in the sales contract that title transfer upon delivery, which under the FOB takes place once the goods are on-board the ocean-going vessel. This can be done. Having said that, in this example nowhere in the Incoterms does it say that the FOB term means that title transfers once the goods are loaded on-board. It has to be a separate understanding or part of the contract between a seller and a buyer. The point again is that Incoterms by themselves do not transfer ownership or title; it is addressed elsewhere in the agreement sales or purchase order. The Incoterms can be used as that point, but only when agreed to as a separate understanding within their overall agreement.

This is a critical point to comprehend in managing Incoterms and managing costs and risks. It is important because numerous companies, countries, and accounting standards use transfer of ownership as one part of an overall standard when revenue can be recognized. This is discussed more in the following section.

While some companies use the Incoterms as the reference point of ownership or title transfer, it is important to note that transfer of ownership and title should occur only once both parties have met the requirements of performance under their agreement.

What are the most basic points of an agreement? One company manufacturers and delivers. The other company pays for that product or service—contract completed—ownership or title transferred.

In another example, what if a company built eyeglass equipment, US$750,000 per unit, sold to eye doctors worldwide from an upstate New York–based manufacturer? In the sales agreement, the company agrees to manufacture to order once a 10% deposit is received. It ships on a DDP to an eye doctor in Brussels, billing the doctor for all costs as part of the overall sales agreement. The eye doctor pays for the equipment only once it in installed by the exporter/manufacturer and a technician has it in working order, has shown the doctor how to use it, and the doctor certifies that everything is A-OK. In this agreement, the exporter would be foolish to transfer ownership upon delivery, which according to the Incoterms is when the goods arrive at the doctor's office unloaded from the arriving conveyance.

The exporter once the balance of the outstanding invoice was paid not only after arrival, but after installation and the doctor OK's the disposition of the goods in working order. Then and only then would it want now to transfer ownership or title to the doctor. If this is done any earlier, it would potentially jeopardize its right of recovery in a payment dispute where title transference was not clear and the law favored possession as 9/10's of most situations.

If the documentation provided ownership once both parties met their responsibilities—the exporter delivered, installed, and has the machine working and the doctor affirmed that everything is OK, then the doctor pays, and now ownership is transferred. Title should always be an issue on all export transactions, where funds will be received at a later date, after delivery has been made.

Importers also have to be concerned about this issue. You could have circumstances where an importer pays a deposit or even in full for the goods and then arranges for a DDP transaction. If the goods never get delivered because of a snafu at the inbound customs station, the importer could potentially never receive its merchandise and be in a very subservient position to take control of the import process, as it does not have ownership. An importer in these circumstances may want to require ownership or title transfer at a much earlier point in the transaction to protect its interests if something was to go wrong impacting clearance or delivery.

This whole subject deals with risk mitigation and reducing exposure to the exporter or importer in an international transaction, so they can agree on ownership and when it gets transferred to protect both their mutual interests.

Revenue Recognition

This subject ties directly in with title and ownership in that Incoterms has little to do with this issue in the global supply chain. Revenue recognition is often a highly debated and contested issue among all chief executive officers, accounting firms, and tax consultants. Each and every country in the world has its own guidelines that impact when a company can earn revenue for an export sale.

Consider the following example. A company in Parsippany, New Jersey, receives a purchase order from a buyer in Barcelona, Spain, for a shipment of retail sporting equipment valued at US$165,00. The U.S. company sells FOB Elizabeth, New Jersey, and arranges for an ocean freight shipment following the instructions of the buyer to deliver the goods on-board a particular vessel in the port of Elizabeth, New Jersey, destined for Spain. The U.S. company will get paid 30 days after delivery in Spain. The calendar will look like this:

April 1: Purchase order is received.
April 2: Manufacturing begins.
April 5: Goods ready for shipping.
April 8: Goods handed over to domestic trucker for delivery to Port Elizabeth.
April 10: Goods loaded on-board vessel.
April 25: Goods arrive at the Port of Barcelona in Spain.
April 28: Goods cleared.
April 29: Goods delivered to consignee.
May 28: Consignee remits funds in full to the exporter in Parsippany by creating an electronic draft from its bank to the shipper's U.S. bank.
May 29: U.S. bank acknowledges payment and transfer of funds is complete. Money available for use.

So the question is: When can the Parsippany company post the revenue: when the PO comes in, when the goods are shipped, when the payment is received, or at some other time? This is where the controversy will start. Keep in mind that every country has its own guidelines in this regard. In the United States

- Companies have their own policies.
- U.S.-based operators of foreign parents have their own guidelines.
- IFRS, GAAP, SEC, IRS, and IAS all have some areas of governance.

Through years of investigation, I have best determined the following for most companies to follow along lines of consistent and correct local governance. For a company to post revenue on an export transaction, the following must be in place:

- The exporter must have received an order from overseas, best demonstrated by receipt of a legitimate PO, Purchase Order.
- The exporter must be capable of meeting the shipping requirements of the purchase order, by either having inventory, work-in-process, or other means to meet the purchase order requirements.
- The exporter must have a reasonable expectation of its ability to get paid for the export.
- Delivery has to have occurred. While delivery is often not clearly defined, through court precedence and trade practices it can best be defined by when the goods are first handed to the carrier whose intent is to move the goods out of the exporting country. This is best evidenced by receipt of a bill of lading or other carrier document evidencing the same.

There is another "standard" that various governing authorities point to for revenue recognition. I find fault in this particular one: in numerous circumstances of global trade this wording would not have a viable application but is offered in being comprehensive to this subject:

- The transfer of property in goods in most cases results in or coincides with the transfer of significant risk and reward of ownership to the buyer.

I find exception here where the title is controlled until payment is received. But shipment, delivery, possession, control, and expectation of payment standards have all been met. In most circumstances the exporter would be in a position to post the export sale. For example, in many countries, car dealers who sell automobiles on credit can post the sale, even though they will retain the title until final payment is made by the buyer. An exporter could be in the same position in meeting all the standards while retaining the title until payment is received in full. He then should be in a position once all other standards are met to receive revenue.

Revenue is defined numerous ways, but the following definition is considered a standard worldwide:

> Revenue is the gross inflow of cash, receivables or other consideration arising in the course of ordinary activities of an enterprise from the sale of goods, from the rendering of services and from the use by others of enterprise resources yielding interest, royalty and dividend. Revenue is measured by the charges made to customers or clients for goods supplied and services rendered to them and by the charges and rewards arising from the use of resources by them. In an agency relationship, the revenue is the amount of commission and not the gross inflow of cash, receivable or other consideration.

Companies across the globe can use this definition only as a guideline. They will need to determine how this works within any governance that is contrary or to modify this model or internal tax, accounting, and supply chain issues that may require different application or modification. Following are some examples of how revenue is recognized in various corporate and government communications.*

One company's website shows the description for revenue recognition.

Kyocera sells various types of products, including fine ceramic parts, semiconductor parts, and telecommunications equipment. Kyocera recognizes revenue upon completion of the earnings process, which occurs when

---

* From International Accounting Standards Board (IASB), http://www.iasplus.com.

products are shipped or delivered to customers in accordance with the terms of an agreement of sale, there is a fixed or determinable selling price, title and risk of loss have been transferred, and collectability is reasonably assured. Most of these conditions are satisfied at the time of delivery to customers in domestic sales (FOB destination) and at the time of shipment (FOB shipping) for export sales.*

Generally accepted accounting principles (GAAP) states:

- GAAP revenue recognition rules are straightforward and relatively simple. Revenue is recognized when a transaction happens that results in income that is (a) realized and (b) earned. For example, company A sells a product to company B for $1,000. Company B promises to pay for the product within 30 days. The revenue can be recorded on the date of sale with the understanding that the cash will be received in the future. Most companies put these terms in writing, as oral agreements can be difficult to substantiate should the transaction not be completed as agreed.
- Companies sell many products and services on credit, generating accounts receivable (agreements to remit the purchase price in the near future) or notes receivable (promises to pay monies due in the short- or longer-term future). In both cases, the companies earning this revenue record the income at the time of sale, not when the payment is received. Therefore, their cash position may or may not reflect the volume of their current sales. GAAP permits this revenue recognition program because the income was earned, although not received, on the date of the sale.†

In addition GAAP puts forth the following:

Evidence of Arrangement

- Accrual basis accounting requires an evidence of arrangement condition. Financial transactions must occur between a buyer and seller in an arms-length transaction. Arms-length transactions occur free from undue pressure and without collusion between the buyer and seller. The evidence of arrangement condition does

---

* From http://www.wikinvest.com/stock/Kyocera_(KYO)/Revenue_Recognition.
† From Pirraglia, W., About GAAP Revenue Recognition, http://www.ehow.com/about_4586143_gaap-revenue-recognition.html

not require a formal written contract. Individuals and businesses engage in these types of arrangements in just about every business environment. Revenue is unrecognizable unless an evidence of arrangement is in place.

Delivery or Services Rendered

- The delivery of goods and rendering of services are another condition of accrual accounting. Delivery of goods usually requires the seller to give full possession of an item to the buyer. The location of delivery (buyer or seller's facilities) is not a factor in this requirement. Rendering services is similar to the delivery of goods. The seller must complete all services in the transaction to ensure it meets accrual basis accounting requirements.

Price Is Fixed or Determinable

- Accrual basis accounting requires the price of goods or services to be fixed or determinable. Buyers and sellers must be unable to change the price once the evidence of arrangement exists. Altering financial information outside of the original agreement can create dangerous business situations. Buyers and seller must both agree to any changes in arms-length financial transactions. This ensures all information relating to a financial transaction is included in the price of the goods or service.

Collectability Is Reasonably Assured

IAS states:

Sale of Goods

Revenue arising from the sale of goods should be recognized when all of the following criteria have been satisfied [IAS 18.14]:

- the seller has transferred to the buyer the significant risks and rewards of ownership
- the seller retains neither continuing managerial involvement to the degree usually associated with ownership nor effective control over the goods sold

- the amount of revenue can be measured reliably
- it is probable that the economic benefits associated with the transaction will flow to the seller, and
- the costs incurred or to be incurred in respect of the transaction can be measured reliably

SEC states:

- Persuasive evidence of an arrangement exists,
- Delivery has occurred or services have been rendered,
- The seller's price to the buyer is fixed or determinable,
- Collectability is reasonably assured.

Revenue recognition is a dicey subject with lots of controversy. Shipments between owned companies from parent to subsidiary add another dynamic for controversy. I suggest the following actions for export revenue recognition:

1. Use the basic model outlined herein as a starting point.
2. Determine which governances your company needs to follow from a regulatory perspective.
3. Interface with both internal and external legal, tax, and accounting expertise to establish corporate SOPs and protocol in export revenue recognition.
4. Work with external consultants and logistics professional to determine what options exist in Incoterms to leverage revenue recognition options.
5. Communicate all agreements to operating staff, vendors, suppliers, and providers.
6. Use agreements consistently.

INCOTERMS AND SARBANES–OXLEY

For public companies in the United States that have to operate under SOX regulations, along with companies striving for world-class and best-practice operations, we recommend the following overview issues to be considered.

Sarbanes–Oxley Act of 2002, also known as the Public Company Accounting Reform and Investor Protection Act of 2002, is a U.S. federal law enacted on July 30, 2002. This law was initiated in response to highly publicized accounting scandals involving major corporations such as Enron, Tyco, and WorldCom. These scandals rocked the public's confidence in the nation's securities markets and cost investors billions of dollars. The legislation was named after sponsors Senator Paul Sarbanes and Representative Michael G. Oxley and was approved by the House in a vote of 423–3 and by the Senate in a vote of 99–0.

To regain the public's confidence, the legislation establishes the standards necessary to monitor and strengthen corporate accounting controls by covering such issues as auditor independence, internal control assessment, and financial disclosure.

SOX is a critical component of the global supply chain, the reasons of which will be made clear shortly. Managing Incoterms is a component of this overall consideration. Incoterms choices will impact the financial integrity of any global transaction and therefore become a SOX concern. The debate continues over the perceived benefits and cost of implementing SOX; however, supporters maintain their position that the legislation is necessary and is a key role in restoring the public's confidence in the securities market.

These regulations have had a huge impact on American public corporations with financial implications having to be reported to senior management. The legislation mandates that senior executives take individual responsibility for the accuracy and completeness of corporate financial findings. Under the legislation, the signing officers must certify that they are responsible for establishing and maintaining internal controls and procedures and can be held accountable for

- All financial statements, both internal and external
- Standard operating procedures
- Accounting practices
- Certification from internal and external auditors

Public companies must make themselves available for scrutiny by outside auditors, the Securities and Exchange Commission, and government investigations. This scrutiny goes beyond the boardroom and failure to meet import and export compliance issues within the global supply chain will result in monetary penalties creating a financial impact on the company. Unfortunately, the global supply chain was not specifically contemplated under SOX leaving corporations vulnerable to the possibility of being in noncompliance. This can lead to fines and penalties, loss of privileges, and delays within the supply chain.

There should not be a disconnection between mandating standard operating procedures for the global supply chain to be in compliance with U.S. import–export and transportation regulations and the need to protect the company's financial security under SOX. This is one misconception a corporation cannot afford to operate by. Standard operating procedures are a basic requirement of U.S. Customs and the Bureau of Industry and Security (government agency that controls the export of dual-use items), and corporations should include these standard operating procedures as part of their SOX management requirements. SOPs and protocol in Incoterms would be an integral part of and SOX trade compliance initiatives.

Guidance and control must also extend to the corporation's domestic and international partners, freight forwarders, and customs brokers. Without proper management of these partners, you cannot have a secure global supply chain. This is considered a lack of due diligence, and their errors can also result in fines and penalties to the corporation. Depending on the nature of a corporation's business, fines and penalties can be assessed by more than one government agency: for example, the U.S. Department of Agriculture for food products; U.S. Food and Drug Administration for pharmaceutical products; and U.S. Department of Transportation for hazardous materials. It would be foolish for a corporation not to be proactive and put procedures in place to mitigate their exposure to such fines and penalties and to ensure a compliant, secure, and efficient supply chain. Globalization is a crucial factor for most companies looking to sell products overseas; therefore, they must acknowledge the necessity to become compliance minded and focused.

Many companies now understand the implication of noncompliance and are thus creating compliance departments, which generally report to corporate counsel or internal audit departments and have an important say in the supply chain and in manufacturing and risk management decisions. Some of the areas of concern within the global supply chain that may result in monetary penalties are incorrect documentation, misclassification and valuation of products, and exporting without a license. In certain instances there could also be a possibility of the loss of import and export privileges. Imagine what an impact that could have on a corporation. A loss of privileges could lead to layoffs, bankruptcy, and pay cuts. Dedication to an aggressive compliance program is a surefire way to help prevent such disastrous results.

Corporations are discovering the importance of a safe, competitive, and secure global supply chain. This also affords the corporation the opportunity to align themselves with Customs Trade Partnership Against Terrorism (C-TPAT), a voluntary security initiative. This enhances a corporation's security program and competitiveness within the global supply chain world while extending these security and financial measures to their global partners. This is a natural alliance that is becoming more and more prevalent in the supply chain. Companies have found that C-TPAT participation has assisted them greatly with their supply chain management and benefits may include a decrease in random inspections, self-auditing, and automatic mitigation in fines and penalties.

Being a C-TPAT member also places a corporation in a more secure position in the eyes of U.S. Customs if such another terror attack should take place on U.S. soil. SOX and C-TPAT are synonymous, so how could you not enter into a partnership that places you in a mitigating circumstance.

In our experience, based on an introspective look, all costs associated with the implementation of SOX and compliance management in the global supply chain is betterment to the bottom line. The benefits are felt within the daily routine with a smoother and more effectively run supply chain. This is a result of managing Incoterms and having internal controls, training, and standard operation procedures in place and are well worth the effort and costs involved.

In summary, the importance of the inclusion of the global supply chain and Incoterms under SOX will result in the protection of the corporation's financial security and the welfare of the investors and employees who work so hard to further maintain the company's future viability and longevity. Operating within SOX guidelines has become another skill set that must be mastered by logistics, traffic, and warehouse managers as well as chief executives and chief financial officers. A company's success in its import and export operations may depend upon it. It is critical when instituting SOX guidelines and requirements that the global supply chain is not left out of the loop and is necessary to maintain and protect the company's integrity and financial security as a whole.

Tax Considerations

When we evaluate where we sell to or where we buy from (i.e., sourcing), we know we have to evaluate landed costs in making good sales and purchasing decisions. Taxes are an integral part of that analysis. The most common form of taxes that we have to consider relate to charges that various government agencies place as goods pass through international borders.

Incoterms tell us who is responsible for paying these costs. Therefore, it is critical for the importer and exporter to understand under the Incoterms who has to pay so they can protect their mutual interests.

These border taxes can be outlines as follows:

- *Ad valorem*
- Value-added

- Supplemental

Additional Tax Issues

Tax concerns also impact exporters on tax-related matters in the country of export. For example, in the United States there are multiple and varied tax consequences on exporters that sell potentially in the following four scenarios.

1. U.S. exporters who export on a direct basis and make export sales to foreign buyers through their own efforts either by responding to foreign inquiries or by sending traveling sales employees overseas.
2. U.S. exporters whose export sales to foreign buyers are made through related intermediaries, such as offshore sales employees, offshore representative offices, offshore branches, or offshore subsidiaries.
3. U.S. exporters whose export sales to foreign buyers are made through unrelated intermediaries, such as dependent sales agents, independent sales agents, dependent distributors, independent distributors, or foreign marketing cooperatives.
4. U.S. exporters who move goods to a bonded warehouse or foreign trade zone overseas before a final sale is made to a foreign entity overseas.

Most countries with export activity have some form of export tax laws that mirrors those in the United States or has some impact on costs. All companies need to weigh these factors into landed cost modeling and understand the favorable and potential harmful impacts of supply chain decisions with Incoterms, title, and revenue recognition that might affect how tax regulations applies to the export.

To truly leverage supply chain choices, all the factors that can potentially impact spend that might not be immediately transparent (e.g., export tax laws) need to eventually be factored in. This requires knowledge and expertise typically found from seeking the advise of outside counsel, accountants, and tax professionals.

Ad Valorem

Ad valorem is a Latin word that means "according to value." Hence, all *ad valorem* taxes are calculated with the value of an asset in mind. Incoterms apply to the movement of freight—typically being an asset and having value. An *ad valorem* tax is imposed on the basis of the monetary value of the taxed item. Traditionally, most customs and excises had "specific" rates; the tax base was defined in terms of physical units such as gallons, pounds, or individual items.

Ad valorem rates, which have come into increased use, have the important advantage of adjusting the tax burden according to the price paid for the taxed items. They thus avoid the serious discrimination of specific rates against the low-priced varieties of the commodities.

The primary difficulty with the *ad valorem* taxation, especially in the case of tariffs, is in establishing a satisfactory value figure. Typical valuation is on a CIF (Cost, Insurance, Freight) basis or alternatively on an FOB (Free on Board) cost basis.

Each country in the world has a different basis for determining this value. As the Incoterms will determine who is responsible to create documents showing evidence of this value, both parties need to communicate how this will be presented at the time goods pass through the border … as it will have cost and risk implications to both companies.

Value-Added Tax

A government levy on the amount that a business firm adds to the price of a commodity during production and distribution of a good. Three major types of value-added tax have been identified, depending on the deductions allowed, but only one—called the "consumption" type—is widely used today.

Calculation of the value-added tax of the consumption type can be made in any of three different ways, but virtually every country imposing the tax uses the "invoice," or "credit," method of computation. Using this method, each seller (the party responsible for collecting the tax and paying it to the government) first calculates the sum of all the taxes that he has collected on goods sold; he then totals the sum of all the taxes that he has paid on goods purchased. His net tax liability is the difference between the tax collected and the tax paid.

It is generally assumed that the burden of the value-added tax, like that of other sales taxes, falls upon the final consumer. Although the tax is collected at each stage of the production-distribution chain, the fact that sellers receive a credit for their tax payments causes the tax, in effect, to be passed on to the final consumer, who receives no credit. The tax can be regressive (i.e., the percentage of income paid in tax rises as income falls), but most countries have at least partly avoided this effect by applying a lower rate to necessities than to luxury items.

In 1954 France was the first country to adopt the value-added tax on a large scale. It served as an improvement on the earlier turnover tax, by which a product was taxed repeatedly at every stage of production and distribution, without relief for taxes paid at previous stages. Although easier to administer, such a tax discriminated heavily against industries and sectors in which products were bought and sold several times, encouraging an undesirable concentration of economic power.

In 1968 West Germany adopted the value-added tax, and since then most other western European nations have followed suit, largely as the result of a desire to harmonize tax systems. All members of the European Union are required to implement value-added taxes that conform to a model prescribed by the union. Many countries in South America, Asia, and Africa have also adopted the tax.

Supplemental Taxes

GST/HST/PST (generalized service tax, harmonized service tax, provincial sales tax) are charged by certain government entities on goods and services imported, purchased or transacted within the country. Below is a sample of the application of such taxes, as conducted in Canada.

Summary

Most goods and services sold or provided in Canada are taxable at the rate of 7% (GST) or 15% (HST). The HST applies in the provinces of New Brunswick, Nova Scotia and Newfoundland and Labrador. Certain items, such as sales of basic groceries and prescription drugs, are also taxable at a rate of 0%. These are referred to as zero-rated goods and services. A limited number of goods and services are exempt from the GST/HST.

The GST/HST applies to most transactions throughout the production and marketing process. Business and organizations required to, or who voluntarily choose to, register for the GST/HST are referred to as registrants. Businesses must register to obtain a Business Number with a GST/HST account. Registrants can claim a credit to recover the GST/HST that is paid or payable on purchases used to provide taxable goods and services. This credit is called an input tax credit and can be claimed for the GST/HST paid or payable for goods or services acquired or imported for use, consumption or supply in their commercial (taxable) activities.

GST/HST registrants who provide taxable goods or services have to charge and collect the GST or HST on their sales. If the GST/HST collected is greater than the GST/HST paid or payable, the difference is sent to the CRA. (Registrants in Quebec send their payment to the ministère du Revenue du Québec). If the GST/HST collected is less than the GST/HST paid or payable, a refund can be claimed.

Every country around the world has different tax considerations. Personnel who operate in the global supply chain need to develop resources with tax professionals to sort out which Incoterms options present the best choices to gain commercial advantages for both the shipper and the consignee.

INTELLECTUAL PROPERTY RIGHTS, TRADEMARKS, AND PATENTS

The protection of patents, trademarks, and other proprietary rights is not addressed by Incoterms. It is necessary for those entering the sales or purchase agreement to address these very specifically.

Companies engaged in global trade also must be aware of how local governments deal with IPR issues and how they support the protection of IPR matters for foreign entities doing business in their country.

The World Trade Organization defines IPR into two categories as follows:

Intellectual property rights are customarily divided into two main areas:

(i) Copyright and rights related to copyright.

The rights of authors of literary and artistic works (such as books and other writings, musical compositions, paintings, sculpture, computer programs and films) are protected by copyright, for a minimum period of 50 years after the death of the author.

Also protected through copyright and related (sometimes referred to as "neighboring") rights are the rights of performers (e.g. actors, singers and musicians), producers of phonograms (sound recordings) and broadcasting organizations. The main social purpose of protection of copyright and related rights is to encourage and reward creative work.

(ii) Industrial property.

Industrial property can usefully be divided into two main areas:

- One area can be characterized as the protection of distinctive signs, in particular trademarks (which distinguish the goods or services of one undertaking from those of other undertakings) and geographical indications (which identify a good as originating in a place where a given characteristic of the good is essentially attributable to its geographical origin).
- The protection of such distinctive signs aims to stimulate and ensure fair competition and to protect consumers, by enabling them to make informed choices between various goods and services. The protection may last indefinitely, provided the sign in question continues to be distinctive.
- Other types of industrial property are protected primarily to stimulate innovation, design, and the creation of technology. In this category fall inventions (protected by patents), industrial designs, and trade secrets.

The social purpose is to provide protection for the results of investment in the development of new technology, thus giving the incentive and means to finance research and development activities.

A functioning intellectual property regime should also facilitate the transfer of technology in the form of foreign direct investment, joint ventures, and licensing.

The World Trade Organization (WTO) deals with the global rules of trade between nations. Its main function is to ensure that trade flows as smoothly, predictably, and freely as possible.

The protection is usually given for a finite term (typically 20 years in the case of patents).

While the basic social objectives of intellectual property protection are as outlined above, it should also be noted that the exclusive rights given are generally subject to a number of limitations and exceptions, aimed at fine-tuning the balance that has to be found between the legitimate interests of right holders and of users.

Companies engaged in global trade need to be aware of IPR issues and make sure they are fully informed on how the countries they do business with treat IPR. They need to build in protections to manage these IPR risks, and a good starting point is in the sales or purchase agreement. This is accomplished irrespective of the Incoterms used.

Carnets and Incoterms[*]

Carnets are an excellent method for moving goods internationally on a temporary basis and accomplishing the transportation with the highest efficiency and at a reduced cost. They ease the clearance process and reduce or eliminate local duty and tax charges.

Countries that allow the use of carnets are as follows:

Algeria	Chile	Germany
Andorra	China	Gibraltar
Antarctica	Corsica	Greece
Aruba	Curacao	Guadeloupe
Australia	Cote d'Ivoire	Guernsey
Austria	Croatia	Hong Kong
Balearic Islands	Cyprus	Hungary
Belarus	Czech Republic	Iceland
Belgium	Denmark	India
Botswana	Estonia	Iran
Bulgaria	European Union	Ireland
Canada	Finland	Isle of Man
Canary Islands	France	Israel
Ceuta	French Guiana	Italy

---

[*] From the United States Council for International Business (USCIB), http://www.uscib.org.

Japan	Mongolia	Singapore
Jersey	Montenegro	Slovakia
Korea (South)	Morocco	Slovenia
Latvia	Namibia	South Africa
Lebanon	The Netherlands	Spain
Lesotho	New Caledonia	Sri Lanka
Liechtenstein	New Zealand	Swaziland
Lithuania	Norway	Sweden
Luxembourg	Pakistan	Switzerland
Macedonia	Poland	Tahiti
Macau	Portugal	Tasmania
Malaysia	Puerto Rico	Taiwan (TECRO/AIT
Malta	Reunion	carnets only)
Martinique	Romania	Thailand
Mauritius	Russia	Tunisia
Mayotte	St. Barthelemy	Turkey
Melilla	St. Martin	Ukraine
Mexico	St. Pierre	United Arab Emirates
Miquelon	Senegal	United Kingdom
Moldova	Serbia (including	United States
Monaco	Kosovo)	Wallis & Futuna

Note: The temporary movement of goods through Taiwan may take place under TECRO/AIT carnets only. Like the ATA carnet system, the AIT carnet allows exporters to avoid paying duties and taxes on temporary imports to Taiwan. AIT carnets also are valid for one year.

Carnet Use

A carnet is a special customs document designed to simplify and streamline customs procedures for business and professional travelers who wish to take commercial samples, advertising material, medical or other professional equipment, accompanied or not, into participating countries. The initials "ATA" are a combination of the French and English words "Admission Temporaire/Temporary Admission."

Customs authorities in participating countries and territories accept carnets as a guarantee that all customs duties and taxes will be paid in the event that any of the items covered by the carnet are not taken out of the country within the time period allowed.

A carnet eliminates extensive customs procedures for temporary imports, including the payment of duties and taxes, registration of goods before departure, and purchase of a temporary import bond for the amount of duties and taxes normally payable. All of these matters involve time, effort, and expense, which the carnet eliminates completely in the countries where the system is in effect.

The carnet, therefore, allows the temporary exporter to make customs arrangements in advance, make the arrangements at a predetermined cost, and use a single document for all customs transactions. Carnets are valid for one year and may be used for unlimited exits from, and entries into, countries that accept the carnet. A carnet can be used for nearly all goods, including commercial samples, professional equipment, and goods for trade shows and exhibitions. Consumable goods such as food and agricultural products, disposable items, and postal shipments are not covered by carnets.

Carnets generally are issued and administered by chambers of commerce in the participating countries through an international arrangement known as the IBCC chain, sponsored by the International Chamber of Commerce in Paris. The U.S. Council for International Business administers the ATA carnet system in the United States. The U.S. Council also administers the TECRO/AIT carnet for the temporary movement of goods through Taiwan.

A multitude of options exist for carnet use, but the most likely choice for an exporter would be DDP, as it would be typically required to ship, export clear, import clear, deliver, and then reverse all of that to bring the merchandise back to origin. The exporter would control the logistics and clearance responsibilities typically provided by its freight forwarders system of offices or agents. Carnets can provide leverage and competitive advantage for goods that move temporarily in global supply chains.

8

Bonded Warehouses and Foreign Trade Zones

Companies all over the world can use bonded warehouses and foreign trade zones to gain competitive advantage in their global supply chains. It is one of the fastest growing areas of growth in multinational corporations to benefit financially in their global supply chains.

These very specialized privileges granted to importers and exporters in most countries around the world offer certain advantages that typically reduce the landed cost to one or both parties involved in international trade. They are one of the fastest growing areas for U.S. corporations to gain leverage in how business is done in North America. Some European and Asian companies that do business in the United States, particularly within the automobile industry (e.g., Mercedes Benz, BMW, Honda, and Toyota) have opened up a bonded and foreign trade zone (FTZ) presence because it benefits both them and their customers.

Providing lower landed costs is a major driving factor in the use of bonded and foreign trade zones both in the United States and overseas.

BONDED WAREHOUSES

Bonded warehouses allow companies to temporarily store goods without entering the economy of the country till a later point in time. They are typically structured under local customs authorities' jurisdictions but owned and operated by private companies. They typically require that no material change takes place on the cargo stored in these facilities. Companies can store, inspect, repack, weigh, and work on goods, but if it enters as a widget it must leave as a widget.

FTZs are usually a much more expansive option in global trade in that they work like bonded warehouses but under a strict set of guidelines allowing formularizations, assembly, ingredient mixing, product change, and assembly and manufacturing in which the products entered will change materially from those that leave.

An important example of FTZs can be found in the automotive industry, where major car manufacturers ship parts and raw materials from overseas to their owned and operated FTZs in foreign countries, where the assembly and manufacturing process takes shape. They then use local labor in the final manufacturing process of an automobile for that market.

In the case of both bonded warehouses and FTZs, there is great economic advantage in handling freight this way, including the following:

- Reduction of both federal and local taxes, duties, VAT, GST, etc.
- Deferral of tax and related obligations
- Localized tax and related relief incentives
- Government incentives such as construction, training, and business development
- Marketing advantage in local economies
- Use of local labor
- Localized manufacturing options
- Leveraged transportation, warehousing, and logistics costs

Bonded warehouses and FTZs vary from one country to another. For example, in Vietnam, their customs describes bonded warehouses as follows.

General Provisions in Vietnam for Bonded Warehouses

- The bonded warehouses are warehouses or yards set up on the Vietnamese territory and separated from the surrounding areas for temporary storage and preservation of, or provision of a number of services for, the goods brought from abroad or from within the country and put into the warehouse under bonded warehouse lease contracts signed between the bonded warehouse owners and the goods owners. Bonded warehouses may be set in the following areas:

- The provinces and centrally run cities which act as goods exchange hubs between Vietnam and foreign countries have favorable conditions for the transportation or export and import goods.
- Industrial parks, high-tech parks, export processing zones, other special economic zones (hereinafter referred to as industrial parks).
- Bonded warehouses, goods, and transport means which enter or leave, or are stored and preserved in bonded warehouses must go through customs procedures and subject to the inspection and supervision by the customs offices.

India[*]

F. No. 473/61/94- LC
Government of India
Ministry of Finance
Department of Revenue, New Delhi
Subject: Public/Private bonded warehouses procedure liberalised

I am directed to state that a review of the existing policy with regard to appointment of public bonded warehouses and licensing of private bonded warehouses has been conducted by the Board. Consequently, it has been decided to liberalize the procedure on the lines indicated in the succeeding paragraphs.

2.0 Appointment of Public Bonded Warehouses:

2.1 The existing policy of appointing only Central Warehousing Corporation and State Warehousing corporations as the customs of the public bonded warehouses, formulated in 1980, will undergo a change in the context of liberalization of the economy. Considering that fact that the management of CFSs and ICDs has been entrusted to private operators, in line with the existing policy of privatization and with a view to raising the efficiency of warehousing services, private operators would now be allowed to

---

[*] From Government of India, New Delhi, http://cbec.gov.in/customs/cs-circulars/cs-circulars95/68-95-cus.htm.

be appointed as custodians of the public bonded warehouses. This relaxation may pave the way for more number of public bonded warehouses coming up in interior locations where these are needed.

2.2 The concerned Commissioner should, however, ensure that while appointing any private operator as a custodian for public bonded warehouse, the application submitted by the latter is very carefully scrutinized and factors such as the feasibility and financial viability of the warehouse operator, his credibility, his financial status, his past record to comply with Customs & Excise Laws, his expertise in warehousing field, etc., should be given due consideration. Besides, operational requirements such as, suitability and security of the premises, availability of customs expertise, proximity to the users, etc., are also to be taken into account while appointing the custodians for the public bonded warehouses. The applicant should agree to take the services of the customs officers on cost-recovery basis, if the services of the officer are required on a continuous basis (i.e., 9 AM to 6 PM), or on payment of MOT/Supervision charges, as the case may be.

United Kingdom*

Definition of a Customs Warehouse

A customs warehouse can either be a defined location (such as premises or place) or an inventory system authorized by us for storing non-Community goods, that are

- chargeable with import duty and/or VAT or
- otherwise not in free circulation.

---

* From UK Import Services Ltd., Public Notice: 232 Customs Warehousing, http://ukimports.org.

Depending on the circumstances, a defined location can be the whole of a building, a small compartment in a building, an open site, a silo, or a storage tank.

United States[*]

What Is a U.S. Customs Bonded Warehouse?

A U.S. Customs Bonded Warehouse is a storage facility licensed by the Customs Bureau to hold products without the payment of duties until removal. In general, the facility must apply, meet the prescribed security and other standards and post a bond to ensure compliance with Customs regulations.

What Are Its Advantages?

U.S. Customs duties are not payable until the products are removed from the Bonded Warehouse and imported into the United States. Products can be repackaged or manufactured in the Bonded Warehouse, and exported duty free. This is attractive for products that are shipped into the United States before actual sale to a buyer, or for interim storage of products that are under a quota.

Incoterms® options must be carefully determined by exporters and importers when they intend to use bonded warehouses or FTZs in their global supply chain operations. For example, an importer may be purchasing product from a supplier overseas that will be transiting through a bonded facility for a certain period before being shipped to a final destination. An importer located in Santa Fe, New Mexico, brings in finished

---

[*] From U.S. Customs and Border Protection, http://www.cbp.gov.

apparel from India through the port of Long Beach, California. It plans to move the goods into a bonded warehouse in Long Beach for a period of time to be determined, possibly as long as nine months, before it decides to ship the goods to Santa Fe or possibly to sell to a potential buyer in Toronto, Canada.

The importer has options and could arrange an Incoterms showing the goods being shipped to the bonded facility in Long Beach or at some prior point. But it would not show an Incoterms option to Santa Fe or Toronto. It might then recreate another transaction showing where the goods' ultimate destination may be at a later point to be agreed upon. The goods may even be shipped back to the origin country, never entering the U.S. commerce at all.

Using the wrong Incoterms could change the nature of the transaction to government agencies that scrutinize the transaction. In the United States, this could be U.S. Customs and Border Patrol, the Internal Revenue Service (IRS), or, for public companies, the U.S. Securities and Exchange Commission (SEC) along with a host of others such as the U.S. Food and Drug Administration (FDA) and the U.S. Bureau of Alcohol, Tobacco, and Firearms (BATF).

Every country around the world has oversight in the import process by various governing agencies. They look at the terms of sale and other supporting documentation as what was the "intent" of the seller and buyer or the exporter and importer that caused goods to be handled in a certain way. This applies to a great deal of issues such as goods that move into bonded warehouses and FTZs.

The *Incoterms 2010* Delivered at Place (DAP) and Delivered at Terminal (DAT) apply here, depending upon where the bonded warehouse or FTZ might be located: inside a terminal, port facility, or at some external location off of the inbound gateway locale.

In the United States, CBP offers the following reasons for gaining advantage with FTZs:[*]

- CBP duty and federal excise tax, if applicable, are paid when the merchandise is transferred from the zone for consumption.
- While in the zone, merchandise is not subject to U.S. duty or excise tax. Certain tangible personal property is generally exempt from state and local *ad valorem* taxes.

---

[*] From About Foreign-Trade Zones and Contact Info, U.S. Customs and Border Protection, http://www.cbp.gov/xp/cgov/trade/cargo_security/cargo_control/ftz/about_ftz.xml.

- Goods may be exported from the zone free of duty and excise tax.
- CBP security requirements provide protection against theft.
- Merchandise may remain in a zone indefinitely, whether or not subject to duty.
- The rate of duty and tax on the merchandise admitted to a zone may change as a result of operations conducted within the zone. Therefore, the zone user who plans to enter the merchandise for consumption to CBP territory may normally elect to pay either the duty rate applicable on the foreign material placed in the zone or the duty rate applicable on the finished article transferred from the zone whichever is to his advantage.
- Merchandise imported under bond may be admitted to a FTZ for the purpose of satisfying a legal requirement of exporting the merchandise. For instance, merchandise may be admitted into a zone to satisfy any exportation requirement of the Tariff Act of 1930, or an exportation requirement of any other Federal law (and many state laws) insofar as the agency charged with its enforcement deems it so.

These all point to cost, an integral component of understanding and managing Incoterms options. Importers and exporters that use these types of locations, whether in the United States or in other countries, must choose Incoterms that reflect the intent of the transaction first to get the goods into the bonded location of the FTZ and then to transport the goods to the point of use or sale. This might mean that potentially two or even more Incoterms and/or sales purchase agreements are used to bring goods in from overseas, move into a bonded or FTZ facility, and then out to be of value in use or in a sale. A back-to-back set of transactions might coincide with multiple Incoterms to ultimately fulfill and bring closure to an international transaction facilitated by bonded or FTZ use.

Mexico*

Mexico uses a program with the United States called the Maquilladora Program. *Maquila* is the Mexican name for manufacturing operations in a free trade zone, where factories import material and equipment on a duty-free and tariff-free basis for assembly, processing, or manufacturing and then re-export the assembled, processed and/or manufactured products, sometimes back to the raw materials' country of origin. This form of FTZ provides great advantage to both U.S. and Mexican companies that use Mexican labor to manufacture products for sale in the United States, Canada, and overseas. Companies that use the Maquilladora Program will employ Incoterms that allow import of components and raw materials into these FTZs and finished products from them.

PACKING, MARKING, AND LABELING

International contracts for sale or purchase need to better detail all the necessary requirements for packing, marking, and labeling. Too often, this does not get addressed until there is a problem. My book *Mastering Import and Export Management*, 2nd edition (New York: AMACOM Books), outlines in detail all the necessary procedures for packing and stowing goods for import and export and is a single source reference for this area of concern.

---

* From Helping U.S. Companies Export, http://export.gov.

A company needs to be concerned about packing, marking, and labeling for a number of reasons:

- Customs and related agencies have packing and labeling regulations (e.g., FDA, BATF, FCC)
- Different trade lanes and modes of transportation have different challenges that test packing and stowage.
- Numerous risks in the global supply chain will impact and test packing and stowage: for example, the transportation voyage, the environment, handling, war, SRCC, carrier and port delays, customs processes.
- They are used for retail sales and shelf and store displays.

When companies are writing their international sale or purchase agreement, these factors should be considered, and then the requirements for packing, marking, and labeling should be written in to meet these regulations and challenges in the global supply chain. This often takes the coordination of many corporate disciplines—logistics, manufacturing, legal, marketing, trade compliance, warehousing, regulatory affairs—and includes all providers, vendors, and suppliers.

9

Global Supply Chain: Best Practices

This chapter provides a blueprint to follow to make the supply chain run better by reducing risks and costs and providing the best opportunity for developing leveraged options.

It provides an action plan for management to follow to make intellectual ideas fall into functional activities that provide competitive deliverables allowing the global supply chain to grow and develop profitably.

SENIOR MANAGEMENT: EXECUTING A BEST PRACTICE STRATEGY

Incoterms Management

As outlined in this chapter, senior management's engagement in Incoterms® is critical to running a successful global supply chain. Senior managers must take a leadership position to ensure that middle managers and operational staff comply with SOPs and best practices in what we refer to as ITM. For senior managers of public companies this is not optional but required.

The following outline demonstrates a higher-level strategy of, for example, chief executive officers, chief operating officers, presidents, and divisional senior executives to implement and follow:

1. Develop ITM into your business processes.
2. Learn the basics of Incoterms.
3. Develop resources for Incoterms expertise.
4. Understand how Incoterms decisions impact the global supply chain and break down fiefdoms.
5. Create integration management into Incoterms decision-making.

6. Learn leverage options in general, and then apply to the specifics in your global supply chain metrics.
7. Establish service provider, supplier, vendor, and other business relationship communications and SOPs.
8. Integrate technology into the Incoterms management process.
9. Create policy guidelines for Incoterms options and trade compliance management. For public companies, SOX Incoterms management is critical.
10. Engage Incoterms lobbying to increase and enhance change to your company's benefit.

Develop ITM into Your Business Processes

Reduce risk and maximize advantage. Gain a senior management commitment. ITM is the new buzz for successfully developing an expertise in Incoterms within an organization and developing processes to gain leverage and competitive advantage in your global supply chain. A commitment from senior management recognizing the importance of Incoterms as a skill set and ability to reduce risk and enhance and impact profits favorably is a corporate behavior that will prove necessary and valuable for long-term sustainability.

Companies allocate funds into personnel, training, and infrastructure. Firms and organizations develop all kinds of protocols and procedures to manage their day-to-day marketing, sales, and operations. Incoterms need to be prioritized among these management decisions and brought into corporate culture, behavior, and decision-making like in any other area of importance.

Learn the Basics of Incoterms

Senior managers do not necessarily need to understand Incoterms with the same detail as mid-level managers and operational staff, but they do need to know the following:

- Incoterms impact risk and cost.
- Companies can choose options that either increase or lower risk and costs.
- Staff making these decisions need to be educated and trained, and monies need to be allocated to this endeavor.

Develop Resources for Incoterms Expertise

Senior managers need to allocate funds and internal resources such as access to CIOs and their staffs for the purpose of obtaining the wealth of information so better decisions about Incoterms and supply chain management can be made.

Understand How Incoterms Decisions Impact the Global Supply Chain and Break Down Fiefdoms

Senior managers need to budget time to interface with operational personnel and observe and scrutinize their Incoterms decisions to assure that their impacts on the global supply chain meet with long-term company objectives. An example might be just how Incoterms options that may benefit logistics choices could unfavorably impact corporate tax issues impacting P&L and balance sheet concerns. Senior management might need to break down the fiefdoms between logistics and finance to come up with compromises that meet both operational concerns and fall in line with company directives and policies. Senior managers in U.S.-based public companies are also typically charged with Sarbanes–Oxley compliance and would also incorporate Incoterms considerations in setting policy decisions in the global supply chain.

Create Integration Management into Incoterms Decision Making

Senior managers need to create a platform within a corporation that not only breaks down walls of distrust but also creates a balance of "integration" and "cooperation" between divisions, disciplines, and the various entities that operate the company's global supply chain.

Learn Leverage Options in General and Then Apply to the Specific Scenarios in Your Global Supply Chain Metrics

Senior managers need to motivate operational personnel to obtain and review and execute Incoterms decisions based upon hard-core information, data, and resources obtained from accounting, freight payment companies, consultants, transportation providers, and carriers. These metrics need to be studied hard and comprehensively, and senior managers should lead the way to decision-making that combines these data with the esoteric more "feely" data that one compiles in making the best Incoterms decisions for the company.

Establish Service Provider, Supplier, Vendor, and Other Business Relationship Communications and Standard Operating Procedures

Senior managers need to lead value proposition management with all those support companies that helps or supports the company in managing all the aspects of their import and export operations. They should stress the value of open, direct, and no-nonsense communications that favorably impact business communications between principals and their vendors/suppliers. And they should encourage the implementation of SOPs between all parties setting up lines of accountability and responsibility. This will assure compliance to best practice levels.

Integrate Technology into the Incoterms Management Process

Information technology can play a very important role in risk management, supply chain operations, and Incoterms management. Senior management needs to set direction and encourage the interface between the IT staff and those who operate the global supply chain to establish common areas of cooperation and utilization. Senior managers need to make sure that IT and supply chain know what each other has as needs and capabilities, and these two should meet somewhere to their mutual benefit. IT can play a huge role in creating tools and options for better Incoterms use that reduces risk and opens opportunity for competitive betterments.

Create Policy Guidelines for Incoterms Options and Trade Compliance Management; for Public Companies, SOX Incoterms Management Is Critical

Senior managers have to create an environment that includes trade compliance management in every Incoterms decision. While Incoterms structure includes compliance, it does so only in a peripheral way. Senior management has to set the guideline for compliance as a major factor in the company's decision-making process. For senior managers leading public companies, this is an absolute because the Incoterms choice at the lowest level of that company could have a huge impact on the financial exposures that company may face.

Engage Incoterms Lobbying to Increase and Enhance Change to Your Company's Benefit

Incoterms don't happen by default. The ICC (http://iccwbo.org) in Paris, France, through its leadership and membership, has numerous outlets for companies to exercise influence on how Incoterms are designed, structured, and eventually implemented. Delegates are lobbied by interested parties to make certain decisions that impact how Incoterms influence risk and costs in the global supply chains of the world. By engaging and joining organizations such as the ICC and the United States Council for International Business (USCIB; http://www.uscib.org) in New York, there are numerous venues, committees, and outreach for companies to lobby those who make Incoterms decisions. So participate and make a difference. The ICC has a complete listing of its member organizations and how to contact them, join in, participate, and make a favorable impact.

GOVERNMENT SECURITY PROGRAMS

Since 9/11, many countries, such as United States, Japan, Europe, Canada, and Mexico, have installed trade compliance and security initiatives for goods and people that move across their borders. This is relevant to Incoterms because the new *Incoterms 2010* specifically outline responsibilities to the seller or buyer to meet security obligations put forth by governments as part of their obligations in the transaction.

Exporters and importers who sell globally need to pay attention to these programs for a number of reasons:

- To meet obligations under their Incoterms
- To create potential advantages in their supply chain
- To assist their governments in thwarting terrorism

Some of the programs work as follows.

United States: C-TPAT*

Customs-Trade Partnership Against Terrorism (C-TPAT) is a joint program between U.S. Customs and Border Protection (CBP) and global trade

---

* From U.S. Customs and Border Protection, http://www.cbp.gov.

stakeholders. The program is designed to strengthen global supply chains and U.S. border security. The goal is to achieve the highest level of cargo security through close cooperation between CBP and businesses related to U.S. import supply chain cargo handling and movement.

C-TPAT is now 10 years old, and for those companies involved in assisting companies join the program are very aware of the greater scrutiny U.S. Customs & Border Protection (CBP) is putting on C-TPAT members as they become validated and revalidated. The C-TPAT program has remained a fluid process and has seen numerous changes in the application and validation process.

Prior to 9/11, the extent to which CBP was interested in a U.S. importer's supply chain was via the clearance process. The events of 9/11 obviously changed that, and C-TPAT has gone through many transformations over the past 10 years, as CBP realized the numerous vulnerabilities associated with the U.S. import supply chain. CBP has become aware that through the process of validation and revalidation, C-TPAT members are not conducting thorough international supply chain security assessments—or at least to the standards that CBP would like to see. While most C-TPAT members were conducting a domestic risk security analysis of their own domestic facility, CBP found that it was not doing the same for its international partners and vendors in dealing with risks in relation to its own import supply chain. This has caused concern for CBP and has created additional processes for U.S. importers to address if they want to remain in the program.

It is now highly recommended, although not required, that C-TPAT members perform an International Supply Chain Risk Assessment to discover the areas of improvement in the supply chain from point of origin to end delivery. This review becomes an integral part of their security profile. This assessment should be done once a company applies to the C-TPAT program since it is part of meeting the minimum security guidelines for joining C-TPAT. Once in the program, these assessments should be performed annually or else expulsion from C-TPAT is a risk. A strongly recommended 5 Step Risk Assessment Program will enable companies to meet these guidelines:*

---

* From U.S. Customs and Border Protection, http://www.cbp.gov.

- Mapping cargo and business partners: This involves monitoring how freight moves from your business partners throughout the supply chain from to point of origin to delivery.
- Conducting a threat assessment: Research any potential vulnerability in your supply chain that can result in potential terrorism.
- Conducting a security vulnerability assessment: Identify any potential areas from your business partners for potential security gaps using the minimum standards guidelines set up by C-TPAT.
- Preparing an action plan to address vulnerabilities: Prepare a written plan to deal with any vulnerabilities that are identified.
- Documenting how the security risk assessment is conducted: Identifying the procedures of the assessment, who will be responsible, and how often it will occur.

It is important to remember that no matter how big or small your company is, if you want to remain a member in good standing in C-TPAT you need to ensure that these risk assessments become an SOP. For an importer to go through the process of applying to the program only to be rejected—or even worse, expelled by not following these steps—is a waste of valuable resources.

Europe: AEO

European
Commission

The countries of Europe in 2005 began a program mirroring some of the principals of C-TPAT and meeting security guidelines tailored to European issues and needing an authorized economic operator (AEO).

One of the main elements of the security amendment of the Community Customs Code (Regulation (EC)648/2005) is the creation of the AEO concept.

On the basis of Article 5a of the security amendments, Member States can grant the AEO status to any economic operator meeting the following common criteria: customs compliance, appropriate record-keeping, financial solvency and, where relevant, security and safety standards.

The status of authorized economic operator granted by one Member State is recognized by the other Member States. This does not automatically allow them to benefit from simplifications provided for in the customs rules in the other Member States. However, other Member States should grant the use of simplifications to authorized economic operators if they meet specific requirements.

Economic operators can apply for an AEO status either to have easier access to customs simplifications or to be in a more favorable position to comply with the new security requirements. Under the security framework, which has been applicable since July 1, 2009, economic operators have to submit pre-arrival and pre-departure information on goods entering or leaving the EU. The security type of AEO certificate and the combined one allow their holders to benefit from facilitations with regard to the new customs controls relating to security.

The detailed provisions are laid down in the amendment (by Regulation 1875/2006) of the Implementing Provisions of the Community Customs Code. These provisions were drafted on the basis of experiences from the AEO Pilot conducted in 2006. Regulation(EC)197/2010 has established new time limits for issuing the AEO certificate

Regulation (EC) No 1192/2008 aligns the rules for granting both the AEO certificate for customs simplifications and the single authorization for simplified procedures (SASP). Being an AEO facilitates the process of achieving a single authorization for simplified procedures as the relevant criteria are deemed to be met.

AEO Guidelines

The AEO Guidelines ensure harmonized implementation of the AEO rules throughout the EU, guaranteeing the equal treatment of economic operators and transparency of the rules.

Part One of the AEO guidelines explains the AEO concept based on the adopted legislation, including:[*]

---

[*] From Authorized Economic Operator (AEO), Taxation and Customs Union, European Commission, http://ec.europa.eu/taxation_customs/customs/policy_issues/customs_security/aeo.

- Explanations about the different categories of AEO
- A specific section dedicated to Small and Medium-sized Enterprises (SME) with guidance on how to examine the AEO requirements if the applicant is an SME
- A section giving advice to customs authorities on how to speed up the authorization process
- Guidance for both customs authorities and trade on how to facilitate the procedure for parent/subsidiary companies
- A description of the AEO benefits with indications on the relevant AEO category and on the timeframe for the application of particular benefit
- A complete explanation on the concept of "business partners' security"
- An explanation, with concrete examples, for determining the competent Member State where the AEO application has to be submitted
- Guidelines for multinational companies and large businesses
- Guidance on how to perform monitoring after an AEO certificate has been issued

Part Two contains the questionnaire, providing a list of points to assist both customs authorities and AEO applicants in assessing whether or not the AEO criteria are met.

Japan

 Japan Customs

Under guidance from the World Trade Organization, Japan has also structured an AEO program. Following the 9/11 terror attacks on the United States, many countries have joined forces to combat terrorism, and C-TPAT and Container Security Initiatives (CSI), introduced by the United States, have been part of this initiative. The European Union amended the Community Customs Code and its implementing provisions in December 2006. They provide traders (AEOs) that meet the compliance criteria for cargo security with preferential customs procedures. On January 1, 2008, the provisions for the Japanese AEO program entered into force. In addition, it became mandatory for traders to provide customs authorities with advance information on goods brought into or out of the EU customs territory from July 1, 2009. AEO certified companies will be granted a streamlined approach to customs procedures, and our European subsidiaries have already applied for and are preparing for this program.

In Japan, the amended Customs Law was enacted in 2007 with the aim of revising the existing Simplified Export Declaration Procedure. This new law is the Japanese version of the AEO and offers preferential treatment to exporters who meet its high standards of compliance as well as a qualification system to obtain the preferential treatment.

Canada Partners in Protection*

Partners in Protection (PIP) is a Canada Border Services Agency (CBSA) program that enlists the cooperation of private industry to enhance border and trade chain security, combat organized crime and terrorism, and help detect and prevent contraband smuggling.

It is a voluntary program with no membership fee that aims to secure the trade chain, one partnership at a time. PIP members agree to implement and adhere to high security standards while the CBSA agrees to assess their security measures, provide information sessions on security issues and offer other benefits. Member companies are recognized as being trusted traders, which allows the CBSA to focus its resources on areas of higher or unknown risk.

Through their partnership with the CBSA, PIP members contribute to the security of the supply chain and the facilitation of legitimate trade.

---

* From Canada Border Services Agency, http://www.cbsa-asfc.gc.ca.

10

Summary

Advanced Incoterms® trade management (ITM) is a new and exciting approach to global trade for those who want to leverage supply chains and become more competitive in international trade. This approach to mastering the terms of sale and trade in global supply chains allows for companies to ultimately be more competitive.

The book has provided a very detailed outline of everything a global supply chain executive needs to know and how to apply this knowledge to leverage the decision-making process for economic benefit. Risk reduction is also a major benefit of ITM. The following summary provides some helpful hints to follow:

- Mastering Incoterms requires comprehensive knowledge of sales and purchase agreements.
- Understanding how the following factors connect to one another and play a role in Incoterms decision-making:
  - Terms of sale
  - Terms of payment
  - Freight
  - Insurance
  - Title
  - Revenue recognition
  - Packaging, marking, and labeling
  - IPR
  - Contractual disputes
- In understanding Incoterms, one needs to read the foreword, introduction, guidance notes, and the following pages after the guidance notes to totally comprehend the meanings and intents of what the ICC Governing Body is trying to convey.

- Incoterms do not complete a sale or purchase. They are only a reference or starting point to dealing with cost, risk, liability, and responsibility.
- Leveraging Incoterms requires intense knowledge and application of global trade to derive economic benefits such as free trade zones, trade compliance, managing freight forwarders, handling documentation, choosing the best carriers, creating standard operating procedures, working trade agreements, localized regulatory and cultural trade issues, logistics implications, and details of cargo insurance.
- ITM requires the support and involvement of senior management along with a concerted effort of all disciplines—for example, manufacturing, operations, legal, finance, customer service—for it to work in harmony and to everyone's benefit.
- Coordination and being sensitive to the needs, capabilities, and expectations of vendors, suppliers, channel partners, and all logistics service providers is critical to ITM.
- Learning local regulatory, cultural, and demographics of all the areas we buy from or sell to.
- Technology is a very robust element of ITM and should be used to leverage all areas of global supply chains inclusive of the best options in Incoterms.

- While all managers and operations personnel are engaged in global import and export sales, purchases and transactions need to acquire the basics of Incoterms, and a point person needs to be developed internally with a higher level of Incoterms capability.
- Resources should be established to consult when questions arise. The preceding chapters outline numerous websites and associations that provide in-depth information and expertise on Incoterms.
- Recognize that ITM is a process; there will be a learning curve, but it can be expedited through resource development, training, and an enhancement of personnel skill sets in all aspects of global supply chain management and the role Incoterms plays.

- Risk management is an important aspect of dealing with exposures in global supply chains tied directly into choosing the best Incoterms that work to avoid pitfalls and the challenges.
- Be proactive in developing an ITM or Incoterms structure before supply chain issues arise.
- Pay attention to world politics, treaties, and current events, all of which can impact business process, regulations, and circumstances and must be factored in when choosing the correct and most competitive Incoterms.
- Logistics or the movement of goods from one place to another through international borders is as much an art as it is a science. Master the skill sets of global logistics, and learn how best to apply the Incoterms to leverage the costs and to mitigate the risks.
- The ICC in Paris is a wonderful advocate and resource for global trade and all the applications of Incoterms that can help companies compete successfully in international sales and purchases.

Appendix

Trademark and Copyright Policies
Glossary
Free Trade Agreements with the United States
Ultimate Consignee
Foreign Trade Zones
U.S. Trade Terms
Institute Cargo Clauses

COPYRIGHT AND TRADEMARK POLICY

While ICC encourages third-party use of the Incoterms rules in sales contracts, it is vigilant about protecting its trademark and copyright ownership to help ensure the integrity and correct use of the rules.

TRADEMARKS

"Incoterms" and the *Incoterms 2010* logo are trademarks of the International Chamber of Commerce (ICC).

It is important to know that "Incoterms" is not a generic name for international trade terms but is a trademark used to designate the rules devised by ICC.

Correct use of the Incoterms rules goes a long way toward providing the legal certainty upon which mutual confidence between business partners must be based. To help trade practitioners use them correctly, ICC—as the originator and developer of the Incoterms rules—issues official publications and provides training on the rules.

ICC protects the name "Incoterms" and the *Incoterms 2010* logo as trademarks to help the trading community identify official and authentic ICC products and services relating to the Incoterms rules.

The rules governing the use of the "Incoterms" trademark and the *Incoterms 2010* logo should be followed when using these trademarks.

To view the communication and legal guidelines for usage of the Incoterms trademark and graphic symbols see http://www.iccbooksusa.com.

GLOSSARY*

A

AA: Always afloat; a contract term requiring that the vessel not rest on the ground. In some ports the ship is aground when approaching or at berth.

AAR: Abbreviation for against all risks (insurance clause) or Association of American Railroads.

Abaft: A point beyond the midpoint of a ship's length, toward the rear or stern.

Abandon: A proceeding wherein a shipper/consignee seeks authority to abandon all or parts of its cargo.

Abatement: A discount allowed for damage or overcharge in the payment of a bill.

ABI: U.S. Customs automated broker interface, by which brokers file importers' entries electronically.

Aboard: Referring to cargo being put, or laden, onto a means of conveyance.

Absorption: One carrier assumes the charges of another without any increase in charges to the shipper.

Acceptance: A time draft (or bill of exchange) that the drawee (payer) has accepted and is unconditionally obligated to pay at maturity. Broadly speaking, any agreement to purchase goods under specified terms.

Accessorial Charges: Charges that are applied to the base tariff rate or base contract rate, such as bunkers, container, currency, destination/delivery.

---

* Compiled from several government websites, including http://www.export.gov and http://www.marad.dot.gov.

Acquiescence: When a bill of lading is accepted or signed by a shipper or shipper's agent without protest, the shipper is said to acquiesce to the terms, giving a silent form of consent.

Acquittance: A written receipt in full, in discharge from all claims.

ACS (A.C.S.) or ACE: U.S. Customs master computer system automated commercial systems. Now being replaced by the automated commercial environment system.

Act of God: An act beyond human control, such as lightning, flood, or earthquake.

Ad Valorem: A term from Latin meaning "according to value." Import duty applied as a percentage of the cargo's dutiable value.

Administrative Law Judge: A representative of a government commission or agency vested with power to administer oaths, examine witnesses, take testimony, and conduct hearings of cases submitted to, or initiated by, that agency. Also called hearing examiner.

Admiralty (Adm.): Refers to marine matters such as an Admiralty Court.

Advance: To move cargo up-line to a vessel leaving sooner than the one booked. *See also Roll.*

Advanced Charge: Transportation charge advanced by one carrier to another to be collected by the later carrier from the consignor or consignee.

Advanced Notice of Arrival (ANOA): Any vessel entering U.S. waters from a foreign port is required to give a 96-hour ANOA. Any vessel of 300 gross registered tonnage and greater is required to give the ANOA to the U.S. Coast Guard's National Vessel Movement Center. Any vessel under 300 gross registered tons is required to give the ANOA to the appropriate captain of the port.

Adventure: Shipment of goods on shipper's own account. A bill of adventure is a document signed by the master of the ship that carries goods at owner's risk. Also a term used in some insurance policies to mean a voyage or a shipment.

Advice of Shipment: A notice sent to a local or foreign buyer advising that shipment has gone forward and containing details of packing, routing, etc. A copy of the invoice is often enclosed and, if desired, a copy of the bill of lading.

Advising Bank: A bank operating in the seller's country that handles letters of credit on behalf of a foreign bank.

AES: U.S. Automated Export System for reporting shipments to the Census Bureau as a requirement for exports from the United States.

Aframax Tanker: A vessel of 70,000 to 119,000 DWT capacity. The largest tanker size in the average freight rate assessment (AFRA) tanker rate system.

Affreightment, Contract of: An agreement by an ocean carrier to provide cargo space on a vessel at a specified time and for a specified price to accommodate an exporter or importer.

Aft: Movement toward the stern (back end) of a ship.

Agency Tariff: A tariff published by an agent on behalf of several carriers.

Agent (Agt.): A person authorized to transact business for and in the name of another person or company. Types of agents are (1) brokers, (2) commission merchants, (3) resident buyers, (4) sales agents, and (5) manufacturer's representatives.

Aggregate Shipment: Numerous shipments from different shippers to one consignee that are consolidated and treated as a single consignment.

Agreed Valuation: The value of a shipment agreed upon to secure a specific freight rate.

Agreed Weight: The weight prescribed by agreement between carrier and shipper for goods shipped in certain packages or in a certain number.

AID: Agency for International Development.

Air Waybill: The forwarding agreement or carrying agreement between shipper and air carrier and is issued only in nonnegotiable form.

All Risk: A form of cargo insurance providing the broadest terms and conditions such as covered under Institute Cargo Clauses A.

All In: The total price to move cargo from origin to destination, inclusive of all charges.

Allowance: In-shipping tolerances allowed for in-weight or measure.

Allision: The striking by a moving vessel against a stationary object.

Alongside: The side of a ship. Goods delivered alongside are to be placed on the dock or barge within reach of the transport ship's tackle so that they can be loaded.

Alternative Rates: Privilege to use the rate producing the lowest charge.

Ambient Temperature: The temperature of a surrounding body. The ambient temperature of a container is the atmospheric temperature to which it is exposed.

American Bureau of Shipping: U.S. classification society that certifies seagoing vessels for compliance to standardized rules regarding construction and maintenance.

AMS: U.S. Customs Automated Manifest System.

Anti-Dumping Duty: A tariff imposed to discourage sale of foreign goods, subsidized to sell at low prices detrimental to local manufacturers.

Any Quantity (AQ): Usually refers to a rating that applies to an article regardless of size or quantity.

Apparent Good Order: When freight appears to be free of damage so far as a general survey can determine.

Appraisement: Determination of the dutiable value of imported merchandise by a customs official who follows procedures outlined in his or her country's tariff, such as the U.S. Tariff Act of 1930.

Appraiser's Stores: The warehouse or public stores to which samples of imported goods are taken to be inspected, analyzed, weighed, etc., by examiners or appraisers.

AQUIS: Australian Quarantine and Inspection Service

Arbitrary: A stated amount over a fixed rate to one point to make a rate to another point.

Arrival Notice: A notification by carrier of ship's arrival to the consignee, the "Notify Party," and when applicable the "Also Notify Party." These parties in interest are listed in blocks 3, 4 and 10, respectively, of the bill of lading.

ASC X12: American Standards Committee X12 responsible for developing EDI standards for the United States.

Assignment: A term commonly used in connection with a bill of lading. It involves the transfer of rights, title, and interest to assign goods by endorsing the bill of lading.

Astern: Behind a vessel or moving in a reverse direction.

ATA: American Trucking Association.

ATDNSHINC: Anytime day or night Sundays and holidays included. A chartering term referring to when a vessel will work.

Athwartships: A direction across the width of a vessel.

Automated Identification System (AIS): Used by ships and Vessel Traffic Service (VTS) principally to identify and locate vessels. Provides a means for ships to electronically exchange ship data including identification, position, course, and speed with other nearby ships and VTS stations.

Average: *See Insurance.*

Avoirdupois Pound: Equal to 0.4535924277 kilograms.

AWWL: Always within institute warranties limits (insurance purpose).

B

BB: Ballast bonus, or special payment above the chartering price when the ship has to sail a long way on ballast to reach the loading port. Also bareboat, or method of chartering of the ship leaving the charterer with almost all the owner's responsibilities.

Backhaul: To haul a shipment back over part of a route it has traveled.

BAF: Bunker adjustment factor. Used to compensate steamship lines for fluctuating fuel costs. Sometimes called fuel adjustment factor (FAF).

Balloon Freight: Light, bulky articles.

Bank Guarantee: Guarantee issued by a bank to a carrier to be used in lieu of lost or misplaced original negotiable bill of lading.

Barratry: An act committed by the master or mariners of a vessel, for some unlawful or fraudulent purpose, contrary to their duty to the owners, whereby the latter sustain injury. It may include negligence, if so gross as to evidence fraud.

Barrel (BBL): A term of measure referring to 42 gallons of liquid at 600 degrees.

Base Rate: A tariff term referring to ocean rate less accessorial charges, or simply the base tariff rate.

BCO: Beneficial cargo owner. Refers to the importer of record, who physically takes possession of cargo at destination and does not act as a third party in the movement of such goods.

Beam: The width of a ship.

Belt Line: A switching railroad operating within a commercial area.

Beneficiary: Entity to whom money is payable and for whom a letter of credit is issued. The seller and the drawer of a draft.

Berth Terms: Shipped-under rate that includes cost from end of ship's tackle at load port to end of ship's tackle at discharge port.

Beyond: Charges assessed for cargo movement past a line–haul terminating point.

Bilateral: A contract term meaning both parties agree to provide something for the other.

Bill of Exchange: Also commonly known as a draft in the United States.

Bill of Lading (B/L): A document that establishes the terms of a contract between a shipper and a transportation company. It serves as a document of title, a contract of carriage, and a receipt for goods.

- Amended B/L: Requires updates that do not change financial status; this is slightly different from corrected B/L.
- B/L terms and conditions: The fine print; defines what the carrier can and cannot do, including the carrier's liabilities and contractual agreements.
- B/L status: Whether the bill of lading has been input, rated, reconciled, printed, or released to the customer.
- B/L type: For example, a memo (ME), original (OBL), non-negotiable, corrected (CBL), or amended (AM) B/L.
- Canceled B/L: B/L status; used to cancel a processed B/L; usually per shipper's request; different from voided B/L.
- Clean B/L: Bears no superimposed clause or notation that declares a defective condition of the goods or the packaging.
- Combined B/L: Covers cargo moving over various transports.
- Consolidated B/L: Combined or consolidated from two or more B/Ls.
- Corrected B/L: Requires any update that results in money or other financially related changes.
- Domestic B/L: Nonnegotiable; primarily contains routing details; usually used by truckers and freight forwarders.
- Duplicate B/L: Another original bill of lading set if first set is lost. Also known as reissued B/L.
- Express B/L: Nonnegotiable; there are no paper copies printed of originals.
- Freight B/L: A contract of carriage between a shipper and forwarder (who is usually a NVOCC); nonnegotiable.
- Government B/L (GBL): A bill of lading issued by the U.S. government.
- Hitchment B/L: Covers parts of a shipment that are loaded at more than one location. Usually consists of two parts: hitchment and hitchment memo. The hitchment portion usually covers the majority of a divided shipment and carries the entire revenue.
- House B/L: Issued by a freight forwarder or consolidator covering a single shipment with the names, addresses and specific description of the goods shipped.

- Intermodal B/L: Covers cargo moving via multimodal means. Also known as combined transport B/L or multimodal B/L.
- Long-form B/L: Contains all terms and conditions written on it. Most B/Ls are short form, which incorporate the long form clauses by reference.
- Memo B/L: Unfreighted; lists no charges.
- Military B/L: Issued by the U.S. military; also known as GBL, or Form DD1252.
- B/L numbers: U.S. Customs standardized B/L numbering format to facilitate electronic communications and to make each B/L number unique.
- Negotiable B/L: A title document to the goods, issued "to the order of" a party, usually the shipper, whose endorsement is required to effect is negotiation. Thus, a shipper's order (negotiable) B/L can be bought, sold, or traded while goods are in transit and is commonly used for letter-of-credit transactions. The buyer must submit the original B/L to the carrier to take possession of the goods.
- Nonnegotiable B/L: See straight B/L. Sometimes means a file copy of a B/L.
- On-board B/L: Validated at the time of loading to transport. Onboard air, boxcar, container, rail, truck, and vessel are the most common types.
- Optional discharge B/L: Covers cargo with more than one discharge point option possibility.
- Order B/L: See negotiable B/L.
- Original B/L (OBL): The part of the B/L set that has value, especially when negotiable; rest are only informational file copies.
- Received for Shipment B/L: Validated at time cargo is received by ocean carrier to commence movement but before being validated as on-board.
- Reconciled B/L: Has completed a prescribed number of edits between the shipper's instructions and the actual shipment received, which makes it very accurate.
- Short-term B/L: Opposite of long-form B/L; does not list terms and conditions. Also known as a Short Form B/L. The terms are incorporated by reference to the long form B/L.

- Split B/L: One of two or more B/L's which have been split from a single B/L.
- Stale B/L: A late B/L; in banking, a B/L which has passed the time deadline of the Letter of Credit (L/C) and is void.
- Straight (Consignment) B/L: Indicates the shipper will deliver the goods to the consignee. It does not convey title (nonnegotiable). Most often used when the goods have been prepaid.
- To-order B/L: See negotiable B/L.
- Unique B/L identifier: U.S. Customs standardization: four-alpha code unique to each carrier placed in front of nine digit B/L number; APL's unique B/L Identifier is "APLU." Sea–land uses "SEAU." These prefixes are also used as the container identification.
- Voided B/L: Related to consolidated B/L; those B/Ls absorbed in the combining process. Different from canceled B/L.

Bill of Lading Port of Discharge: Port where cargo is discharged from means of transport.

Bill of Sale: Confirms the transfer of ownership of certain goods to another person in return for money paid or loaned.

Bill to Party: Customer designated as party paying for services.

Billed Weight: The weight shown in a waybill and freight bill, i.e., the invoiced weight.

BIMCO: The Baltic and International Maritime Council, the world's largest private shipping organization.

Blanket Bond: A bond covering a group of persons, articles, or properties.

Blanket Rate: A rate applicable to or from a group of points; a special rate applicable to several different articles in a single shipment.

Blanket Waybill: A waybill covering two or more consignments of freight.

Blind Shipment: A B/L wherein the paying customer has contracted with the carrier that shipper or consignee information is not given.

Block Stowage: Stowing cargo destined for a specific location close together to avoid unnecessary cargo movement.

Blocked Trains: Railcars grouped in a train by destination so that segments (blocks) can be uncoupled and routed to different destinations as the train moves through various junctions. Eliminates the need to break up a train and sort individual railcars at each junction.

Blocking or Bracing: Wood or metal supports to keep shipments in place to prevent cargo shifting. *See also Dunnage.*

Bls.: Bales.

Board: To gain access to a vessel.

Board Feet: The basic unit of measurement for lumber. One board foot is equal to a 1-inch board, 12 inches wide and 1 foot long. Thus, a board 10 feet long, 12 inches wide, and 1 inch thick contains 10 board feet.

Boat: A relatively small, usually open craft/vessel a small, often open vessel for traveling on water An inland vessel of any size.

Bobtail: Movement of a tractor, without trailer, over the highway.

Bogie: A set of wheels built specifically as rear wheels under the container.

Bolster: A device fitted on a chassis or railcar to hold and secure the container.

Bond: In international trade the security posted with customs to allow freight access to that market.

Bond Port: Port of initial customs entry of a vessel to any country. Also known as first port of call.

Bonded Freight: Freight moving under a bond to U.S. Customs or to the Internal Revenue Service, to be delivered only under stated conditions.

Bonded Warehouse: A warehouse authorized by customs authorities for storage of goods on which payment of duties is deferred until the goods are removed.

Booking: Arrangements with a carrier for the acceptance and carriage of freight, i.e., a space reservation.

Booking Number: Reservation number used to secure equipment and act as a control number prior to completion of a B/L.

Bottom Side Rails: Structural members on the longitudinal sides of the base of the container.

Bottom-Air Delivery: A type of air circulation in a temperature control container. Air is pulled by a fan from the top of the container, passed through the evaporator coil for cooling, and then forced through the space under the load and up through the cargo. This type of airflow provides even temperatures.

Bow: The front of a vessel.

Boxcar: A closed rail freight car.

Break Bulk: To unload and distribute a portion or all of the contents of a rail car, container, trailer, or ship. Loose, noncontainerized mark and count cargo. Packaged cargo that is not containerized.

Bridge Point: An inland location where cargo is received by the ocean carrier and then moved to a coastal port for loading.

Bridge Port: A port where cargo is received by the ocean carrier and stuffed into containers but then moved to another coastal port to be waded on a vessel.

Broken Stowage: The loss of space caused by irregularity in the shape of packages. Any void or empty space in a vessel or container not occupied by cargo.

Broker: A person who arranges for transportation of loads for a percentage of the revenue from the load.

Brokerage: Freight forwarder/broker compensation as specified by ocean tariff or contract.

Bulk Cargo: Not in packages or containers; shipped loose in the hold of a ship without mark and count. Grain, coal, and sulfur are usually bulk freight.

Bulk-Freight Container: A container with a discharge hatch in the front wall; allows bulk commodities to be carried.

Bulkhead: A partition separating one part of a ship, freight car, aircraft, or truck from another part.

Bull Rings: Cargo-securing devices mounted in the floor of containers; allow lashing and securing of cargo.

Bunker Charge: An extra charge sometimes added to steamship freight rates; justified by higher fuel costs. Also known as fuel adjustment factor (FAF).

Bunkers: A maritime term referring to fuel used aboard the ship. In the past, fuel coal stowage areas aboard a vessel were in bins or bunkers.

Bureau Veritas: A French classification society that certifies seagoing vessels for compliance to standardized rules regarding construction and maintenance.

C

C&F Terms of Sale, or Incoterms: Obsolete, although heavily used, term of sale meaning "cargo and freight" whereby Seller pays for cost of goods and freight charges up to destination port. In July 1990 the International Chamber of Commerce replaced C&F with CFR.

Cabotage: Water transportation term applicable to shipments between ports of a nation; commonly refers to coastwise or intercoastal navigation or trade. Many nations, including the United States, have cabotage laws which require national flag vessels to provide domestic interport service.

CAF: Abbreviation for "Currency Adjustment Factor." A charge, expressed as a percentage of a base rate, that is applied to compensate ocean carriers of currency fluctuations.

Capesize Vessel: A dry bulk vessel above 80,000 dwt or whose beam precludes passage via the Panama Canal and thus forces them to pass around Cape Horn or the Cape of Good Hope.

Captain's Protest: A document prepared by the captain of a vessel on arriving at port; shows conditions encountered during voyage, generally for the purpose of relieving ship owner of any loss to cargo and shifting responsibility for reimbursement to the insurance company.

Car Pooling: Use of individual carrier/rail equipment through a central agency for the benefit of carriers and shippers.

Car Seal: Metal strip and lead fastener used for locking freight car or truck doors. Seals are numbered for record purposes.

Carfloat: A barge equipped with tracks on which up to approximately 12 railroad cars are moved in harbors or inland waterways.

Cargo: Freight loaded into a ship.

Cargo Manifest: A manifest that lists all cargo carried on a specific vessel voyage.

Cargo NOS: Cargo Not Otherwise Specified. Usually the rate entry in a tariff that can apply to commodities not covered under a specific item or sub-item in the applicable tariff.

Cargo Preference: Cargo reserved by a nation's laws for transportation only on vessels registered in that nation. Typically the cargo is moving due to a direct or indirect support or activity of the government.

Cargo Tonnage: Most ocean freight is billed on the basis of weight or measurement tons (W/M). Weight tons can be expressed in short tons of 2,000 pounds, long tons of 2,240 pounds or metric tons of 1,000 kilos (2,204.62 pounds). Measurement tons are usually expressed as cargo measurement of 40 cubic feet (1.12 meters) or cubic meters (35.3 cubic feet.)

Carload Rate: A rate applicable to a carload of goods.

Carnet: A customs document permitting the holder to temporarily carry or send merchandise into certain foreign countries (for display, demonstration or similar purposes) without paying duties or posting bonds. Any of various Customs documents required for crossing some international borders.

Carrier: Any person or entity who, in a contract of carriage, undertakes to perform or to procure the performance of carriage by rail, road, sea, air, inland waterway or by a combination of such modes.

Carrier's Certificate: A certificate required by U.S. Customs to release cargo properly to the correct party.

Cartage: Usually refers to intra-city hauling on drays or trucks. Same as drayage.

Cartment: Customs form permitting in-bond cargo to be moved from one location to another under Customs control, within the same Customs district. Usually in motor carrier's possession while draying cargo.

Cash Against Documents (CAD): Method of payment for goods in which documents transferring title are given the buyer upon payment of cash to an intermediary acting for the seller, usually a commission house.

Cash in Advance (CIA): A method of payment for goods in which the buyer pays the seller in advance of the shipment of goods. Usually employed when the goods, such as specialized machinery, are built to order.

Cash With Order (CWO): A method of payment for goods in which cash is paid at the time of order and the transaction becomes binding on both buyer and seller.

CBM (CM): Abbreviation for "Cubic Meter."

CE: Abbreviation for "Consumption Entry." The process of declaring the importation of foreign-made goods for use in the United States.

Cells: The construction system employed in container vessels; permits ship containers to be stowed in a vertical line with each container supporting the one above it

Center of Gravity: The point of equilibrium of the total weight of a containership, truck, train or a piece of cargo.

Certificate of Inspection:

- A document certifying that merchandise (such as perishable goods) was in good condition immediately prior to its shipment.
- The document issued by the U.S. Coast Guard certifying an American
- Flag vessel's compliance with applicable laws and regulations.

Certificate of Origin: A certified document showing the origin of goods; used in international commerce.

CFS: Abbreviation for "Container Freight Station." A shipping dock where cargo is loaded ("stuffed") into or unloaded ("stripped") from containers. Generally, this involves less than container load shipments, although small shipments destined to same consignee are often consolidated. Container reloading from/to rail or motor carrier equipment is a typical activity. These facilities can be located in container yards, or off dock.

Charter Party: A written contract between the owner of a vessel and the person desiring to employ the vessel (charterer); sets forth the terms of the arrangement, such as duration of agreement, freight rate, and ports involved in the trip.

Chassis: A frame with wheels and container locking devices in order to secure the container for movement.

Chock: A piece of wood or other material placed at the side of cargo to prevent rolling or moving sideways.

CCC Mark: A mark or label indicating the cargo conforms to standards required by China for certain products.

CE Mark: A mark or label indicating the cargo conforms to standards required by the European Union for certain products.

CI: Abbreviation for "Cost and Insurance." A price that includes the cost of the goods, the marine insurance, and all transportation charges except the ocean freight to the named point of destination.

CIF (Named Port): Abbreviation for "Cost, Insurance, Freight." (Named Port) Same as C&F or CFR except seller also provides insurance to named destination.

CIF&C: Price includes commission as well as CIF.

CIF&E: Abbreviation for "Cost, Insurance, Freight and Exchange."

CIFCI: Abbreviation for "Cost, Insurance, Freight, Collection and Interest."

CIFI&E: Abbreviation for "Cost, Insurance, Freight, Interest and Exchange."

CKD: Abbreviation for "Completely Knocked Down." Parts and sub-assemblies being transported to an assembly plant.

CL: Abbreviation for "Carload" and "Containerload."

Claim: A demand made upon a transportation line for payment on account of a loss sustained through its alleged negligence.

Classification: A publication, such as Uniform Freight Classification (railroad) or the National Motor Freight Classification (motor carrier), that assigns ratings to various articles and provides bill of lading descriptions and rules.

Classification Rating: The designation provided in a classification by which a class rate is determined.

Classification Society: An organization maintained for the surveying and classing of ships so that insurance underwriters and others may know the quality and condition of the vessels offered for insurance or employment. *See also ABS, BV, DNV, LR, and NK.*

Classification Yard: A railroad yard with many tracks used for assembling freight trains.

Clayton Act: An anti-trust act of the U.S. Congress making price discrimination unlawful.

Clean Bill of Lading: A receipt for goods issued by a carrier with an indication that the goods were received in "apparent good order and condition," without damage or other irregularities. If no notation or exception is made, the B/L is assumed to be "cleaned."

Cleaning in Transit: The stopping of articles, such as peanuts, etc., for cleaning at a point between the point of origin and destination.

Clearance Limits: The size beyond which cars or loads cannot use bridges, tunnels, etc.

Cleat: A strip of wood or metal used to afford additional strength, to prevent warping, or to hold in place.

Clip-On: Refrigeration equipment attachable to an insulated container that does not have its own refrigeration unit.

CM: Abbreviation for "Cubic Meter" (capital letters).

cm: Abbreviation for "centimeter."

Coastwise: Water transportation along the coast.

COD: Abbreviation for
- collect (cash) on Delivery.
- carried on Docket (pricing).

COFC: Abbreviation for the Railway Service "Container On Flat Car."

COGSA: Carriage of Goods by Sea Act. U.S. federal codification passed in 1936 which standardizes carrier's liability under carrier's bill of lading. U.S. enactment of The Hague Rules.

Collecting: A bank that acts as an agent to the seller's bank (the presenting bank). The collecting bank assumes no responsibility for either the documents or the merchandise.

Collection: A draft drawn on the buyer, usually accompanied by documents, with complete instructions concerning processing for payment or acceptance.

Combination Export Mgr.: A firm that acts as an export sales agent for more than one non-competing manufacturer.

Combination Rate: A rate made up of two or more factors, separately published.

Commercial Invoice: Represents a complete record of the transaction between exporter and importer with regard to the goods sold. Also reports the content of the shipment and serves as the basis for all other documents relating to the shipment.

Commercial Transport Vessel: Any ship which is used primarily in commerce

- for transporting persons or goods to or from any harbor(s) or port(s) or between places within a harbor area;
- in connection with the construction, change in construction, servicing, maintenance, repair, loading, unloading, movement, piloting, or salvaging of any other ship or vessel.

Commodity: Article shipped. For dangerous and hazardous cargo, the correct commodity identification is critical.

Commodity Rate: A rate published to apply to a specific article or articles.

Common Carrier: A transportation company which provides service to the general public at published rates.

Common Law: Law that derives its force and authority from precedent, custom and usage rather than from statutes, particularly with reference to the laws of England and the United States.

Company Security Officer: Is the person designated by the company for ensuring that a ship security assessment is carried out and that a ship security plan is developed, submitted for approval, and thereafter implemented and maintained for liaison with port facility security officers and the ship security officer.

Compulsory Ship: Any ship which is required to be equipped with radio telecommunication equipment in order to comply with the radio or radio-navigation provisions of a treaty or statute to which the vessel is subject.

Concealed Damage: Damage that is not evident from viewing the unopened package.

Conference: An association of ship owners operating in the same trade route who operate under collective conditions and agree on tariff rates.

Confirmed Letter of Credit: A letter of credit, issued by a foreign bank, whose validity has been confirmed by a domestic bank. An exporter with a confirmed letter of credit is assured of payment even if the foreign buyer or the foreign bank defaults.

Confirming Bank: The bank that adds its confirmation to another bank's (the issuing bank's) letter of credit and promises to pay the beneficiary upon presentation of documents specified in the letter of credit.

Connecting Carrier: A carrier which has a direct physical connection with, or forms a link between two or more carriers.

Consignee: A person or company to whom commodities are shipped.

Consignee Mark: A symbol placed on packages for identification purposes; generally a triangle, square, circle, etc., with letters and/or numbers and port of discharge.

Consignment: (1) A stock of merchandise advanced to a dealer and located at his place of business, but with title remaining in the source of supply. (2) A shipment of goods to a consignee.

Consignor: A person or company shown on the bill of lading as the shipper.

Connecting Carrier Agreement: A connecting carrier agreement is a contract between the originating carrier and a second party, where the second party agrees to carry goods to a final destination on a through Bill of Lading.

Consolidation: Cargo containing shipments of two or more shippers or suppliers. Container load shipments may be consolidated for one or more consignees, often in container load quantities.

Consolidator: A person or firm performing a consolidation service for others. The consolidator takes advantage of lower full carload (FCL) rates, and passes on the savings to shippers.

Construction Differential Subsidy: A program whereby the U.S. government attempted to offset the higher shipbuilding cost in the U.S. by paying up to 50% of the difference between cost of U.S. and non-U.S. construction. The difference went to the U.S. shipyard. It is unfunded since 1982.

Consul: A government official residing in a foreign country who represents the interests of her or his country and its nationals.

Consular Declaration: A formal statement describing goods to be shipped; filed with and approved by the consul of the country of destination prior to shipment.

Consular Invoice: A document, certified by a consular official, is required by some countries to describe a shipment. Used by Customs of the foreign country, to verify the value, quantity and nature of the cargo.

Consular Visa: An official signature or seal affixed to certain documents by the consul of the country of destination.

Consumption Entry (CE): The process of declaring the importation of foreign-made goods into the United States for use in the United States.

Container: A truck trailer body that can be detached from the chassis for loading into a vessel, a rail car or stacked in a container depot. Containers may be ventilated, insulated, refrigerated, flat rack, vehicle rack, open top, bulk liquid or equipped with interior devices. A container may be 20 feet, 40 feet, 45 feet, 48 feet or 53 feet in length, 8′0″ or 8′6″ in width, and 8′6″ or 9′6″ in height.

Container Booking: Arrangements with a steamship line to transport containerized cargo.

Container Freight Station: *See CFS.*

Container Manifest: Document showing contents and loading sequence, point of origin, and point of destination for a container. Vessels are required by law to carry such a document for each container carried.

Container Pool: An agreement between parties that allows the efficient use and supply of containers. A common supply of containers available to the shipper as required.

Container Security Initiative (CSI): A U.S. cargo security program whereby containerized cargoes destined for the United States may be inspected on a selective basis at many foreign ports before loading on a vessel. As of October 2007, there were 51 approved ports. A multinational program, aligned with the President's "Strategy for Homeland Security," that extends the United States' zone of security by pre-screening containers that pose a potential security risk before they leave foreign ports for U.S. seaports.

Container Terminal: An area designated for the stowage of cargoes in container; usually accessible by truck, railroad, and marine transportation. Here containers are picked up, dropped off, maintained, and housed.

Container Yard (CY): A materials-handling/storage facility used for completely unitized loads in containers and/or empty containers. Commonly referred to as CY.

Containerizable Cargo: Cargo that will fit into a container and result in an economical shipment.

Containerization: Stowage of general or special cargoes in a container for transport in the various modes.

Container Load: A load sufficient in size to fill a container either by cubic measurement or by weight.

Contingency Cargo Insurance (Unpaid Vendor): A form of cargo insurance to protect a party not responsible to insure a shipment but has potential financial exposure in the transaction.

Contraband: Cargo that is prohibited.

Contract: A legally binding agreement between two or more persons/organizations to carry out reciprocal obligations or value.

Contract Carrier: Any person not a common carrier who, under special and individual contracts or agreements, transports passengers or property for compensation.

Controlled Atmosphere: Sophisticated, computer-controlled systems that manage the mixtures of gases within a container throughout an intermodal journey reducing decay.

Corner Posts: Vertical frame components fitted at the corners of the container, integral to the corner fittings and connecting the roof and floor structures. Containers are lifted and secured in a stack using the castings at the ends.

Correspondent Bank: A bank that, in its own country, handles the business of a foreign bank.

Cost, Insurance and Freight (CIF): Cost of goods, marine insurance, and all transportation (freight) charges are paid to the foreign point of delivery by the seller.

Countervailing Duty: An additional duty imposed to offset export grants, bounties, or subsidies paid to foreign suppliers in certain countries by the government of that country for the purpose of promoting export.

Cross Member: Transverse members fitted to the bottom side rails of a container, which support the floor.

C–TPAT (Customs–Trade Partnership Against Terrorism): A voluntary supply chain security partnership established by U.S. Customs and Border Protection in November 2001. Meeting the C–TPAT standards allows cargo owners faster processing through customs formalities and inspections.

Cu.: An abbreviation for "Cubic." A unit of volume measurement.

Cube Out: When a container or vessel has reached its volumetric capacity before its permitted weight limit.

Cubic Foot: 1,728 cubic inches. A volume contained in a space measuring one foot high, one foot wide, and one foot long.

Customhouse: A government office where duties are paid, import documents filed, etc., on foreign shipments.

Customhouse Broker: A person or firm, licensed by the treasury department of their country when required, engaged in entering and clearing goods through Customs for a client (importer).

Customs: Government agency charged with enforcing the rules passed to protect the country's import and export revenues.

Customs Bonded Warehouse: A warehouse authorized by Customs to receive duty-free merchandise.

Customs Entry: All countries require that the importer make a declaration on incoming foreign goods. The importer then normally pays a duty on the imported merchandise. The importer's statement is compared against the carrier's vessel manifest to ensure that all foreign goods are properly declared.

Customs Invoice: A form requiring all data in a commercial invoice along with a certificate of value and/or a certificate of origin. Required in a few countries (usually former British territories) and usually serves as a seller's commercial invoice.

Customs of the Port (COP): A phrase often included in charter parties and freight contracts referring to local rules and practices which may impact upon the costs borne by the various parties.

Customs–Trade Partnership Against Terrorism (C–TPAT): It is a voluntary supply chain security program, launched in November 2001 and led by U.S. Customs and Border Protection (CBP) which focuses on improving the security of private companies' supply chains with respect to terrorism. In exchange for companies participation CBP will provide reduced inspections at the port of arrival, expedited processing at the border and penalty mitigation.

Cut-Off Time: The latest time cargo may be delivered to a terminal for loading to a scheduled train or ship.

Cwt.: Hundred weight (United States, 100 pounds; U.K., 112).

CY: Abbreviation for:

- Container Yard.
- The designation for full container receipt/delivery.

D

D&H: Abbreviation for "Dangerous and Hazardous" cargo.

D.B.A.: Abbreviation for "Doing Business As." A legal term for conducting business under a registered name.

DDC: Abbreviation for "Destination Delivery Charge." A charge, based on container size that is applied in many tariffs to cargo. This charge is considered accessorial and is added to the base ocean freight. This charge covers crane lifts off the vessel, drayage of the container within the terminal and gate fees at the terminal operation.

Deadhead: One leg of a move without a paying cargo load. Usually refers to repositioning an empty piece of equipment.

Deadweight Cargo: A long ton of cargo that can be stowed in less than 40 cubic feet.

Deadweight Tonnage (DWT): The number of tons of 2,240 pounds that a vessel can transport of cargo, stores and bunker fuel. It is the difference between the number of tons of water a vessel displaces "light" and the number of tons it displaces when submerged to the "load line." An approximate conversion ratio is 1NT = 1.7GT and 1GT = 1.5DWT.

Deconsolidation Point: Place where loose or other non-containerized cargo is ungrouped for delivery.

Deficit Weight: The weight by which a shipment is less than the minimum weight.

Delivery Instructions: Order to pick up goods at a named place and deliver them to a pier. Usually issued by exporter to trucker but may apply to a railroad, which completes delivery by land. Use is limited to a few major U.S. ports. Also known as shipping delivery order.

DEMDES: Demurrage/Despatch money. (Under vessel chartering terms, the amount to be paid if the ship is loading/discharging slower/faster than foreseen.)

Demurrage: A penalty charge against shippers or consignees for delaying the carrier's equipment or vessel beyond the allowed free time. The free time and demurrage charges are set forth in the charter party or freight tariff. *See also Detention and Per Diem.*

Density: The weight of cargo per cubic foot or other unit.

Depot, Container: Container freight station or a designated area where empty containers can be picked up or dropped off.

Despatch: An incentive payment paid by the vessel to the charterer for loading and unloading the cargo faster than agreed. Usually negotiated only in charter parties. Also called "dispatch."

Destination: The place to which a shipment is consigned. The place where carrier actually turns over cargo to consignee or his agent.

Destination Control Statements: Various statements that the U.S. government requires to be displayed on export shipments. The statements specify the authorized destinations.

Det Norske Veritas: A Norwegian classification society which certifies seagoing vessels for compliance to standardized rules regarding construction and maintenance.

Detention: A penalty charge against shippers or consignees for delaying carrier's equipment beyond allowed time. Demurrage applies to cargo; detention applies to equipment. *See Per Diem.*

Devanning: The unloading of a container or cargo van.

DF Car: Damage-Free Car. Boxcars equipped with special bracing material.

Differential: An amount added or deducted from base rate to make a rate to or from some other point or via another route.

Discrepancy Letter of Credit: When documents presented do not conform to the requirements of the letter of credit (L/C), it is referred to as a "discrepancy." Banks will not process L/C's which have discrepancies. They will refer the situation back to the buyer and/or seller and await further instructions.

Dispatch: *See Despatch.*

Displacement: The weight, in tons of 2,240 pounds, of the vessel and its contents. Calculated by dividing the volume of water displaced in cubic feet by 35, the average density of sea water.

Diversion: A change made either in the route of a shipment in transit (see Reconsignment) or of the entire ship.

Division: Carriers' practice of dividing revenue received from rates where joint hauls are involved. This is usually according to agreed formulae.

Dock: For ships, a cargo handling area parallel to the shoreline where a vessel normally ties up. For land transportation, a loading or unloading platform at an industrial location or carrier terminal.

Dock Receipt: A form used to acknowledge receipt of cargo and often serves as basis for preparation of the ocean bill of lading.

Dockage: Refers to the charge assessed against the vessel for berthing at the facility or for morring to a vessel so berthed.

Docket: Present a rate proposal to a conference meeting for adoption as a conference group rate.

Documents Against Acceptance (D/A): Instructions given by a shipper to a bank indicating that documents transferring title to goods should be delivered to the buyer only upon the buyer's acceptance of the attached draft.

Documents Against Payment (D/P): An indication on a draft that the documents attached are to be released to the drawee only on payment.

Dolly: A set of wheels that support the front of a container; used when the automotive unit is disconnected.

Door-to-Door: Through transportation of a container and its contents from consignor to consignee. Also known as House to House. Not necessarily a through rate.

D.O.T.: U.S. Department of Transportation. The executive branch department that coordinates and oversees transportation functions in the United States.

Draft:

- The number of feet that the hull of a ship is beneath the surface of the water.
- An unconditional order in writing, addressed by one party (drawer) to another party (drawee), requiring the drawee to pay at a fixed or determinable future date a specified sum in lawful currency to the order of a specified person.

Draft, Bank: An order issued by a seller against a purchaser; directs payment, usually through an intermediary bank. Typical bank drafts are negotiable instruments and are similar in many ways to checks on checking accounts in a bank.

Draft, Clean: A draft to which no documents are attached.

Draft, Date: A draft that matures on a fixed date, regardless of the time of acceptance.

Draft, Discounted: A time draft under a letter of credit that has been accepted and purchased by a bank at a discount.

Draft, Sight: A draft payable on demand upon presentation.

Draft, Time: A draft that matures at a fixed or determinable time after presentation or acceptance.

Drawback: A partial refund of an import fee. Refund usually results because goods are re-exported from the country that collected the fee.

Drawee: The individual or firm that issues a draft and thus stands to receive payment.

Drayage: Charge made for local hauling by dray or truck. Same as Cartage.

DRFS: Abbreviation for "Destination Rail Freight Station." Same as CFS at destination, except a DRFS is operated by the rail carrier participating in the shipment.

DSU: Delay in Startup Insurance is a policy to protect the seller of a construction project from penalties if the project is not completed on time. See "Liquidated Damages."

Dry Cargo: Cargo that is not liquid and normally does not require temperature control.

Dry-Bulk Container: A container constructed to carry grain, powder, and other free-flowing solids in bulk. Used in conjunction with a tilt chassis or platform.

Dumping: Attempting to import merchandise into a country at a price less than the fair market value, usually through subsidy by exporting country.

Dunnage: Any material or objects utilized to protect cargo. Examples of dunnage are blocks, boards, burlap and paper.

Duty: Collected tax by Customs.

Dutiable Value: The amount on which an *Ad Valorem* or customs duty is calculated.

DWT: *See Deadweight Tonnage.*

E

E.C.M.C.A.: Eastern Central Motor Carriers Association.

ECMC: The U.S. Exporters Competitive Maritime Council. An association primarily of U.S. engineering, procurement, and construction companies and their freight forwarders that was formed jointly by the Maritime Administration in 1997 to seek solutions to transportation problems and enhance the export of U.S. project cargoes.

Edge Protector: An angle piece fitted over the edge of boxes, crates, bundles, and other packages to prevent the pressure from metal bands or other types from cutting into the package.

EDI: Abbreviation for "Electronic Data Interface." Generic term for transmission of transactional data between computer systems. EDI is typically via a batched transmission, usually conforming to consistent standards.

EDIFACT: International data interchange standards sponsored by the United Nations. *See UN/EDIFACT.*

Elevating:

- A charge for services performed in connection with floating elevators.
- Charges assessed for the handling of grain through grain elevators.

Elkins Act: An act of Congress (1903) prohibiting rebates, concession, misbilling, etc., and providing specific penalties for such violations.

Embargo: Order to restrict the hauling of freight.

Eminent Domain: The sovereign power to take property for a necessary public use, with reasonable compensation.

Empty Repo: Contraction for Empty Repositioning. The movement of empty containers.

Endorsement: A legal signature usually placed on the reverse of a draft; signifies transfer of rights from the holder to another party.

Entry: Customs documents required to clear an import shipment for entry into the general commerce of a country.

Equalization: A monetary allowance to the customer for picking up or delivering at a point other than the destination shown on the bill of lading. This provision is covered by tariff publication.

Equipment Interchange Receipt (EIR): A document transferring a container from one carrier to another, or to/from a terminal.

ETA, C, D, R, S:

- Estimated Time of Arrival, Completion, Departure, Readiness, or Sailing.
- Estimated Time of Availability. That time when a tractor/ partner carrier is available for dispatch.

Ethylene: A gas produced by many fruits and vegetables that accelerates the ripening and aging processes.

E.W.I.B.: Eastern Weighing and Inspection Bureau.

"Ex Dec": Contraction for "Shipper's Export Declaration."

Ex—"From": When used in pricing terms such as "Ex Factory" or "Ex Dock," it signifies that the price quoted applies only at the point of origin indicated.

Exception: Notations made when the cargo is received at the carrier's terminal or loaded aboard a vessel. They show any irregularities in packaging or actual or suspected damage to the cargo. Exceptions are then noted on the bill of lading.

EXIM Bank: Abbreviation for Export–Import Bank of the United States. An independent U.S. government agency which facilitates exports of U.S. goods by providing loan guarantees and insurance for repayment of bank-provided export credit.

Expiry Date: Issued in connection with documents such as letters of credit, tariffs, etc., to advise that stated provisions will expire at a certain time.

Export: Shipment of goods to a foreign country.

Export Declaration: A government document declaring designated goods to be shipped out of the country. To be completed by the exporter and filed with the U.S. government.

Export License: A government document which permits the "Licensee" to engage in the export of designated goods to certain destinations.

Export Rate: A rate published on traffic moving from an interior point to a port for transshipment to a foreign country.

Ex-Works: An Incoterm of sale meaning the seller delivers to the buyer at seller's named premises.

F

Factor: A factor is an agent who will, at a discount (usually 5% to 8% of the gross), buy receivables.

FAK: Abbreviation for "Freight All Kinds." Usually refers to full container loads of mixed shipments.

False Billing: Misrepresenting freight or weight on shipping documents.

FAS: Abbreviation for "Free Alongside Ship."

FCL: Abbreviation for "Full Container Load."

FD: Abbreviation for "Free Discharge."

F.D.A.: Food and Drug Administration.

Feeder Service: Cargo to/from regional ports are transferred to/from a central hub port for a long-haul ocean voyage.

Feeder Vessel: A short-sea vessel which transfers cargo between a central "hub" port and smaller "spoke" ports.

FEU: Abbreviation for "Forty-Foot Equivalent Units." Refers to container size standard of 40 feet. Two 20-foot containers or TEU's equal one FEU.

Fifth Wheel: The semi-circular steel coupling device mounted on a tractor which engages and locks with a chassis semi-trailer.

FIO: *See Free In and Out.*

Firkin: A capacity measurement equal to one-fourth of a barrel.

Fixed Costs: Costs that do not vary with the level of activity. Some fixed costs continue even if no cargo is carried. Terminal leases, rent and property taxes are fixed costs.

Flat Car: A rail car without a roof and walls.

Flat Rack/Flat Bed Container: A container with no sides and frame members at the front and rear. Container can be loaded from the sides and top.

FMC (F.M.C.): Federal Maritime Commission. The U.S. governmental regulatory body responsible for administering maritime affairs including the tariff system, freight forwarder licensing, enforcing the conditions of the Shipping Act and approving conference or other carrier agreements.

FOB: *See Free On Board. See also Terms of Sale, FOB.*

FOR: Abbreviation for "Free on Rail."

Force Majeure: The title of a common clause in contracts, exempting the parties for non-fulfillment of their obligations as a result of conditions beyond their control, such as earthquakes, floods or war.

Fore and Aft: The direction on a vessel parallel to the center line.

Foreign Sales Corporation: Under U.S. tax law, a corporation created to obtain tax exemption on part of the earnings of U.S. products in foreign markets. Must be set-up as a foreign corporation with an office outside the United States.

FPPI: Foreign Principal Party of Interest The party to whom final delivery or end use of the exported goods will be made, usually the buyer.

Foreign Trade Zone: A free port in a country divorced from Customs authority but under government control. Merchandise, except that which is prohibited, may be stored in the zone without being subject to import duty regulations.

Fork Lift: A machine used to pick up and move goods loaded on pallets or skids.

Foul Bill of Lading: A receipt for goods issued by a carrier with an indication that the goods were damaged when received. Compare Clean Bill of Lading.

Four-Way Pallet: A pallet designed so that the forks of a fork lift truck can be inserted from all four sides. See Fork lift.

Forwarder Compensation: *See Brokerage.*

F.P.A.: *See Free of Particular Average.*

Free Alongside (FAS): The seller must deliver the goods to a pier and place them within reach of the ship's loading equipment. See Terms of Sale.

Free Astray: An astray shipment (a lost shipment that is found) sent to its proper destination without additional charge.

Free Carrier (FCA): An Incoterm of sale meaning the seller has delivered when the cargo is given to the carrier nominated by the buyer at the named place.

Free In and Out (FIO): Cost of loading and unloading a vessel is borne by the charterer/shipper.

Free of Particular Average (FPA): A marine insurance term meaning that the assurer will not allow payment for partial loss or damage to cargo shipments except in certain circumstances, such as stranding, sinking, collision or fire.

Free on Board (FOB—U.S. Domestic Use): Shipped under a rate that includes costs of delivery to and the loading onto a carrier at a specified point.

- FOB Freight Allowed: The same as FOB named inland carrier, except the buyer pays the transportation charge and the seller reduces the invoice by a like amount.
- FOB Freight Prepaid: The same as FOB named inland carrier, except the seller pays the freight charges of the inland carrier.
- FOB Named Point of Exportation: Seller is responsible for the cost of placing the goods at a named point of exportation.

> Some European buyers use this form when they actually mean FOB vessel.
> - FOB Vessel: Seller is responsible for goods and preparation of export documentation until actually placed aboard the vessel.

Free on Board (Int'l Use): *See Terms of Sale.*

Free Out (FO): Cost of unloading a vessel is borne by the charterer.

Free Port: A restricted area at a seaport for the handling of duty-exempted import goods. Also called a Foreign Trade Zone.

Free Sale Certificate: The U.S. government does not issue certificates of free sale. However, the Food and Drug Administration, Silver Spring, Maryland, will issue, upon request, a letter of comment to the U.S. manufacturers whose products are subject to the Federal Food, Drug and Cosmetic Act or other acts administered by the agency. The letter can take the place of the certificate.

Free Time: That amount of time that a carrier's equipment may be used without incurring additional charges. (See Storage, Demurrage or Per Diem.)

Free Trade Zone: A port designated by the government of a country for duty-free entry of any non-prohibited goods. Merchandise may be stored, displayed, used for manufacturing, etc., within the zone and re-exported without duties.

Freight: Refers to either the cargo carried or the charges assessed for carriage of the cargo.

Freight Bill: A document issued by the carrier based on the bill of lading and other information; used to account for a shipment operationally, statistically, and financially. An Invoice.

Freight Forwarder: A person whose business is to act as an agent on behalf of the shipper. A freight forwarder frequently makes the booking reservation. In the United States, freight forwarders are now licensed by the FMC as "Ocean Intermediaries."

Freighters: *See Ships.*

Full Shipload Lot: The amount of cargo a vessel carries or is able to carry. Practically, it is the amount of cargo which induces the specific voyage. While the cargo lot may take up the majority of the vessel's space or tonnage capacity, it does not require a vessel's volume and weight capacity to be fully utilized.

Full and Down: An expression to describe a loaded vessel carrying cargoes of such a volume and weight that it fills all the vessel's spaces and also brings her down to her tonnage loadline. A rare but optimum revenue condition for a vessel operator.

G

Gateway: Industry-related: A point at which freight moving from one territory to another is interchanged between transportation lines.

GATT: Abbreviation for "General Agreement on Tariffs and Trade." A multilateral treaty to help reduce trade barriers between the signatory countries and to promote trade through tariff concessions. The World Trade Organization (WTO) superseded GATT in 1994.

GBL: Abbreviation for "Government Bill of Lading."

GDSM: Abbreviation for "General Department Store Merchandise." A classification of commodities that includes goods generally shipped by mass-merchandise companies. This commodity structure occurs only in service contracts.

General Order (G.O.): When U.S. Customs orders shipments without entries to be kept in their custody in a bonded warehouse.

Generator Set (Gen Set): A portable generator which can be attached to a refrigerated container to power the refrigeration unit during transit.

Global Maritime Intelligence Integration (GMII): It is within the Office of the Director of National Intelligence, with the mission to ensure government-wide access to maritime information and data critical to intelligence production and to serve as the focal point and oversight agent for maritime specific information issues.

Go-Down: In the Far East, a warehouse where goods are stored and delivered.

Gooseneck: The front rails of the chassis that raise above the plane of the chassis and engage in the tunnel of a container leading to the connection to tractor.

GRI: Abbreviation for "General Rate Increase." Used to describe an across-the-board tariff rate increase implemented by conference members and applied to base rates.

Gross Tonnage (GT): Applies to vessels, not to cargo $(0.2 + 0.02 \log_{10} V)$ where V is the volume in cubic meters of all enclosed spaces on the vessel. Since 1994, it replaces "Gross Registered Tonnage." An approximate conversion ratio is 1NT = 1.7GT and 1GT = 1.5DWT.

Gross Weight: Entire weight of goods, packaging and freight car or container, ready for shipment. Generally, 80,000 pounds maximum container, cargo, and tractor for highway transport.

Groupage: A consolidation service, putting small shipments into containers for shipment.

GVW: Abbreviation for "Gross Vehicle Weight." The combined total weight of a vehicle and its container, inclusive of prime mover.

H

Hague Rules, The: A multilateral maritime treaty adopted in 1921 (at The Hague, Netherlands). Standardizes liability of an international carrier under the Ocean B/L. Establishes a legal "floor" for B/L. See COGSA.

Handymax Vessel: A dry bulk vessel of 35,000 to 49,000dwt. (Note that a "Handy" dry bulk carrier is from 10,000 to 34,000dwt.) A "Handy max Tanker" is a liquid bulk carrier of 10,000 to 60,000dwt.

Harbor: Any place to which ships may resort for shelter, or to load or unload passengers or goods, or to obtain fuel, water, or supplies. This term applies to such places whether proclaimed public or not and whether natural or artificial.

Harbor Master: An official responsible for construction, maintenance, operation, regulation, enforcement, administration, and management pertaining to marinas, ports, and harbors.

Harmonized System of Codes (HS): An international goods classification system for describing cargo in international trade under a single commodity-coding scheme. Developed under the auspices of the Customs Cooperations Council (CCC), an international Customs organization in Brussels, this code is a hierarchically structured product nomenclature containing approximately 5,000 headings and subheadings.

It is organized into 99 chapters arranged in 22 sections. Sections encompass an industry (e.g., Section XI, Textiles and Textile Articles); chapters encompass the various materials and products of the industry (e.g., Chapter 50, Silk; Chapter 55, Manmade Staple Fibers; Chapter 57, Carpets).

The basic code contains four-digit headings and six-digit subheadings. Many countries add digits for Customs tariff and statistical purposes. In the United States, duty rates will be the eight-digit level; statistical suffixes will be at the ten-digit level.

The Harmonized System (HS) is the current U.S. tariff schedule (TSUSA) for imports and is the basis for the ten-digit Schedule B export code.

Hatch: The opening in the deck of a vessel; gives access to the cargo hold.

HAZMAT: An industry abbreviation for "Hazardous Material."

Heavy-Lift Charge: A charge made for lifting articles too heavy to be lifted by a ship's normal tackle.

High-Density Compression: Compression of a flat or standard bale of cotton to approximately 32 pounds per cubic foot. Usually applies to cotton exported or shipped coastwise.

Hitchment: The marrying of two or more portions of one shipment that originate at different locations, moving under one bill of lading, from one shipper to one consignee. Authority for this service must be granted by tariff publication. See Bill of Lading.

Hopper Barge: A barge which loads material dumped into it by a dredger and discharges the cargo through the bottom.

House-to-House: *See Door-to-Door.*

House-to-Pier: Cargo loaded into a container by the shipper under shipper's supervision. When the cargo is exported, it is unloaded at the foreign pier destination.

Humping: The process of connecting a moving rail car with a motionless rail car within a rail classification yard in order to make up a train. The cars move by gravity from an incline or "hump" onto the appropriate track.

I

I/A: Abbreviation for "Independent Action." The right of a conference member to publish a rate of tariff rule that departs from the Agreement's common rate or rule.

ICC: Abbreviation for
- Interstate Commerce Commission
- International Chamber of Commerce

IE: Stands for "Immediate Exit." In the United States, Customs IE Form is used when goods are brought into the United States and are to be immediately re-exported without being transported within the United States.

I.M.C.O.: International Maritime Consultative Organization. A forum in which most major maritime nations participate and through which recommendations for the carriage of dangerous goods, bulk commodities, and maritime regulations become internationally acceptable.

I.M.D.G. Code: International Maritime Dangerous Goods Code. The regulations published by the IMO for transporting hazardous materials internationally.

Immediate Exportation: An entry that allows foreign merchandise arriving at one port to be exported from the same port without the payment of duty.

Import: To receive goods from a foreign country.

Import License: A document required and issued by some national governments authorizing the importation of goods.

In Bond: Cargo moving under Customs control where duty has not yet been paid.

In Gate: The transaction or interchange that occurs at the time a container is received by a rail terminal or water port from another carrier.

In Transit: In transit, or in passage.

In-Transit Entry (I.T.): Allows foreign merchandise arriving at one port to be transported in bond to another port, where a superseding entry is filed.

Incentive Rate: A lower-than-usual tariff rate assessed because a shipper offers a greater volume than specified in the tariff. The incentive rate is assessed for that portion exceeding the normal volume.

IncoTerms: The recognized abbreviation for the International Chamber of Commerce Terms of Sale. These terms were last amended, effective July 1, 1990.

Indemnity Bond: An agreement to hold a carrier harmless with regard to a liability.

Independent Action: Setting rate within a conference tariff that is different from the rate(s) for the same items established by other conference members.

Independent Tariff: Any body of rate tariffs that are not part of an agreement or conference system.

Inducement: Placing a port on a vessel's itinerary because the volume of cargo offered at that port justifies the cost of routing the vessel.

Inherent Vice: An insurance term referring to any defect or other characteristic of a product that could result in damage to the product without external cause (for example, instability in a chemical that could cause it to explode spontaneously). Insurance policies may exclude inherent vice losses.

Inland Carrier: A transportation line that hauls export or import traffic between ports and inland points.

Inspection Certificate: A certificate issued by an independent agent or firm attesting to the quality and/or quantity of the merchandise being shipped. Such a certificate is usually required in a letter of credit for commodity shipments.

Installment Shipments: Successive shipments are permitted under letters of credit. Usually they must take place within a given period of time.

Insulated Container: A container insulated on the walls, roof, floor, and doors, to reduce the effect of external temperatures on the cargo.

Insulated Container Tank: The frame of a container constructed to hold one or more thermally insulated tanks for liquids.

Insurance with Average-clause: This type of clause covers merchandise if the damage amounts to three percent or more of the insured value of the package or cargo. If the vessel burns, sinks, or collides, all losses are fully covered. In marine insurance, the word average describes partial damage or partial loss.

Insurance, All-risk: This type of insurance offers the shipper the broadest coverage available, covering against all losses that may occur in transit.

Insurance, General-Average: In water transportation, the deliberate sacrifice of cargo to make the vessel safe for the remaining cargo. Those sharing in the spared cargo proportionately cover the loss.

Insurance, Particular Average: A marine insurance term which refers to partial loss on an individual shipment from one of the perils insured against, regardless of the balance of the cargo. Particular-average insurance can usually be obtained, but the loss must be in excess of a certain percentage of the insured value of the shipment, usually 3% to 5%, before a claim will be allowed by the company.

Interchange Point: A location where one carrier delivers freight to another carrier.

Intercoastal: Water service between two coasts; in the United States, this usually refers to water service between the Atlantic and Pacific or Gulf Coasts.

Interline Freight: Freight moving from origin to destination over the Freight lines of two or more transportation carriers.

Intermediate Point: A point located en route between two other points.

Intermodal: Used to denote movements of cargo containers interchangeably between transport modes, i.e., motor, rail, water, and air carriers, and where the equipment is compatible within the multiple systems.

International Ship and Port Security Code (ISPS): It is an amendment to the Safety of Life at Sea (SOLAS) Convention (1974/1988) on minimum security arrangements for ships, ports and government agencies. Having come into force in 2004, it prescribes responsibilities to governments, shipping companies, shipboard personnel, and port/facility personnel to "detect security threats and take preventative measures against security incidents affecting ships or port facilities used in international trade."

In-Transit Entry (IT): Allows foreign merchandise arriving at one port to be transported in bond to another port, where a superseding entry is filed.

Invoice: An itemized list of goods shipped to a buyer, stating quantities, prices, shipping charges, etc.

Inward Foreign Manifest (IFM): A complete listing of all cargo entering the country of discharge. Required at all world ports and is the primary source of cargo control, against which duty is assessed by the receiving country.

IPI: Abbreviation for "Inland Point Intermodal." Refers to inland points (non-ports) that can be served by carriers on a through bill of lading.

Irrevocable Letter of Credit: Letter of credit in which the specified payment is guaranteed by the bank if all terms and conditions are met by the drawee and which cannot be revoked without joint agreement of both the buyer and the seller.

I.S.O.: International Standards Organization which deals in standards of all sorts, ranging from documentation to equipment packaging and labeling.

Issuing Bank: Bank that opens a straight or negotiable letter of credit and assumes the obligation to pay the bank or beneficiary if the documents presented are in accordance with the terms of the letter of credit.

Issuing Carrier: The carrier issuing transportation documents or publishing a tariff.

I.T.: Abbreviation for "Immediate Transport." The document (prepared by the carrier) allows shipment to proceed from the port of entry in the U.S. to Customs clearing at the destination. The shipment clears Customs at its final destination. Also called an "In-Transit" Entry.

J

Jacket: A wood or fiber cover placed around such containers as cans and bottles.

Jacob's Ladder: A rope ladder suspended from the side of a vessel and used for boarding.

Jettison: Act of throwing cargo or equipment (jetsam) overboard when a ship is in danger.

JIT: Abbreviation for "Just In Time." In this method of inventory control, warehousing is minimal or nonexistent; the container is the movable warehouse and must arrive "just in time;" not too early nor too late.

Joint Rate: A rate applicable from a point on one transportation line to a point on another line, made by agreement and published in a single tariff by all transportation lines over which the rate applies.

K

KT: Kilo or metric ton. 1,000 kilos or 2,204.6 pounds.

Kilogram: 1,000 grams or 2.2046 pounds.

King Pin: A coupling pin centered on the front underside of a chassis; couples to the tractor.

Knocked Down (KD): Articles which are taken apart to reduce the cubic footage displaced or to make a better shipping unit and are to be re-assembled.

Knot: One nautical mile (6,076 feet or 1,852 meters) per hour. In the days of sail, speed was measured by tossing overboard a log which was secured by a line. Knots were tied into the line at intervals of approximately six feet. The number of knots measured was then compared against time required to travel the distance of 1,000 knots in the line.

Known Loss: A loss discovered before or at the time of delivery of a shipment.

L

L/C: Abbreviation for "Letter of Credit."

Laden: Loaded aboard a vessel.

Lading: Refers to the freight shipped; the contents of a shipment.

Landbridge: Movement of cargo by water from one country through the port of another country, thence, using rail or truck, to an inland point in that country or to a third country. As example, a through movement of Asian cargo to Europe across North America.

Landed Cost: The total cost of a good to a buyer, including the cost of transportation.

Lanemeter: Primarily used to indicate the cargo capacity of a roll-on/roll-off car carrier. It is one meter of deck with a width of 2.5 to 3.0 meters.

Landing Certificate: Certificate issued by consular officials of some importing countries at the point or place of export when the subject goods are exported under bond.

Landing Gear: A support fixed on the front part of a chassis (which is retractable); used to support the front end of a chassis when the tractor has been removed.

LASH: A maritime industry abbreviation for "Lighter Aboard Ship." A specially constructed vessel equipped with an overhead crane for lifting specially designed barges and stowing them into cellular slots in an athwartship position.

LAYCAN: Laydays/Cancelling (date): Range of dates within the hire contract must start.

LCL: Abbreviation for "Less than Container Load." The quantity of freight which is less than that required for the application of a container load rate. Loose Freight.

Less Than Truckload: Also known as LTL or LCL.

Letter of Credit (LC): A document, issued by a bank per instructions by a buyer of goods, authorizing the seller to draw a specified sum of money under specified terms, usually the receipt by the bank of certain documents within a given time. Some of the specific descriptions are:

- Back-to-Back: A new letter of credit issued to another beneficiary on the strength of a primary credit. The second L/C uses the first L/C as collateral for the bank. Used in a three-party transaction.
- Clean: A letter of credit that requires the beneficiary to present only a draft or a receipt for specified funds before receiving payment.
- Confirmed: An L/C guaranteed by both the issuing and advising banks of payment so long as seller's documents are in order, and the L/C terms are met. Only applied to irrevocable L/C's. The confirming bank assumes the credit risk of the issuing bank.
- Deferred Payment: A letter of credit issued for the purchase and financing of merchandise, similar to acceptance-type letter of credit, except that it requires presentation of sight drafts payable on an installment basis.
- Irrevocable: An instrument that, once established, cannot be modified or cancelled without the agreement of all parties concerned.
- Non cumulative: A revolving letter of credit that prohibits the amount not used during the specific period from being available afterwards.
- Restricted: A condition within the letter of credit which restricts its negotiation to a named bank.
- Revocable: An instrument that can be modified or cancelled at any moment without notice to and agreement of the beneficiary, but customarily includes a clause in the credit to the effect that any draft negotiated by a bank prior to the receipt of a notice of revocation or amendment will be honored by the issuing bank. Rarely used since there is no protection for the seller.
- Revolving: An irrevocable letter issued for a specific amount; renews itself for the same amount over a given period.
- Straight: A letter of credit that contains a limited engagement clause which states that the issuing bank promises to pay the beneficiary upon presentation of the required documents at its counters or the counters of the named bank.

- Transferable: A letter of credit that allows the beneficiary to transfer in whole or in part to another beneficiary any amount which, in aggregate, of such transfers does not exceed the amount of the credit. Used by middlemen.
- Unconfirmed: A letter of credit forwarded to the beneficiary by the advising bank without engagement on the part of the advising bank.

Letter of Indemnity: In order to obtain the clean bill of lading, the shipper signs a letter of indemnity to the carrier on the basis of which may be obtained the clean bill of lading, although the dock or mate's receipt showed that the shipment was damaged or in bad condition.

Licenses:

- Some governments require certain commodities to be licensed prior to exportation or importation. Clauses attesting to compliance are often required on the B/L.
- Various types issued for export (general, validated) and import as mandated by government(s).

Lien: A legal claim upon goods for the satisfaction of some debt or duty.

Lightening: A vessel discharges part of its cargo at anchor into a lighter to reduce the vessel's draft so it can then get alongside a pier.

Lighter: An open or covered barge towed by a tugboat and used mainly in harbors and inland waterways to carry cargo to/from alongside a vessel.

Lighterage: Refers to carriage of goods by lighter and the charge assessed there from.

Liner: A vessel advertising sailings on a specified trade route on a regular basis. It is not necessary that every named port be called on every voyage.

Line-Haul: Transportation from one city to another as differentiated from local switching service.

List: The amount in degrees that a vessel tilts from the vertical.

Liter: 1.06 liquid U.S. quarts or 33.9 fluid ounces.

Liquidated Damages: The penalty a seller must pay if the construction project does not meet contractual standards or deadlines.

Lloyds' Registry: An organization maintained for the surveying and classing of ships so that insurance underwriters and others may know the quality and condition of the vessels offered for insurance or employment.

LNG (Liquefied Natural Gas): Natural gas will liquefy at a temperature of approximately –259°F or –160°C at atmospheric pressure. One cubic foot of liquefied gas will expand to approximately 600 cubic feet of gas at atmospheric pressure.

LNGC (LNG Carrier): An ocean-going ship specially constructed to carry LNG in tanks at 160°C. Current average carrying capacity of LNGs is 125,000 cubic meters. Many LNGCs presently under construction or on order are in the 210,000–215,000 cubic meter range.

Load Line: The waterline corresponding to the maximum draft to which a vessel is permitted to load, either by freeboard regulations, the conditions of classification, or the conditions of service. *See also Plimsoll Mark.*

Local Cargo: Cargo delivered to/from the carrier where origin/destination of the cargo is in the local area.

Long Ton: 2,240 pounds.

Longshoreman: Individual employed in a port to load and unload ships.

Loose: Without packing.

Low-Boy: A trailer or semi-trailer with no sides and with the floor of the unit close to the ground.

M

Malpractice: A carrier giving a customer illegal preference to attract cargo. This can take the form of a money refund (rebate); using lower figures than actual for the assessment of freight charges (under-cubing); misdeclaration of the commodity shipped to allow the assessment of a lower tariff rate; waiving published tariff charges for demurrage, CFS handling or equalization; providing specialized equipment to a shipper to the detriment of other shippers, etc.

Mandamu: A writ issued by a court; requires that specific things be done.

Manifest: Document that lists in detail all the bills of lading issued by a carrier or its agent or master for a specific voyage. A detailed summary of the total cargo of a vessel. Used principally for Customs purposes.

Marine Insurance: Broadly, insurance covering loss or damage of goods at sea. Marine insurance typically compensates the owner of merchandise for losses sustained from fire, shipwreck, etc., but excludes losses that can be recovered from the carrier.

Maritime: Business pertaining to commerce or navigation transacted upon the sea or in seaports in such matters as the court of admiralty has jurisdiction.

Maritime Domain: It is all areas and things of, on, under, relating to, adjacent to, or bordering on a sea, ocean, or other navigable waterway, including all maritime related activities, infrastructure, people, cargo, and vessels and other conveyances.

Maritime Domain Awareness (MDA): It is the effective understanding of anything associated with the global maritime domain that could impact the security, safety, economy, or environment of the United States.

Maritime Security and Safety Information System (MSSIS): It shares and displays vessel Automated Identification System (AIS) data real-time with multiple international users through a web-based, password-protected system.

MarView: It is an integrated, data-driven environment providing essential information to support the strategic requirements of the United States Marine Transportation System and its contribution to economic viability of the nation.

Marking: Letters, numbers, and other symbols placed on cargo packages to facilitate identification. Also known as marks.

Marlinespike: A pointed metal spike, used to separate strands of rope in splicing.

Master Inbound: U.S. Customs' automated program under AMS. It allows for electronic reporting of inbound (foreign) cargoes in the U.S.

Mate's Receipt: An archaic practice. An acknowledgement of cargo receipt signed by a mate of the vessel. The possessor of the mate's receipt is entitled to the bill of lading, in exchange for that receipt.

MBM: 1,000 board feet. One MBM equals 2,265 C.M.

MCFS: Abbreviation for "Master Container Freight Station." See CFS.

Measurement Cargo: Freight on which transportation charges are calculated on the basis of volume measurement.

Measurement Ton: 40 cubic feet.

Mechanically Ventilated Container: A container fitted with a means of forced air ventilation.

Megaports Initiative: It is a National Nuclear Security Administration (NNSA) initiative, started in 2003. It teams up with other countries to enhance their ability to screen cargo at major international seaports. The Initiative provides radiation detection equipment and trains their personnel to specifically check for nuclear or other radioactive materials. In return, NNSA requires that data be shared on detections and seizures of nuclear or radiological material that resulted from the use of the equipment provided.

Memorandum Bill of Lading: An in-house bill of lading. A duplicate copy.

Memorandum Freight Bill: See *Multiple Container Load Shipment.*

Meter: 39.37 inches (approximately).

Metric Ton: 2,204.6 pounds or 1,000 kilograms.

Microbridge: A cargo movement in which the water carrier provides a through service between an inland point and the port of load/discharge. The carrier is responsible for cargo and costs from origin on to destination. Also known as IPI or Through Service.

Mile: A unit equal to 5,280 feet on land. A nautical mile is 6,076.115 feet.

Mini Landbridge: An intermodal system for transporting containers by ocean and then by rail or motor to a port previously served as an all-water move (e.g., Hong Kong to New York over Seattle).

Minimum Bill of Lading: A clause in a bill of lading which specifies the least charge that the carrier will make for issuing a lading. The charge may be a definite sum or the current charge per ton for any specified quantity.

Minimum Charge: The lowest charge that can be assessed to transport a shipment.

Mixed Container Load: A container load of different articles in a single consignment.

MLB: Abbreviation for "Mini Landbridge."

M.M.F.B.: Middlewest Motor Freight Bureau.

Modified Atmosphere: A blend of gases tailored to replace the normal atmosphere within a container.

MSA: Maritime Security Act.

MSP: A U.S. Department of Transportation program that helps to assure sufficient sealift to support the United States Armed Forces and U.S. emergency sealift needs, using commercial ships.

MT: Abbreviation for "Metric Ton."

MTSA: The Maritime Transportation Security Act of 2002, is designed to protect ports and waterways from terrorists attacks. The law is the U.S. equivalent of the International Ship and Port Facility Security Code (ISPS), and was fully implemented on July 1, 2004. It requires vessels and port facilities to conduct vulnerability assessments and develop security plans that may include passenger, vehicle, and baggage screening procedures; security patrols; establishing restricted areas; personnel identification procedures; access control measures; and/or installation of surveillance equipment.

Multimodal: Synonymous for all practical purposes with "Intermodal."

MultiTank Container: A container frame fitted to accommodate two or more separate tanks for liquids.

N

National Strategy for Maritime Security: In December 2004 the president directed the secretaries of the Department of Defense and Homeland Security to lead the federal effort to develop a comprehensive National Strategy for Maritime Security, to better integrate and synchronize the existing department-level strategies and ensure their effective and efficient implementation. The strategy includes eight supporting plans to address the specific threats and challenges of the maritime environment and combined they present a comprehensive national effort to promote global economic stability and protect legitimate activities while preventing hostile or illegal acts within the maritime domain.

- The National Plan to Achieve Maritime Domain Awareness lays the foundation for an effective understanding of anything associated with the Maritime Domain and identifying threats as early and as distant from our shores as possible.
- The Global Maritime Intelligence Integration Plan uses existing capabilities to integrate all available intelligence regarding potential threats to U.S. interests in the Maritime Domain.
- The Maritime Operational Threat Response Plan facilitates coordinated U.S. government response to threats against the United States and its interests in the Maritime Domain by establishing roles and responsibilities, which enable the government to respond quickly and decisively.

- The International Outreach and Coordination Strategy provides a framework to coordinate all maritime security initiatives undertaken with foreign governments and international organizations, and solicits international support for enhanced maritime security.
- Maritime Infrastructure Recovery Plan recommends procedures and standards for the recovery of the maritime infrastructure following attack or similar disruption.
- Maritime Transportation System Security Plan responds to the president's call for recommendations to improve the national and international regulatory framework regarding the maritime domain.
- Maritime Commerce Security Plan establishes a comprehensive plan to secure the maritime supply chain.
- The Domestic Outreach Plan engages non-federal input to assist with the development and implementation of maritime security policies resulting from National Security Presidential Directive 41/HSPD–13.

Nautical Mile: Distance of one minute of longitude at the equator, approximately 6,076.115 feet. The metric equivalent is 1,852 meters.

Naval Cooperation and Guidance for Shipping (NCAGS): It is a naval organization with members who are trained to establish and provide advice for safe passage of merchant ships worldwide, during times of peace, tension, crisis, and war. NCAGS personnel act as a liaison between military commanders and the civil authorities. During war, the NCAGS organization may be responsible for establishing a convoy.

NCB: National Cargo Bureau, established in 1952 as a nonprofit marine surveying organization that inspects and surveys ships and cargoes incidental to loading and discharging. It issues certificates as evidence of compliance with the provisions of the Dangerous Cargo Act and the Rules and Regulations for Bulk Grain Cargo.

N.C.I.T.D.: National Committee on International Trade Documentation.

NEC: Abbreviation for "Not Elsewhere Classified."

Negotiable Instruments: A document of title (such as a draft, promissory note, check, or bill of lading) transferable from one person to another in good faith for a consideration. Non-negotiable bills of lading are known as "straight consignment." Negotiable bills are known as "order b/l's."

NES: Abbreviation for "Not Elsewhere Specified."

Nested: Articles packed so that one rests partially or entirely within another, thereby reducing the cubic-foot displacement.

Net Tare Weight: The weight of an empty cargo-carrying piece of equipment plus any fixtures permanently attached.

Net Tonnage (NT): The replacement, since 1994, for "Net Register Tonnage." Theoretically the cargo capacity of the ship. Sometimes used to charge fees or taxes on a vessel. The formula is $(0.2 + 0.02 \log_{10}(Vc))$ Vc $(4d/3D)^2$; for passenger ships the following formula is added: 1.25 (GT+10000)/10,000 (N1+(N2/10)), where Vc is the volume of cargo holds, D is the distance between ship's bottom and the uppermost deck, d is the draught, N1 is the number of cabin passengers, and N2 is the number of deck passengers. "Ton" is figured as a 100 cubic foot ton. An approximate conversion ratio is 1NT = 1.7GT and 1GT = 1.5DWT.

Net Weight: Weight of the goods alone without any immediate wrappings, e.g., the weight of the contents of a tin can without the weight of the can.

Neutral Body: An organization established by the members of an ocean conference acts as a self-policing force with broad authority to investigate tariff violations, including authority to scrutinize all documents kept by the carriers and their personnel. Violations are reported to the membership and significant penalties are assessed.

Nippon Kaiji Kyokai (NK): A Japanese classification society which certifies seagoing vessels for compliance to standardized rules regarding construction and maintenance.

N.M.F.C.: National Motor Freight Classification.

NOI: Abbreviation for "Not Otherwise Indexed."

NOIBN: Abbreviation for "Not Otherwise Indexed By Name."

Nomenclature of the Customs Cooperation Council: The Customs tariff used by most countries worldwide. It was formerly known as the Brussels Tariff Nomenclature and is the basis of the commodity coding system known as the Harmonized System.

Non-Dumping Certificate: Required by some countries for protection against the dumping of certain types of merchandise or products.

Non-Vessel Operating Common Carrier (NVOCC): A cargo consolidator in ocean trades who will buy space from a carrier and sub-sell it to smaller shippers. The NVOCC issues bills of lading, publishes tariffs and otherwise conducts itself as an ocean common carrier, except that it will not provide the actual ocean or intermodal service.

NOR: Notice of Readiness (when the ship is ready to load).

NOS: Abbreviation for "Not Otherwise Specified."

Nose: Front of a container or trailer-opposite the tail.

No-show: Cargo which has been booked but does not arrive in time to be loaded before the vessel sails. See also "Windy Booking."

N.P.C.F.B.: North Pacific Coast Freight Bureau.

NRT—Net Register Tons: Theoretically the cargo capacity of the ship. Sometimes used to charge fees or taxes on a vessel. See *Net Tonnage*.

O

Ocean Bill of Lading (Ocean B/L): A contract for transportation between a shipper and a carrier. It also evidences receipt of the cargo by the carrier. A bill of lading shows ownership of the cargo and, if made negotiable, can be bought, sold or traded while the goods are in-transit.

OCP: *See Overland Common Points.*

ODS: Abbreviation for "Operating Differential Subsidy." An amount of money the U.S. government paid U.S. shipping companies that qualify for this subsidy. The intent was to help offset the higher subsidy. The intent was to help offset the higher cost of operating a U.S.–flag vessel. The ODS program is administered by the U.S. Maritime Administration and is being phased out.

O.E.C.D.: Organization of Economic Cooperation and Development, headquartered in Paris with membership consisting of the world's developed nations.

Office of Global Maritime Situational Awareness (OGMSA): It is the United States initiative to establish a world-wide maritime information exchange that encompasses both public and private sector entities with maritime interests. The GMSA supports maritime domain awareness by making maritime related information available and searchable.

On-board: A notation on a bill of lading that cargo has been loaded on board a vessel. Used to satisfy the requirements of a letter of credit, in the absence of an express requirement to the contrary.

On Deck: A notation on a bill of lading that the cargo has been stowed on the open deck of the ship.

Open Account: A trade arrangement in which goods are shipped to a foreign buyer without guarantee of payment.

Open Insurance Policy: A marine insurance policy that applies to all shipments made by an exporter over a period of time rather than to one shipment only.

Open Sea: The water area of the open coast seaward of the ordinary low-water mark, or seaward of inland waters.

Open Top Container: A container fitted with a solid removable roof, or with a tarpaulin roof so the container can be loaded or unloaded from the top.

Operating Ratio: A comparison of a carrier's operating expense with its net sales. The most general measure of operating efficiency.

O.P.I.C.: Overseas Private Investment Corporation, an agency of the U.S. government which helps U.S. businesses invest overseas.

Optimum Cube: The highest level of cube utilization that can be achieved when loading cargo into a container.

Order–Notify (O/N): A bill of lading term to provide surrender of the original bill of lading before freight is released; usually associated with a shipment covered under a letter of credit.

ORFS: Abbreviation for "Origin Rail Freight Station." Same as CFS at origin except an ORFS is operated by the rail carrier participating in the shipment.

Origin: Location where shipment begins its movement.

Original Bill of Lading (OBL): A document which requires proper signatures for consummating carriage of contract. Must be marked as "original" by the issuing carrier.

OS&D: Abbreviation for "Over, Short, or Damaged" Usually discovered at cargo unloading.

Out Gate: Transaction or interchange that occurs at the time a container leaves a rail or water terminal.

Overcharge: To charge more than the proper amount according to the published rates.

Overheight Cargo: Cargo more than eight feet high which thus cannot fit into a standard container.

Overland Common Point (OCP): A term stated on the bills of lading offering lower shipping rates to importers east of the Rockies, provided merchandise from the Far East comes in through the West Coast ports. OCP rates were established by U.S. West Coast steamship companies in conjunction with western railroads so that cargo originating or destined for the American Midwest and East would be competitive with all-water rates via the U.S. Atlantic and Gulf ports. Applies to eastern Canada.

Owner Code (SCAC): Standard Carrier Abbreviation Code identifying an individual common carrier. A three letter carrier code followed by a suffix identifies the carrier's equipment. A suffix of "U" is a container and "C" is a chassis.

P

P&I: Abbreviation for "Protection and Indemnity," an insurance term.

Packing List: Itemized list of commodities with marks/numbers but no cost values indicated.

PADAG: Abbreviation for "Please Authorize Delivery Against Guarantee." A request from the consignee to the shipper to allow the carrier or agent to release cargo against a guarantee, either bank or personal. Made when the consignee is unable to produce original bills of lading.

Paired Ports: A U.S. Customs program wherein at least two designated Customs ports will enter cargo that arrives at either port without the necessity of an in-bound document.

Pallet: A platform with or without sides, on which a number of packages or pieces may be loaded to facilitate handling by a lift truck.

Panamax Tanker: A liquid cargo vessel of 50,000 to 70,000dwt.

Panamax Vessel: The largest size vessel that can traverse the Panama Canal. Current maximum dimensions are: Length 294.1 meters (965 feet); width 32.3 meters (106 feet); draft 12.0 meters (39.5 feet) in tropical fresh water; height 57.91 meters (190 feet) above the water.

Paper Ramp: A technical rail ramp, used for equalization of points not actually served.

Paper Rate: A published rate that is never assessed because no freight moves under it.

Parcel Receipt: An arrangement whereby a steamship company, under rules and regulations established in the freight tariff of a given trade, accepts small packages at rates below the minimum bill of lading, and issues a parcel receipt instead of a bill of lading.

Partial Shipments: Under letters of credit, one or more shipments are allowed by the phrase "partial shipments permitted."

Particular Average: *See Insurance, Particular Average.*

Payee: A party named in an instrument as the beneficiary of the funds. Under letters of credit, the payee is either the drawer of the draft or a bank.

Payer: A party responsible for the payment as evidenced by the given instrument. Under letters of credit, the payer is the party on whom the draft is drawn, usually the drawee bank.

Per Diem: A charge, based on a fixed daily rate.

Perils of the Sea: Those causes of loss for which the carrier is not legally liable. The elemental risks of ocean transport.

Phytosanitary Inspection Certificate: A certificate issued by the U.S. Department of Agriculture to satisfy import regulations of foreign countries; indicates that a U.S. shipment has been inspected and found free from harmful pests and plant diseases.

Pickup: The act of calling for freight by truck at the consignor's shipping platform.

Pier: The structure perpendicular to the shoreline to which a vessel is secured for the purpose of loading and unloading cargo.

Pier-to-House: A shipment loaded into a container at the pier or terminal, thence to the consignee's facility.

Pier-to-Pier: Containers loaded at port of loading and discharged at port of destination.

Piggy Packer: A mobile container-handling crane used to load/unload containers to/from railcars.

Piggyback: A transportation arrangement in which truck trailers with their loads are moved by train to a destination. Also known as Rail Pigs.

Place of Delivery: Place where cargo leaves the care and custody of carrier.

Place of Receipt: Location where cargo enters the care and custody of carrier.

Plimsoll Mark: A series of horizontal lines, corresponding to the seasons of the year and fresh or saltwater, painted on the outside of a ship marking the level which must remain above the surface of the water for the vessel's stability.

POD: Abbreviation for:
- Port of Discharge.
- Port of Destination.
- Proof of Delivery. A document required from the carrier or driver for proper payment.

Point of Origin: The place at which a shipment is received by a carrier from the shipper.

POL: Abbreviation for:

- Port of Loading.
- Petroleum, Oil, and Lubricants.

Pomerene Act, Also known as (U.S.) Federal Bill of Lading Act of 1916: U.S. federal law enacting conditions by which a B/L may be issued. Penalties for issuing B/L's containing false data include monetary fines and/or imprisonment.

Port:

- Harbor with piers or docks.
- Left side of a ship when facing forward.
- Opening in a ship's side for handling freight.

Port of Call: Port where a ship discharges or receives traffic.

Port of Entry: Port where cargo is unloaded and enters a country.

Port of Exit: Place where cargo is loaded and leaves a country.

PPI: Principal Party of Interest (see USPPI and FPPI).

Port Facility Security Officer: Is the person designated as responsible for the development, implementation, revision and maintenance of the port facility security plan and for liaison with the ship security officers and company security officers.

Port Facility Security Plan: Is a plan developed to ensure the application of measures designed to protect persons on board, cargo, cargo transport units and ship's stores within the port facility from the risks of a security incident.

Port Security: It is the defense, law and treaty enforcement, and counterterrorism activities that fall within the port and maritime domain. It includes the protection of the seaports themselves, the protection and inspection of the cargo moving through the ports, and maritime security.

Port Security Grant Program (PSGP): As a result of the Department of Homeland Security Appropriations Act of 2005, fiscal year grant funding is provided annually to the Nation's most at-risk seaports for physical security enhancements to be used in the protection of critical port infrastructure from terrorism. PSGP funds help ports enhance their risk management capabilities, domain awareness, training and exercises, and capabilities to prevent, detect, respond to, and recover from attacks involving improvised explosive devices and other non-conventional weapons.

Pratique Certificate: Lifts temporary quarantine of a vessel; granted pratique by Health Officer.

Pre-cooling: A process employed in the shipment of citrus fruits and other perishable commodities. The fruit is packed and placed in a cold room from which the heat is gradually extracted. The boxes of fruit are packed in containers that have been thoroughly cooled and transported through to destination without opening the doors.

Prepaid (Ppd.): Freight charges paid by the consignor (shipper) prior to the release of the bills of lading by the carrier.

Product Tanker: A liquid cargo vessel of 10,000 to 60,000 dwt. Also referred to as a Handymax Tanker. Often built with many segregated cargo tanks and thus sometimes called a "drugstore tanker."

Pro Forma: A Latin term meaning "For the sake of form."

Pro Forma Invoice: An invoice provided by a supplier prior to the shipment of merchandise, informing the buyer of the kinds and quantities of goods to be sent, their value, and specifications (weight, size, etc.).

Pro Rata: A Latin term meaning "In proportion."

Project Rate: Single tariff item, established to move multiple commodities needed for a specified project, usually construction.

Public Service Commission: A name usually given to a State body having control or regulation of public utilities.

Publishing Agent: Person authorized by transportation lines to publish tariffs or rates, rules, and regulations for their account.

Pulp Temperature: Procedure where carrier tests the temperature of the internal flesh of refrigerated commodities to assure that the temperature at time of shipment conforms to prescribed temperature ranges.

Pup: A short semi-trailer used jointly with a dolly and another semi-trailer to create a twin trailer.

Q

Quarantine: A restraint placed on an operation to protect the public against a health hazard. A ship may be quarantined so that it cannot leave a protected point. During the quarantine period, the Q flag is hoisted.

Quoin: A wedge-shaped piece of timber used to secure barrels against movement.

Quota: The quantity of goods that may be imported without restriction during a set period of time.

Quotation: An offer to sell goods at a stated price and under stated terms.

Quay: A structure attached to land to which a vessel is moored. See also Pier and Dock.

R

Rag Top: A slang term for an open-top trailer or container with a tarpaulin cover.

Rail Division: The amount of money an ocean carrier pays to the railroad for overland carriage.

Rail Grounding: The time that the container was discharged (grounded) from the train.

Ramp: Railroad terminal where containers are received or delivered and trains loaded or discharged. Originally, trailers moved onto the rearmost flatcar via a ramp and driven into position in a technique known as "circus loading." Most modern rail facilities use lifting equipment to position containers onto the flatcars.

Ramp-to-Door: A movement where the load initiates at an origin rail ramp and terminates at a consignee's door.

Ramp-to-Ramp: A movement of equipment from an origin rail ramp to a destination rail ramp only.

Rate Basis: A formula of the specific factors or elements that control the making of a rate. A rate can be based on any number of factors (i.e., weight, measure, equipment type, package, box, etc.).

Reasonableness: Under ICC and common law, the requirement that a rate not be higher than is necessary to reimburse the carrier for the actual cost of transporting the traffic and allow a fair profit.

Rebate: An illegal form of discounting or refunding that has the net effect of lowering the tariff price. See also Malpractice.

Reconsignment: Changing the consignee or destination on a bill of lading while shipment is still in transit. Diversion has substantially the same meaning.

Recourse: A right claim against the guarantors of a loan or draft or bill of exchange.

Red Label: A label required on shipments of flammable articles.

Reefer: Refrigerated container.

Related Points: A group of points to which rates are made the same as or in relation to rates to other points in group.

RFP: Request for Proposal

RFQ: Request for quotation.

Relay: To transfer containers from one ship to another when both vessels are controlled by the same network (carrier) manager.

Remittance: Funds sent by one person to another as payment.

Restricted Articles: Articles handled only under certain conditions.

Revenue Ton (RT): A ton on which the shipment is freighted. If cargo is rated as weight or measure (W/M), whichever produces the highest revenue will be considered the revenue ton. Weights are based on metric tons and measures are based on cubic meters. RT = 1 MT or 1 CBM.

Reverse IPI: An inland point provided by an all-water carrier's through bill of lading in the U.S. by first discharging the container in an East Coast port.

"Ro/Ro": A shortening of the term, "Roll On/Roll Off." A method of ocean cargo service using a vessel with ramps which allows wheeled vehicles to be loaded and discharged without cranes. Also refers to any specialized vessel designed to carry Ro/Ro cargo.

Roll: To re-book cargo to a later vessel.

Rolling: The side-to-side (athwartship) motion of a vessel.

Route: The manner in which a shipment moves; i.e., the carriers handling it and the points at which the carriers interchange.

Running Gear: Complementary equipment for terminal and over-the-road handling containers.

RVNX: Abbreviation for "Released Value Not Exceeding." Usually used to limit the value of goods transported. The limitation refers to carrier liability when paying a claim for lost or damaged goods.

S

Sanction: An embargo imposed by a government against another country.

SAFE Port Act: Is the Security and Accountability For Every Port Act of 2006 which is an Act of Congress in the United States that covers port security.

S/D: Abbreviation for
- Sight draft.
- Sea damage.

SCAC Code: *See Owner Code.*

Schedule B: The Statistical Classification of Domestic and Foreign Commodities Exported from the United States.

Sea-Bee Vessels: Ocean vessels constructed with heavy-duty submersible hydraulic lift or elevator system at the stern of the vessel. The Sea-Bee system facilitates forward transfer and positioning of barges. Sea-Bee barges are larger than LASH barges. The Sea-Bee system is no longer used.

Sea Waybill: Document indicating the goods were loaded onboard when a document of title (b/L) is not needed. Typically used when a company is shipping goods to itself.

Seawaymax Vessel: The largest vessel that can transit the locks of the St. Lawrence Seaway. Length is 226 meters (740 feet); beam is 24 meters (78 feet); draft is 7.92 meters (26 feet).

Seaworthiness: The fitness of a vessel for its intended use.

Secure Freight Initiative (SFI): It is a key provision of the SAFE Port Act of 2006 and is part of the International Container Security scanning project. It builds on its current partnership between the Container Security Initiative and the Megaports Initiative. It expands the use of scanning and imaging equipment to examine more U.S. bound containers, not just those determined to be high risk.

Security Level 1: Is the level for which minimum appropriate protective security measures shall be maintained at all times.

Security Level 2: Is the level for which appropriate additional protective security measures shall be maintained for a period of time as a result of heightened risk of a security incident.

Security Level 3: Is the level for which further specific protective security measures shall be maintained for a limited period of time when a security incident is probable or imminent, although it may not be possible to identify the specific target.

SED: U.S. Commerce Department document, "Shipper's Export Declaration."

Service: A string of vessels which makes a particular voyage and serves a particular market.

Service Contract: As provided in the Shipping Act of 1984, a contract between a shipper (or a shippers association) and an ocean common carrier (or conference) in which the shipper makes a commitment to provide a certain minimum quantity of cargo or freight revenue over a fixed time period, and the ocean common carrier or conference commits to a certain rate or rate schedule as well as a defined service level (such as assured space, transit time, port rotation or similar service features). The contract may also specify provisions in the event of nonperformance on the part of either party.

SHEX: Saturday and Holidays Excluded.

SHINC: Saturday and Holidays Included.

Ship:

- A vessel of considerable size for deep-water navigation.
- A sailing vessel having three or more square-rigged masts.

Ship Chandler: An individual or company selling equipment and supplies for ships.

Ship Demurrage: A charge for delaying a steamer beyond a stipulated period.

Ship's Bells: Measure time onboard ship. One bell sounds for each half hour. One bell means 12:30, two bells mean 1:00, three bells mean 1:30, and so on until 4:00 (eight bells). At 4:30 the cycle begins again with one bell.

Ship Load: The amount of cargo a ship carries or is able to carry. *See also Full Shipload Lot and Full and Down.*

Ship's Manifest: A statement listing the particulars of all shipments loaded for a specified voyage.

Shipment: The tender of one lot of cargo at one time from one shipper to one consignee on one bill of lading.

Ship Security Officer: Is the person on board the vessel, accountable to the master, designated by the company as responsible for the security of the ship, including implementation and maintenance of the ship security plan and for the liaison with the company security officer and the port facility security officers.

Ship Security Plan: Is a plan developed to ensure the application of measures on board the ship and designed to protect persons on board, cargo, cargo transport units, ship's stores or the ship from the risks of a security incident.

Ship Types:

- Barge Carriers: Ships designed to carry barges; some are fitted to act as full containerships and can carry a varying number of barges and containers at the same time. At present this class includes two types of vessels LASH and Sea-Bee.
- Bulk Carriers: All vessels designed to carry bulk homogeneous cargo without mark and count such as grain, fertilizers, ore, and oil.
- Combination Passenger and Cargo Vessels: Ships with a capacity for 13 or more passengers and any form of cargo or freight.
- Freighters: Breakbulk vessels both refrigerated and unrefrigerated, containerships, partial containerships, roll-on/roll-off vessels, and barge carriers. A general cargo vessel designed to carry heterogeneous mark and count cargoes.
- Full Containerships: Ships equipped with permanent container cells, with little or no space for other types of cargo.
- General Cargo Carriers: Breakbulk freighters, car carriers, cattle carriers, pallet carriers and timber carriers. A vessel designed to carry heterogeneous mark and count cargoes.
- Partial Containerships: Multipurpose containerships where one or more but not all compartments are fitted with permanent container cells. Remaining compartments are used for other types of cargo.
- Roll-on/Roll-off vessels: Ships specially designed to carry wheeled containers or trailers using interior ramps. Includes all forms of car and truck carriers.
- Tankers: Ships fitted with tanks to carry liquid bulk cargo such as crude petroleum and petroleum products, chemicals, Liquefied gasses (LNG and LPG), wine, molasses, and similar product tankers.

Ship's Tackle: All rigging, cranes, etc., utilized on a ship to load or unload cargo.

Shipper: The person or company who is usually the supplier or owner of commodities shipped. Also called Consignor.

Shippers Association: A non-profit entity that represents the interests of a number of shippers. The main focus of shippers associations is to pool the cargo volumes of members to leverage the most favorable service contract rate levels.

Shipper's Export Declaration—SED, "Ex Dec": A joint Bureau of the Census' International Trade Administration form used for compiling U.S. exports. It is completed by a shipper and shows the value, weight, destination, etc., of export shipments as well as Schedule B commodity code.

Shipper's Instructions: Shipper's communication(s) to its agent and/or directly to the international water-carrier. Instructions may be varied, e.g., specific details/clauses to be printed on the B/L, directions for cargo pickup and delivery.

Shipper's Letter of Instructions for Issuing an Air Waybill: The document required by the carrier or freight forwarders to obtain (besides the data needed) authorization to issue and sign the air waybill in the name of the shipper.

Shipper's Load & Count (SL&C): Shipments loaded and sealed by shippers and not checked or verified by the carriers.

Shipping Act of 1916: The act of the U.S. Congress (1916) that created the U.S. Shipping Board to develop water transportation, operate the merchant ships owned by the government, and regulate the water carriers engaged in commerce under the flag of the United States. As of June 18, 1984, applies only to domestic offshore ocean transport.

Shipping Act of 1984: Effective June 18, 1984, describes the law covering water transportation in the U.S. foreign trade.

Shipping Act of 1998: Amends the Act of 1984 to provide for confidential service contracts and other items.

Shipping Order: Shipper's instructions to carrier for forwarding goods; usually the triplicate copy of the bill of lading.

Shore: A prop or support placed against or beneath anything to prevent sinking or sagging.

Short Sea Shipping—SSS (European-EU): Short Sea Shipping means the movement of cargo by sea between ports situated in geographical Europe or between those ports situated in non-European countries having a coastline on the enclosed seas bordering Europe (Baltic, Mediterranean, and Black). It is a successful mode of transport in Europe.

Short Ton (ST): A weight unit of measure equal to 2,000 pounds.

Shrink Wrap: Polyethylene or similar substance heat-treated and shrunk into an envelope around several units, thereby securing them as a single pack for presentation or to secure units on a pallet.

Side Loader: A lift truck fitted with lifting attachments operating to one side for handling containers.

Side-Door Container: A container fitted with a rear door and a minimum of one side door.

Sight Draft: A draft payable upon presentation to the drawee.

SIGTTO: Society of International Gas Transport and Terminal Operators, an industry organization promoting the exchange of safety information concerning the processing, transporting, and handling of liquefied gases.

Skids: Battens, or a series of parallel runners, fitted beneath boxes or packages to raise them clear of the floor to permit easy access of forklift blades or other handling equipment.

SL/W: Shippers load and count. All three clauses are used as needed on the bill of lading to exclude the carrier from liability when the cargo is loaded by the shipper.

Sleepers: Loaded containers moving within the railroad system that are not clearly identified on any internally generated reports.

Sling: A wire or rope contrivance placed around cargo and used to load or discharge it to/from a vessel.

Slip: A vessel's berth between two piers.

SPA: Abbreviation for "Subject to Particular Average." *See also Particular Average.*

Spine Car: An articulated five-platform railcar. Used where height and weight restrictions limit the use of stack cars. It holds five 40-foot containers or combinations of 40- and 20-foot containers.

Spotting: Placing a container where required to be loaded or unloaded.

Spreader: A piece of equipment designed to lift containers by their corner castings.

SSHEX: Abbreviation for Saturdays, Sundays, and Holidays Excepted. Refers to loading and discharging of cargo as agreed to in the charter party. This indicates when time does not count in the calculation of demurrage and despatch.

Stability: The force that holds a vessel upright or returns it to upright position if keeled over. Weight in the lower hold increases stability. A vessel is stiff if it has high stability, tender if it has low stability. In a ship, stability is indicated by several characteristics. Initial stability is measured by the metacentric height; also known as "GM." If GM is low, the vessel makes long slow rolls, and is considered tender. When GM is too high, the vessel is considered stiff, and may return violently to the upright position when rolling, with possible damage to cargo and injury to passengers and crew. Other stability considerations include the vessel's range of stability, maximum righting arm, and the angle of heel at which the maximum righting arm occurs.

Stack Car: An articulated five-platform rail car that allows containers to be double stacked. A typical stack car holds ten 40-foot equivalent units (FEU).

Stacktrain: A rail service whereby rail cars carry containers stacked two high on specially operated unit trains. Each train includes up to 35 articulated multi-platform cars. Each car is comprised of 5 well-type platforms upon which containers can be stacked. No chassis accompany containers.

Standard Industrial Classification (SIC): A standard numerical code used by the U.S. government to classify products and services.

Standard International Trade Classification (SITC): A standard numeric code developed by the United Nations to classify commodities used in international trade, based on a hierarchy.

Standard Operating Procedures (SOPs): Protocols and procedures internal in a company for following best practice and well established guidelines to operate in. Follows corporate governance.

Starboard: The right side of a ship when facing the bow.

Statute of Limitation: A law limiting the time in which claims or suits may be instituted.

STCC: Abbreviation for "Standard Transportation Commodity Code."

Steamship Conference: A group of vessel operators joined together for the purpose of establishing freight rates.

Steamship Guarantee: An indemnity issued to the carrier by a bank; protects the carrier against any possible losses or damages arising from release of the merchandise to the receiving party. This instrument is usually issued when the bill of lading is lost or is not available.

Stern: The end of a vessel. Opposite of bow.

Stevedore: Individual or firm that employs longshoremen and who contracts to load or unload the ship.

Store-Door Pick-up Delivery: A complete package of pick up or delivery services performed by a carrier from origin to final consumption point.

Stowage: A marine term referring to loading freight into ships' holds.

STC: Said to contain.

Straddle Carrier: Mobile truck equipment with the capacity for lifting a container within its own framework.

Straight Bill of Lading: A non-negotiable bill of lading which states a specific identity to whom the goods should be delivered. See Bill of Lading.

Stripping: Removing cargo from a container (devanning).

Stuffing: Putting cargo into a container.

STW: Said to weigh.

Subrogate: To put in place of another; i.e., when an insurance company pays a claim it is placed in the same position as the payee with regard to any rights against others.

Suezmax Tanker: A tanker of 120,000 to 199,000dwt.

Surface Transportation Board (STB): The U.S. federal body charged with enforcing acts of the U.S. Congress that affect common carriers in interstate commerce. STB replaced the Interstate Commerce Commission (ICC) in 1997.

Sufferance Wharf: A wharf licensed and attended by Customs authorities.

Supply Chain: A logistical management system which integrates the sequence of activities from delivery of raw materials to the manufacturer through to delivery of the finished product to the customer into measurable components. "Just in Time" is a typical value-added example of supply chain management.

Surcharge: An extra or additional charge

Surtax: An additional extra tax.

T

T&E: Abbreviation for "Transportation and Exportation." Customs form used to control cargo movement from port of entry to port of exit, meaning that the cargo is moving from one country, through the United States, to another country.

Tail: Rear of a container or trailer-opposite the front or nose.

Tare Weight: In railcar or container shipments, the weight of the empty railcar or empty container.

Tariff (Trf.): A publication setting forth the charges, rates, and rules of transportation companies.

Telex: Used for sending messages to outside companies. Messages are transmitted via Western Union, ITT, and RCA. Being replaced by fax and internet.

Temperature Recorder: A device to record temperature in a container while cargo is en route.

Tender: The offer of goods for transportation or the offer to place cars or containers for loading or unloading.

Tenor: Time and date for payment of a draft.

Terminal: An assigned area in which containers are prepared for loading into a vessel, train, truck, or airplane or are stacked immediately after discharge from the vessel, train, truck, or airplane.

Terminal Charge: A charge made for a service performed in a carrier's terminal area.

Terms of Sale: The point at which sellers have fulfilled their obligations so the goods in a legal sense could be said to have been delivered to the buyer. They are shorthand expressions that set out the rights and obligations of each party when it comes to transporting the goods. Following are the 13 terms of sale in international trade as Terms of Sale reflected in the recent amendment to the International Chamber of Commerce Terms of Trade (INCOTERMS), effective July 1990: exw, fca, fas, fob, cfr, cif, cpt, cip, daf, des, deq, ddu and ddp.

- EXW (Ex Works) (...Named Place): A Term of Sale which means that the seller fulfills the obligation to deliver when he or she has made the goods available at his/her premises (i.e., works, factory, warehouse, etc.) to the buyer. In particular, the seller is not responsible for loading the goods in the vehicle provided by the buyer or for clearing the goods for export, unless otherwise agreed. The buyer bears all costs and risks involved in taking the goods from the seller's premises to the desired destination. This term thus represents the minimum obligation for the seller.

- FCA (Free Carrier) (... Named Place): A Term of Sale which means the seller fulfills their obligation when he or she has handed over the goods, cleared for export, into the charge of the carrier named by the buyer at the named place or point. If no precise point is indicated by the buyer, the seller may choose, within the place or range stipulated, where the carrier should take the goods into their charge.

- FAS (Free Alongside Ship) (…Named Port of Shipment): A Term of Sale which means the seller fulfills his obligation to deliver when the goods have been placed alongside the vessel on the quay or in lighters at the named port of shipment. This means that the buyer has to bear all costs and risks of loss of or damage to the goods from that moment.

- FOB (Free On Board) (…Named Port of Shipment): An International Term of Sale that means the seller fulfills his or her obligation to deliver when the goods have passed over the ship's rail at the named port of shipment. This means that the buyer has to bear all costs and risks to loss of or damage to the goods from that point. The FOB term requires the seller to clear the goods for export. (Note: The U.S. government sometimes uses a made-up term "FOB Destination" to require the seller to take responsibility for delivering the goods at destination rather than the correct Incoterm of DDP.)

- CFR (Cost and Freight) (…Named Port of Destination): A Term of Sale where the seller pays the costs and freight necessary to bring the goods to the named port of destination, Terms of Sale but the risk of loss of or damage to the goods, as (continued) well as any additional costs due to events occurring after the time the goods have been delivered on board the vessel, is transferred from the seller to the buyer when the goods pass the ship's rail in the port of shipment. The CFR term requires the seller to clear the goods for export.

- CIF (Cost, Insurance and Freight) (…Named Place of Destination): A Term of Sale where the seller has the same obligations as under the CFR but also has to procure marine insurance against the buyer's risk of loss or damage to the goods during the carriage. The seller contracts for insurance and pays the insurance premium. The CIF term requires the seller to clear the goods for export.

- CPT (Carriage Paid To) (…Named Place of Destination): A Term of Sale which means the seller pays the freight for the carriage of the goods to the named destination. The risk of loss of or damage to the goods, as well as any additional costs due to events occurring after the time the goods have been delivered to the carrier, is transferred from the seller to the buyer when the goods have been delivered into the custody of the carrier. If subsequent carriers are used for the carriage to the agreed upon destination, the risk passes when the goods have been delivered to the first carrier. The CPT term requires the seller to clear the goods for export.

- CIP (Carriage and Insurance Paid To) (...Named Place of Destination): A Term of Sale which means the seller has the same obligations as under CPT, but with the addition that the seller has to procure cargo insurance against the buyer's risk of loss of or damage to the goods during the carriage. The seller contracts for insurance and pays the insurance premium. The buyer should note that under the CIP term the seller is required to obtain insurance only on minimum coverage. The CIP term requires the seller to clear the goods for export.

- DAF (Delivered At Frontier) (...Named Place): A Term of Sale which means the sellers fulfill their obligation to deliver when the goods have been made available, cleared for export, at the named point and placed at the frontier, but before the customs Terms of Sale border of the adjoining country.

- DDU (Delivered Duty Unpaid) (...Named Port of Destination): A Term of Sale where the seller fulfills his obligation to deliver when the goods have been made available at the named place in the country of importation. The seller has to bear the costs and risks involved in bringing the goods thereto (excluding duties, taxes and other official charges payable upon importation) as well as the costs and risks of carrying out customs formalities. The buyer has to pay any additional costs and to bear any risks caused by failure to clear the goods for in time.

- DDP (Delivered Duty Paid) (...Named Port of Destination): "Delivered Duty Paid" means that the seller fulfills his obligation to deliver when the goods have been made available at the named place in the country of importation. The seller has to bear the risks and costs, including duties, taxes and other charges of delivering the goods thereto, clear for importation. While the EXW term represents the minimum obligation for the seller, DDP represents the maximum.

- DES (Delivered Ex Ship) (...Named Port of Destination): A Term of Sale where the seller fulfills his/her obligation to deliver when the goods have been made available to the buyer on board the ship, uncleared for import at the named port of destination. The seller has to bear all the costs and risks involved in bringing the goods to the named port destination.

- DEQ (Delivered Ex Quay, [Duty Paid]) (…Named Port of Destination): A Term of Sale which means the DDU term has been fulfilled when the goods have been available to the buyer on the quay (wharf) at the named port of destination, cleared for importation. The seller has to bear all risks and costs including duties, taxes and other charges of delivering the goods thereto.

TBN: To Be Nominated (when the name of a ship is still unknown).

TEU: Abbreviation for "Twenty foot Equivalent Unit."

Third Party Logistics (3PL): A company that provides logistics services to other companies for some or all of their logistics needs. It typically includes warehousing and transportation services. Most 3PL's also have freight forwarding licenses.

Through Rate: The total rate from the point of origin to final destination.

Throughput Charge: The charge for moving a container through a container yard off or onto a ship.

Time Charter: A contract for leasing between the ship owners and the lessee. It would state, e.g., the duration of the lease in years or voyages.

Time Draft: A draft that matures either a certain number of days after acceptance or a certain number of days after the date of the draft.

TIR: Transport International par la Route. Road transport operating agreement among European governments and the United States for the international movement of cargo by road. Display of the TIR carnet allows sealed container loads to cross national frontiers without inspection.

TL: Abbreviation for "Trailer Load."

TOFC: Abbreviation for "Trailer on Flat Car." The movement of a highway trailer on a railroad flatcar. Also known as Piggyback.

Ton-Mile:

- A unit used in comparing freight earnings or expenses. The amount earned from the cost of hauling a ton of freight one mile.
- The movement of a ton of freight one mile.

Tonnage: 100 cubic feet. Generally refers to freight handled.

Top-Air Delivery: A type of air circulation in a container. In top-air units, air is drawn from the bottom of the container, filtered through the evaporator for cooling, and then forced through the ducted passages along the top of the container. This type of airflow requires a special loading pattern.

Towage: The charge made for towing a vessel.

Tractor: Unit of highway motive power used to pull one or more trailers/containers.

Trade Acceptance: A time or a date draft that has been accepted by the buyer (the drawee) for payment at maturity.

Traffic: Persons and property carried by transport lines.

Trailer: The truck unit into which freight is loaded as in tractor trailer combination. *See Container.*

Tramp Line: An ocean carrier company operating vessels not on regular runs or schedules. They call at any port where cargo may be available.

Transport: To move cargo from one place to another.

Transportation & Exit (T&E): Allows foreign merchandise arriving at one port to be transported in bond through the U.S. to be exported from another port, without paying duty.

Transportation Worker Identification Credential (TWIC): Established by Congress through the Maritime Transportation Security Act (MTSA) and is administered by the Transportation Security Administration (TSA) and U.S. Coast Guard. TWICs are tamper–resistant biometric credentials that will be issued to all credentialed merchant mariners and to workers who require unescorted access to secure areas of ports, vessels or outer continental shelf facilities.

Transship: To transfer goods from one transportation line to another, or from one ship to another.

Transshipment Port: Place where cargo is transferred to another carrier.

Trust Receipt: Release of merchandise by a bank to a buyer while the bank retains title to the merchandise. The goods are usually obtained for manufacturing or sales purposes. The buyer is obligated to maintain the goods (or the proceeds from their sales) distinct from the remainder of the assets and to hold them ready for repossession by the bank.

Turnaround: In water transportation, the time it takes between the arrival of a vessel and its departure.

Twist Locks: A set of four twistable bayonet type shear keys used as part of a spreader to pick up a container or as part of a chassis to secure the containers.

Two-Way Pallet: A pallet so designed that the forks of a fork lift truck can be inserted from two sides only.

U

UCP: Abbreviation for the "Uniform Customs and Practice for Documentary Credits," published by the International Chamber of Commerce. This is the most frequently used standard for making payments in international trade; e.g., paying on a Letter of Credit. It is most frequently referred to by its shorthand title: UCP No. 500. This revised publication reflects recent changes in the transportation and banking industries, such as electronic transfer of funds.

UFC: Abbreviation for "Uniform Freight Classification."

ULCC: Ultra Large Crude Carrier. A tanker in excess of 320,000dwt.

Ullage: The space not filled with liquid in a drum or tank.

UN/EDIFACT: United Nations EDI for Administration, Commerce and Transport. EDI Standards are developed and supported by the UN for electronic message (data) interchange on an international level.

Unclaimed Freight: Freight that has not been called for or picked up by the consignee or owner.

Undercharge: To charge less than the proper amount.

Underway: A vessel is underway when it is not at anchor, made fast to the shore, or aground.

Uniform Customs and Practices for Documentary Credits (UCP): Rules for letters of credit drawn up by the Commission on Banking Technique and Practices of the International Chamber of Commerce in consultation with the banking associations of many countries. See Terms of Payment.

Unit Load: Packages loaded on a pallet, in a crate or any other way that enables them to be handled at one time as a unit.

Unit Train: A train of a specified number of railcars, perhaps 100, which remain as a unit for a designated destination or until a change in routing is made.

Unitization:
- The consolidation of a quantity of individual items into one large shipping unit for easier handling.
- Loading one or more large items of cargo onto a single piece of equipment, such as a pallet.

Unloading: Removal of a shipment from a vessel.

U.S. Consular Invoice: A document required on merchandise imported into the United States.

USPPI—United States Principal Party of Interest: The party that receives the primary benefit from an export transaction, usually the seller of the goods.

V

Validated Export License: A document issued by the U.S. government; authorizes the export of commodities for which written authorization is required by law.

Validation: Authentication of B/L and when B/L becomes effective.

Vanning: A term for stowing cargo in a container.

Variable Cost: Costs that vary directly with the level of activity within a short time. Examples include costs of moving cargo inland on trains or trucks, stevedoring in some ports, and short-term equipment leases. For business analysis, all costs are either defined as variable or fixed. For a business to break even, all fixed costs must be covered. To make a profit, all variable and fixed costs must be recovered plus some extra amount.

Ventilated Container: A container designed with openings in the side and/or end walls to permit the ingress of outside air when the doors are closed.

Vessel Supplies for Immediate Exportation (VSIE): Allows equipment and supplies arriving at one port to be loaded on a vessel, aircraft, etc., for its exclusive use and to be exported from the same port.

Vessel Manifest: The international carrier is obligated to make declarations of the ship's crew and contents at both the port of departure and arrival. The vessel manifest lists various details about each shipment by B/L number. Obviously, the B/L serves as the core source from which the manifest is created.

VISA: Voluntary Intermodal Sealift Agreement. Provides the U.S. defense community with "assured access" to commercial intermodal capacity to move sustainment cargoes during time of war or national emergency. In return, during peacetime, the carriers receive preference in the carriage of DOD cargoes.

Viz.: Namely. Used in tariffs to specify commodities.

VLCC: Very Large Crude Carrier. A tanker of 200,000 to 319,000dwt. It can carry about 2 million barrels of crude oil.

VLFO—Vessel Load Free Out: The loading and discharge terms for the cargo to be shipped, as agreed to in the charter party. The vessel (carrier) pays for the loading of the cargo on board the ship and the receiver pays for the discharge of the cargo from the ship to the pier.

Voluntary Ship: Any ship which is not required by treaty or statute to be equipped with radio telecommunication equipment.

W

War Risk: Insurance coverage for loss of goods resulting from any act of war.

Warehouse: A place for the reception, delivery, consolidation, distribution, and storage of goods/cargo.

Warehouse Entry: Document that identifies goods imported when placed in a bonded warehouse. The duty is not imposed on the products while in the warehouse but will be collected when they are withdrawn for delivery or consumption.

Warehouse Withdrawal for Transportation Immediate Exportation (WDEX): Allows merchandise that has been withdrawn from a bonded warehouse at one U.S. port to be exported from the same port exported without paying duty.

Warehouse Withdrawal for Transportation (WDT): Allows merchandise that has been withdrawn from a bonded warehouse at one port to be transported in bond to another port, where a superseding entry will be filed.

Warehouse Withdrawal for Transportation Exportation (WDT&E): Allows merchandise that has been withdrawn from a bonded warehouse at one port to be transported in bond through the

United States to be exported from another port, without paying duty.

Warehousing: The storing of goods/cargo.

Waybill (WB): A document prepared by a transportation line at the point of a shipment; shows the point of the origin, destination, route, consignor, consignee, description of shipment and amount charged for the transportation service. It is forwarded with the shipment or sent by mail to the agent at the transfer point or waybill destination. Abbreviation is WB. Unlike a bill of lading, a waybill is *not* a document of title.

Weight Cargo: A cargo on which the transportation charge is assessed on the basis of weight.

Weights and Measures/Measurement Ton:
- 40 cubic ft or one cubic meter
- Net ton/short ton—2,000 lbs
- Gross ton/long ton—2,240 lbs
- Metric ton/kilo ton—2,204.6 lbs
- Cubic meter—35.314 cubic ft

Well Car: Also known as stack car. A drop–frame rail flat car.

Wharf: A structure built on the shore of a harbor extending into deep water so that vessels may lie alongside. See also Dock and Pier.

Wharfage (Whfge.): Charge assessed by a pier or dock owner against freight handled over the pier or dock or against a steamship company using the pier or dock.

WIBON: Whether In Berth or Not.

Windy Booking: A freight booking made by a shipper or freight forwarder to reserve space but not actually having a specific cargo at the time the booking is made. Carriers often overbook a vessel by 10% to 20% in recognition that "windy booking" cargo will not actually ship.

Without Recourse: A phrase preceding the signature of a drawer or endorser of a negotiable instrument; signifies that the instrument is passed onto subsequent holders without any liability to the endorser in the event of nonpayment or non-delivery.

W.M. (W/M): Abbreviation for "Weight or Measurement;" the basis for assessing freight charges. Also known as "worm." The rate charged under W/M will be whichever produces the highest revenue between the weight of the shipment and the measure of the shipment. The comparison is based on the number of metric tons the cargo weights compared to the number of cubic meters of space the cargo measures. The prior English method was one long ton compared to forty cubic feet.

WPA: Abbreviation for "With Particular Average."

W.T.L.: Western Truck Lines.

WWD: Weather Working Days.

Y

Yard: A classification, storage or switching area.

York–Antwerp Rules of 1974: Established the standard basis for adjusting general average and stated the rules for adjusting claims.

Z

Zulu Time: Time based on Greenwich Mean Time.

U.S. TRADE TERMS

Institute Cargo Clauses
Global Foreign-Trade Zones:
Routed Freight Transaction
IncoTerms Use

U.S. FREE TRADE AGREEMENTS

Why Should You Care about Free Trade Agreements (FTAs)?

If you are looking to export your product or service, the United States may have negotiated favorable treatment for your service or product through an FTA. This treatment should make it easier to export your product to or offer your service in the FTA country's market. It may also give your product or service a competitive advantage versus products from other countries.

What Is an FTA Negotiated by the United States?

An FTA is an agreement between two or more countries where the countries agree on certain behaviors that affect trade in goods and services, and protections for investors and intellectual property rights, among other topics. For the United States, the main goal of trade agreements is to reduce barriers to U.S. exports, and protect U.S. interests, and enhance the rule of law in the FTA partner country. The reduction of trade barriers and the creation of a more stable and transparent trading and investment environment make it easier and cheaper for U.S. companies to export their products and services to trading partner markets. Forty-one percent of U.S. goods exports went to FTA partner countries in 2010, with exports to those countries growing at a faster rate than exports to the rest of the world from 2009 to 2010, 23% vs. 20%.

FTAs usually build off of the agreements negotiated in the World Trade Organization (WTO). For example, in the WTO, each country agrees to issue, at the request of the importer or exporter, binding advance determinations on where a product will be viewed as coming from, since many products are made up of parts from multiple countries. Under an FTA, importers and exporters can obtain determinations for a broader set of issues, including finding what tariff line the product will be classified under, and value that will use to calculate the tariff.

Other countries also negotiate FTAs and the behaviors covered may not be the same as those negotiated by the United States.

What Types of Behaviors Are Addressed in a U.S. FTA?

U.S. FTAs typically address a wide variety of government activity. One example is the eventual elimination of tariffs charged on all products coming from the other country, if the product meets the rules of origin spelled out in the agreement. For example, a country that normally charges a tariff of 5% of the value of the incoming product will eliminate that tariff for products they can certify come from the United States. The rules of origin can make using the FTA negotiated tariffs a bit more complicated, but help to ensure that U.S. exports, rather than exports from other countries, receive the benefits of the agreement.

Some other types of commitments frequently found in FTAs include

- the right for a U.S. company to bid on certain government procurements in the FTA partner country;
- the right for a U.S. investors to get adequate compensation if its investment in the FTA partner country is taken by the government (e.g., expropriated);
- the right for U.S. service suppliers to supply their services in the FTA partner country;
- protection and enforcement of American-owned intellectual property rights in the FTA partner country; and
- the right for U.S. exporters to participate in the development of product standards in the FTA partner country.

With Which Countries Does the United States Have an FTA?

The United States has 11 FTAs in force with 17 countries. In addition, the United States has negotiated FTAs with Korea, Panama, and Colombia, but these agreements have not yet entered into force. The United States is also in the process of negotiating a regional FTA, the Trans-Pacific Partnership, with Australia, Brunei Darussalam, Chile, Malaysia, New Zealand, Peru, Singapore, and Vietnam.

U.S. FTA Partner Countries

- Australia
- Bahrain
- Chile
- DR-CAFTA: Costa Rica, Dominican Republic, El Salvador, Guatemala, Honduras, and Nicaragua
- Israel
- Jordan
- Morocco
- NAFTA: Canada and Mexico
- Oman
- Peru
- Singapore

How Can U.S. Companies Identify Tariffs on Exports to FTA Partner Countries?

The FTA Tariff Tool can help you determine the tariff, or tax at the border, that certain foreign countries will collect when a U.S. exported product enters the country. You can look up the tariff rate for a given product today, as well as identify when in the future the tariff rate will go down further or be eliminated altogether.

If you would like more information on exporting to FTA partner countries, please contact the Trade Information Center at 1-800-872-8723.

ULTIMATE CONSIGNEE VERIFICATION[*]

Overview

There are many U.S. companies who are not aware of the responsibility towards import compliance management that is associated with the designation of ultimate consignee. There are instances in which a U.S. party may be defined as ultimate consignee that are commonly overlooked due to common practice interpretations such as the act of causing the importation. Generally, the ultimate consignee designation is assigned to the U.S. party who purchases the imported merchandise from the foreign supplier, whether or not designated as importer of record. There are exceptions to this general rule which should be clarified to ensure that there does not exist additional unsupervised compliance responsibilities within any aspect of an importer's supply chain process. It is necessary to verify this issue and identify import circumstances that do not meet ultimate consignee responsibilities as well as those that do. For those circumstances that do not meet ultimate consignee defined parameters, there exists no compliance responsibility. For instances that do meet the ultimate consignee definition parameters, a compliance structure of adherence will be required to be implemented.

Objective

To identify and verify procurement circumstances, inclusive of purchased and non-purchased items, in which *U.S. party* may be defined as ultimate

---

[*] From U.S. Free Trade Agreements, Helping U.S. Companies Export, http://export.gov/fta.

consignee and therefore responsible for import compliance management activities.

Definition

The Ultimate Consignee at the time of entry or release is defined as the party in the United States, to whom the overseas shipper sold the imported merchandise. If at the time of entry or release the imported merchandise has not been sold, then the Ultimate Consignee at the time of entry or release is defined as the party in the United States to whom the overseas shipper consigned the imported merchandise. If the merchandise has not been sold or consigned to a U.S. party at the time of entry or release, then the Ultimate Consignee at the time of entry or release is defined as the proprietor of the U.S. premises to which the merchandise is to be delivered.

Verification Questions as Affirmation of Ultimate Consignee Designation*

1. Does U.S. party purchase merchandise directly from the overseas manufacturer of imported merchandise?
2. Does U.S. party knowingly cause the importation or transportation or storage of merchandise carried or held under bond into or from the territory of the United States?
3. Does U.S. party act as a U.S. agent of any company who knowingly caused the importation of merchandise to the United States?
4. Does U.S. party own the merchandise at the time of import entry or customs entry release?
5. Will the imported merchandise be consigned to U.S. party on any import related transportation documents such as a commercial/proforma invoice, contract of carriage (bill of lading or airway bill), letter of credit, purchase order confirmation?
6. If not owned or consigned at the time of entry or customs release, will the goods be delivered to U.S. party designated receiving location?
7. If not purchased at the time of initial import entry, is it possible that U.S. party will purchase the imported merchandise within 10 days from the date of import entry presentation and or release?

---

* From U.S. Customs and Border Protection, http://www.cbp.gov.

U.S. Customs and Border Protection Office of Strategic Trade Regulatory Audit Division Treatment of Ultimate Consignee Transactions in a Focused Assessment

Introduction

A Focused Assessment (FA) provides U.S. Customs and Border Protection (CBP) with the ability to review and verify information disclosed to CBP for accuracy and completeness. During an audit, the auditor may review records where the auditee is the Importer of Record (IOR) and/or the Ultimate Consignee (UC). Many issues can arise during an audit involving the auditee's responsibilities for reporting entry information to CBP and for record keeping. This document addresses IOR and UC responsibilities and audit procedures.

Background

The entry statute (19 U.S.C. 1484 (a)) establishes responsibilities of the IOR as follows:

(a) Requirement and time
  (1) Except as provided in sections 1490, 1498, 1552, and 1553 of this title, one of the parties qualifying as "importer of record" under paragraph (2) (B), either in person or by an agent authorized by the party in writing, shall, using reasonable care—
    (A) make entry therefor by filing with the Customs Service—
      (i) such documentation or, pursuant to an electronic data interchange system, such information as is necessary to enable the Customs Service to determine whether the merchandise may be released from customs custody, and
      (ii) notification whether an import activity summary statement will be filed; and
    (B) complete the entry by filing with the Customs Service the declared value, classification and rate of duty applicable to the merchandise, and such other documentation or, pursuant to an electronic data interchange system, such other information as is necessary to enable the Customs Service to—
      (i) properly assess duties on the merchandise,
      (ii) collect accurate statistics with respect to the merchandise, and

(iii) determine whether any other applicable requirement of
law (other than a requirement relating to release from
customs custody) is met.

The statute (19 U.S.C. 1484(a)(2)(B)) defines the term "importer of record" as the owner or purchaser of the merchandise or a licensed customs broker appropriately designated by the owner, purchaser or consignee of the merchandise. Statutory obligations make the IOR "accountable" for the declarations made at entry. However, while the entry statute clearly identifies the "accountable "party, liability for penalties may attach to any culpable party under civil penalty statute, 19 U.S.C. 1592 (a).

In some instances, in order to meet the burden of using reasonable care when making declarations at entry, the IOR or his agent must necessarily seek information from another source. Sometimes that is the UC. For example, the IOR may not be the owner or purchaser of the merchandise, but rather, a customs broker retained by a UC. In such a case, it is unlikely that the IOR will have sufficient information to meet its reasonable care obligation without obtaining information about the transaction from another party. The IOR is always "accountable." If the UC provides the IOR with information that is material and false and that information is used to make entry, the UC may be culpable under 19 U.S.C. 1592.

In addition to responsibilities as IOR, auditees may be subject to record-keeping requirements in 19 U.S.C. 1508, which state:

(a) Requirements: Any
  (1) Owner, importer, consignee, importer of record, entry filer, or
  other party who—
     (A) imports merchandise into the customs territory of the
     United States, files a drawback claim, or transports or stores
     merchandise carried or held under bond, or
     (B) knowingly causes the importation or transportation or storage of merchandise carried or held under bond into or from
     the customs territory of the United States;
  (2) agent of any party described in paragraph (1); or
  (3) person whose activities require the filing of a declaration or
  entry, or both; shall make, keep, and render for examination and
  inspection records (which for purposes of this section include,
  but are not limited to, statements, declarations, documents and
  electronically generated or machine readable data) which—

(A) pertain to any such activity, or to the information contained in the records required by this chapter in connection with any such activity; and

(B) are normally kept in the ordinary course of business.

Procedures

During an audit, the FA team will primarily address issues related to responsibilities of the auditee as IOR. Issues related to auditee's responsibilities as the UC will be addressed as needed on a case-by-case basis. The IOR will be held "accountable" for the declarations made at entry. Both the IOR and UC will be held responsible for maintaining records required by 19 U.S.C. 1508. If the UC provides the IOR with information that is material and false, that information is used to make entry, and the resulting errors have significant impact, the auditors will refer the information to appropriate action officials for possible action under provisions of 19 U.S.C. 1592.

The following three scenarios provide guidance to the auditors when the auditee is the UC but *not* the IOR.

Consolidated Entries with Multiple Ultimate Consignees

In the past, shippers and importers used consolidated release and entry summary for shipments that had multiple UCs arriving at the border in a single conveyance. But CBP's automated system has limitations that allow for the submission of only a single UC. Because only one UC can be designated for the consolidated shipment, a company may be listed as the UC on the consolidated entry summary in CBP's automated system but may not be responsible for all portions of the consolidated entry summary.

An audit sample may include a consolidated entry that identifies the auditee as the UC when other UCs are responsible for part of the consolidated shipment. When this occurs and the auditee is not the IOR, the auditee must arrange with the entry filer to provide information to CBP to prove that the auditee is not the UC responsible for all portions of the consolidated entry. The auditee is only responsible for those portions of the consolidated entry for which he is the UC. Under provisions of 19 U.S.C. 1508, the auditee must maintain records related to those portions of the entry for which he was the UC.

Unsolicited Merchandise on Entries Listing a Company as UC

Sometimes companies are listed as the UC on an entry when the company does not initiate or have any information about the specific import transaction. For example, a related company may send unsolicited prototypes or samples. This may also occur if unrelated entities send unsolicited merchandise (such as returned merchandise) to a company listed as UC on the entry. During an audit, the sample may include unsolicited entries where the auditee is listed as the UC but is not the IOR. If the auditee did not initiate the import transaction, has no records related to the importation, and can adequately explain the circumstances and its lack of records to support this transaction, the auditee will not be held responsible for records required by 19 U.S.C. 1508 or for accuracy or completeness of entry information.

Entries Initiated by the UC but Another Entity Is IOR

In some cases, a company initiates an import or is in some way responsible for information related to the import, is listed as UC, but is not the IOR. For example, this may occur when the overseas supplier (or other entity) is IOR and handles the details of the importation. If these entries are included in an audit sample, the UC is responsible for maintaining and making available records required by 19 U.S.C. 1508.

The IOR is always accountable for entry information. However, if the UC provides the IOR with information, which is material and false, and that information is used to make entry, the UC may be culpable under 19 U.S.C. 1592.

Aside from the record keeping obligations and the situation where the UC may be liable under 19 U.S.C. 1592 for false statements or omissions, the auditee will be responsible for entry information or internal control of entry information provided to CBP only when designated as the IOR.

Routed Freight Transactions

Routed and Nonrouted Export Transactions

Primary responsibility for compliance with the EAR falls on the *principal parties in interest (PPI)* in a transaction. Generally, the PPIs in an export transaction are the U.S. seller and foreign buyer. See the following parts and sections of the EAR for additional information: section 748.5, regarding parties to a transaction; part 758 on export clearance; and relevant definitions in part 772.

In a *routed export transaction*, in which the foreign PPI authorizes a U.S. agent to facilitate the export of items from the United States, the U.S. PPI obtains from the foreign PPI a writing in which the foreign PPI expressly assumes responsibility for determining licensing requirements and obtaining authorization for the export. In this case, the U.S. agent acting for the foreign PPI is the "exporter" under the EAR, and is responsible for determining licensing authority and obtaining the appropriate license or other authorization for the export.

An agent representing the foreign PPI in this type of routed export transaction must obtain a power of attorney or other written authorization in order to act on behalf of the foreign PPI.

In this type of routed export transaction, if the U.S. PPI does not obtain from the foreign PPI the writing described above, then the U.S. PPI is the "exporter" and must determine licensing authority and obtain the appropriate license or other authorization. This is true even if the transaction is considered a routed export transaction for purposes of filing electronic export information pursuant to the Foreign Trade Regulations (15 C.F.R. part 30).

In a routed export transaction in which the foreign PPI assumes responsibility for determining the appropriate authorization for the export, the U.S. PPI obtains from the foreign PPI a writing wherein the foreign PPI expressly assumes responsibility for determining licensing requirements and obtaining licensing authority. The EAR requires the U.S. PPI to furnish the foreign PPI and its agent, upon request, with the correct Export Control Classification Number (ECCN) or sufficient technical information to determine the ECCN. In addition, the U.S. PPI must provide the foreign PPI and its agent with any information that it knows will affect the determination of license authority. The U.S. PPI also has responsibility under the Foreign Trade Regulations (15 C.F.R. part 30) to provide certain data to the agent for the purposes of filing electronic export information.

In a transaction that is not a routed export transaction, if the U.S. PPI authorizes an agent to prepare and file the export declaration on its behalf, the U.S. PPI is the "exporter" under the EAR and is required to

(A) **provide the agent with the information necessary to complete the AES submission;**
(B) **authorize the agent to complete the AES submission by power of attorney or other written authorization; and**

(C) **maintain documentation to support the information provided to the agent for completing the AES submission.**

If authorized by either the U.S. or foreign PPI, the agent is responsible for

(A) **preparing the AES submission based on information received from the U.S. PPI;**
(B) **maintaining documentation to support the information reported on the AES submission; and**
(C) **upon request, providing the U.S. PPI with a copy of the AES filed by the agent.**

Both the agent and the PPI who has authorized the agent are responsible for the correctness of each entry made on an AES submission. Good faith reliance on information obtained from the PPI can help protect an agent, but the careless use of "No License Required," or unsupported entries, can get an agent into trouble. Agents without the appropriate technical expertise should avoid making commodity classifications and should obtain support documentation for ECCNs.

Additionally, upon written request, Census will provide companies with 12 months of AES data free of charge every 365 days. The Census Bureau's Foreign Trade Division currently provides U.S. PPIs, and other filers requesting their AES data, with all 10 data elements required in routed export transactions.

TAX RATES*

EU Countries

Country	Standard Rate	Reduced Rate	Abbr.	Name
Austria	20% [22]	12% or 10%	MwSt./ USt.	Mehrwertsteuer/ Umsatzsteuer
Belgium	21% [22]	12% or 6% or 0% in some cases	BTW	Belasting over de toegevoegde waarde
			TVA	Taxe sur la Valeur Ajoutée
			MWSt	Mehrwertsteuer
Bulgaria	20% [22]	7% or 0%	ДДС	Данък добавена стойност
Cyprus	15% [22]	5% (8% for taxi and bus transportation)	ΦΠΑ	Φόροσ Προστιθέμενησ Αξίασ
Czech Republic	20% [22]	14%	DPH	Daň z přidané hodnoty
Denmark	25% [22][23]	0%	Moms	Meromsætningsafgift
Estonia	20% [22]	9%	Km	käibemaks
Finland	23% [22][24]	13% or 9%	ALV	Arvonlisävero (Finnish)
			Moms	Mervärdesskatt (Swedish)
France	19.6% [22]	5.5% or 2.1% or 7%	TVA	Taxe sur la valeur ajoutée
Germany	19% (Helgoland 0%)[22]	7% or 0% (Helgoland always 0%)	MwSt./ USt.	Mehrwertsteuer/ Umsatzsteuer
Greece	23% [22][25]	13% (6.5% for hotels and pharmacies)		
	(16% on Aegean islands)	(8% and 4% on Aegean islands)	ΦΠΑ	Φόροσ Προστιθέμενησ Αξίασ

continued

---

* From the Bureau of Industry and Security, U.S. Department of Commerce, http://www.bis.doc. gov.

Country	Standard Rate	Reduced Rate	Abbr.	Name
Hungary	27% [26]	18% or 5%	ÁFA	Általános forgalmi adó
Ireland	23% [22][27]	13.5% or 9.0% or 4.8% or 0%	CBL	Cáin Bhreisluacha (Irish)
			VAT	Value Added Tax (English)
Italy	21% [22] (23% from 2012)	10% or 4%	IVA	Imposta sul Valore Aggiunto
Latvia	22% [22]	12% or 0%	PVN	Pievienotās vērtības nodoklis
Lithuania	21% [22]	9% or 5%	PVM	Pridėtinės vertės mokestis
Luxembourg	15% [22]	12% or 9% or 6% or 3%	TVA	Taxe sur la Valeur Ajoutée
Malta	18% [22]	5% or 0%	VAT	Taxxa tal-Valur Miżjud
Netherlands	19% [22]	6% or 0%	BTW	Belasting over de toegevoegde waarde
Poland	23% [28]	8% or 5% or 0%	PTU/VAT	Podatek od towarów i usług
Portugal	23% [29]	13% or 6%	IVA	Imposto sobre o Valor Acrescentado
	16% in Madeira and Azores (Minimum 70% of mainland rate)[30]	9% or 4% in Madeira and Azores (Minimum 70% of mainland rate) [30]		
Romania	24% [31]	9% (medication and books) or 5% (first time buyers of new homes under special conditions)	TVA	Taxa pe valoarea adăugată
Slovakia	20% [22]	10%	DPH	Daň z pridanej hodnoty
Slovenia	20% [22]	8.5%	DDV	Davek na dodano vrednost
Spain	18% [22][32]	8% or 4% [22] [33]	IVA	Impuesto sobre el Valor Añadido

Country	Standard Rate	Reduced Rate	Abbr.	Name
	5% in Canary Islands	2% or 0% in CanaryIslands	IGIC	Impuesto General Indirecto Canario
Sweden	25% [22]	12% (e.g., food, hotels and restaurants) or 6% (e.g., public transport)	Moms	Mervärdesskatt
United Kingdom	20% [34] (0% on Channel Islands and Gibraltar)	5% for home energy and renovations and 0% for life necessities—groceries, water, prescription medications, medical supplies and equipment, children clothing, public transport, books and periodicals	VAT	Value Added Tax

Non-EU Countries

Country	Standard Rate	Reduced Rate	Local Name
Albania	20%	10% (pharmacies), 0%	TVSH = *Tatimi mbi Vlerën e Shtuar*
Andorra[35]	4.5%	1%	IVA = *Impost sobre el Valor Afegit*
Azerbaijan	18%	10.5% or 0%	ƏDV = *Əlavə dəyər vergisi*
Argentina	21%	10.5% or 0%	IVA = *Impuesto al Valor Agregado*
Armenia	20%	0%	AAH = *Avelac'vaç aržek'i hark*
Australia	10%	0%	GST = Goods and Services Tax

continued

Country	Standard Rate	Reduced Rate	Local Name
Belarus	18%	10% or 0.5%	ПДВ = *Падатак на дададзеную вартасьць*
Barbados	17.5%		VAT = Value Added Tax
Bosnia and Herzegovina	17%	0%	PDV = *Porez na dodanu vrijednost*
Brazil	12% + 25% + 5%	0%	*IPI—12% = Imposto sobre produtos industrializados (Tax over industrialized products)—Federal Tax* ICMS—25% = *Imposto sobre circulação e serviços (Tax over commercialization and services)—State Tax* ISS—5% = *Imposto sobre serviço de qualquer natureza (Tax over any service)—City tax* *IPI = Imposto sobre produtos industrializados (Tax over industrialized products) can reach 60% over imported products.*
Bolivia	13%		IVA = *Impuesto al Valor Agregado*
Canada	5% + 0–10% HST (GST + PST)	5%/0%[2]	GST = Goods and Services Tax, TPS = *Taxe sur les produits et services*; HST[1] = *Harmonized Sales Tax*, TVH = *Taxe de vente harmonisée*
Chile	19%		IVA = *Impuesto al Valor Agregado*
Colombia	16%		IVA = *Impuesto al Valor Agregado*
People's Republic of China [3]	17%	13% for foods, printed matter, and households fuels; 6% or 3%	增值税 (pinyin:*zēng zhí shuì*)
Croatia	23%	10% or 0%	PDV = *Porez na dodanu vrijednost*

Country	Standard Rate	Reduced Rate	Local Name
Dominican Republic	16%	12% or 0%	ITBIS = *Impuesto sobre Transferencia de Bienes Industrializados y Servicios*
Ecuador	12%		IVA = *Impuesto al Valor Agregado*
Egypt	10%		VAT = *Value Added Tax* (الضريبة على القيمة المضافة)
El Salvador	13%		IVA = *Impuesto al Valor Agregado* o "Impuesto a la Transferencia de Bienes Muebles y a la Prestación de Servicios"
Ethiopia	15%		VAT = *Value Added Tax*
Fiji	15%	0%	VAT = *Value Added Tax*
Faroe Islands	25%		MVG = *Meirvirðisgjald*
Georgia	18%	0%	DGhG = *Damatebuli Ghirebulebis gdasakhadi*
Guatemala	12%		IVA = *Impuesto al Valor Agregado*
Guyana[36]	16%	0%	VAT = *Value Added Tax*
Iran	4%		VAT = *Value Added Tax* (مالیات بر ارزش افزوده)
Iceland	25.5%	7%[4]	VSK, VASK = *Virðisaukaskattur*
India [5]	13.5%	5%, 1%, or 0%	VAT = *Valued Added Tax*
Indonesia	10%	5%	PPN = *Pajak Pertambahan Nilai*
Israel [6]	16%[7] (Eilat 0%)	0% (fruits and vegetables, tourism services, diamonds, flights and apartments renting)	Ma'am = מס ערך מוסף
Japan	5%		Consumption tax = 消費税

continued

Country	Standard Rate	Reduced Rate	Local Name
South Korea	10%		VAT = 부가세 (附加稅, *Bugase*) = 부가가치세(附加價值稅, *Bugagachise*)
Jersey [8]	5%	0%	GST = *Goods and Services Tax*
Jordan	16%		GST = *Goods and Sales Tax*
Kazakhstan	12%		ҚСҚ = *Қосымша салық құны* (Kazakh) НДС = *Налог на добавленную стоимость* (Russian) VAT = *Value Added Tax*
Lebanon	10%		TVA = *Taxe sur la valeur ajoutée*
Liechtenstein	7.6%	3.6% (lodging services) or 2.4%	MWST = *Mehrwertsteuer*
Morocco	20%		GST = *Goods and Sales Tax* (الضريبة على القيمة المضافة)
Moldova	20%	8%, 5% or 0%	TVA = *Taxa pe Valoarea Adăugată*
Macedonia	18%	5%	ДДВ = *Данок на Додадена Вредност*, DDV = *Danok na Dodadena Vrednost*
Malaysia [9]	10%		GST = *Goods and Services Tax* (Government Tax)
Maldives	6%	0%	GST = *Goods and Services Tax* (Government Tax)
Mexico	16%	11%, 0%	IVA = *Impuesto al Valor Agregado*
Monaco [38]	19.6%	5.6%	TVA = *Taxe sur la valeur ajoutée*
Montenegro	17%		PDV = *Porez na dodatu vrijednost*
Mauritius	15%		VAT = *Value Added Tax*
Namibia	15%	0%	VAT = *Value Added Tax*
Nepal	13%	0%	VAT = *Value Added Taxes*
New Zealand	15%		GST = *Goods and Services Tax*

Country	Standard Rate	Reduced Rate	Local Name
Norway	25%	15% or 8%	MVA = *Merverdiavgift* (bokmål) or *meirverdiavgift* (nynorsk) (informally *moms*)
Palestinian territories	14.5%		VAT = *Value Added Tax*
Pakistan	16%	1% or 0%	GST = *General Sales Tax*
Panama	7%		ITBMS = *Impuesto de Transferencia de Bienes Muebles y Servicios*
Paraguay	10%	5%	IVA = *Impuesto al Valor Agregado*
Peru	16%+2%		IGV—16% = *Impuesto General a la Ventas* IPM—2% *Impuesto de Promocion Municipal*
Philippines	12%[10]		RVAT = *Reformed Value Added Tax*, locally known as *Karagdagang Buwis/ Dungag nga Buhis*
Russia	18%	10% or 0%	НДС = *Налог на добавленную стоимость*, NDS = *Nalog na dobavlennuyu stoimost'*
Saint Kitts and Nevis	17%		VAT = *Value Added Tax*
Serbia	18%	8% or 0%	ПДВ = *Порез на додату вредност*, PDV = *Porez na dodatu vrednost*
Singapore	7%		GST = Goods and Services Tax
South Africa	14%	0%	VAT = *Valued Added Tax*
Sri Lanka	12%	0%	VAT = *Valued Added Tax* has been in effect in Sri Lanka since 2001. On the 2001 budget, the rates have been revised to 12% and 0% from the previous 20%, 12% and 0%

continued

Country	Standard Rate	Reduced Rate	Local Name
Switzerland	8%[39]	3.8% (hotel sector) and 2.5% (essential foodstuffs, books, newspapers, medical supplies)[39]	MWST = *Mehrwertsteuer*, TVA = *Taxe sur la valeur ajoutée*, IVA = *Imposta sul valore aggiunto*, TPV = *Taglia sin la Plivalur*
Taiwan	5%		
Thailand	7%		VAT = *Value Added Tax*,
Trinidad and Tobago	15%	0%	
Turkey	18%	8% or 1%	KDV = *Katma değer vergisi*
Ukraine	20% (17% from January 2014)	0%	ПДВ = *Податок на додану вартість*, PDV = *Podatok na dodanu vartist'*.
Uruguay	22%	10%	IVA = *Impuesto al Valor Agregado*
Uzbekistan	20%		НДС = Налог на добавленную стоимость
Vietnam	10%	5% or 0%	GTGT = *Giá Trị Gia Tăng*
Venezuela	12%	11%	IVA = *Impuesto al Valor Agregado*

Note 1: HST is a combined federal/provincial VAT collected in some provinces. In the rest of Canada, the GST is a 5% federal VAT and if there is a *Provincial Sales Tax* (PST) it is a separate non-VAT tax.

Note 2: No real "reduced rate," but rebates generally available for new housing effectively reduce the tax to 4.5%.

Note 3: These taxes do not apply in Hong Kong and Macau, which are financially independent as specialadministrativeregions.

Note 4: The reduced rate was 14% until 1 March 2007, when it was lowered to 7%. The reduced rate applies to heating costs, printed matter, restaurant bills, hotel stays, and most food.

Note 5: VAT is not implemented in 2 of India's 28 states.

Note 6: Except Eilat, where VAT is not raised.[40]

Note 7: The VAT in Israel is in a state of flux. It was reduced from 18% to 17% on March 2004, to 16.5% on September 2005, then to 15.5% on July 2006. It was then raised back to 16.5% in July 2009 only to be lowered to its current rate of 16% on January 1, 2010.

Note 8: The introduction of a goods and sales tax of 3% on 6 May 2008 was to replace revenue from Company Income Tax following a reduction in rates.

Note 9: In the 2005 Budget, the government announced that GST would be introduced in January 2007. Many details have not yet been confirmed but it has been stated that essential goods and small businesses would be exempted or zero rated. Rates have not yet been established as of June 2007.

Note 10: The President of the Philippines has the power to raise the tax to 12% after January 1, 2006. The tax was raised to 12% on February 1.[41]

VAT Registered

Belgian VAT Receipt

VAT registered means registered for VAT purposes, i.e., entered into an official VAT payers register of a country. Both natural persons and legal entities can be VAT registered. Countries that use VAT have established different thresholds for remuneration derived by natural persons/legal entities during a calendar year (or a different period), by exceeding which the VAT registration is compulsory. Natural persons/legal entities that are VAT registered are obliged to calculate VAT on certain goods/services that they supply and pay VAT into a particular state budget. VAT registered persons/entities are entitled to a VAT deduction under legislative regulations of a particular country. The introduction of a VAT can reduce the cash economy because businesses that wish to buy and sell with other VAT registered businesses must themselves be VAT registered.[*]

As of November 2011, 11 countries and 9 territories under 2 countries remain VAT free in the world.

---

[*] From Encyclopedia, Nation Master, http://www.nationmaster.com/encyclopedia/value-addedtax#vatregister-ed.

Country	Remark
United States	
Bahamas	
San Marino	
Saudi Arabia	Gulf Cooperation Council
Qatar	Gulf Cooperation Council
United Arab Emirates	Gulf Cooperation Council
Kuwait	Gulf Cooperation Council
Bahrain	Gulf Cooperation Council
Oman	Gulf Cooperation Council
Libya	
Brunei	
Maldives	
Hong Kong	special administrative region of China
Macau	special administrative region of China
British Virgin Islands	British Overseas Territory
Bermuda	British Overseas Territory
Cayman Islands	British Overseas Territory
Anguilla	British Overseas Territory
Gibraltar	British Overseas Territory
Turks and Caicos Islands	British Overseas Territory
Guernsey	British Crown Dependency

Source: Compiled from World Tax Rates, http://www.taxrates.cc/index.html.

Index

For Product Safety Concerns and Information please contact our EU representative GPSR@taylorandfrancis.com Taylor & Francis Verlag GmbH, Kaufingerstraße 24, 80331 München, Germany

T - #0005 - 230425 - C0 - 234/156/22 [24] - CB - 9781466595781 - Gloss Lamination